Human Dignity and Managerial Responsibility

Corporate Social Responsibility Series

Series Editors:
Professor Güler Aras, Yildiz Technical University, Istanbul, Turkey
Professor David Crowther, DeMontfort University, Leicester, UK

Presenting applied research from an academic perspective on all aspects of corporate social responsibility, this global interdisciplinary series includes books for all those with an interest in ethics and governance, corporate behaviour and citizenship, regulation, protest, globalization, responsible marketing, social reporting and sustainability.

Recent titles in this series:

Wealth, Welfare and the Global Free Market
Ibrahim Ozer Ertuna
ISBN: 978-0-566-08905-3

Global Perspectives on Corporate Governance and CSR
Edited by Güler Aras and David Crowther
ISBN: 978-0-566-08830-8

A Handbook of Corporate Governance and Social Responsibility
Edited by Güler Aras and David Crowther
ISBN: 978-0-566-08817-9

Making Ecopreneurs
Edited by Michael Schaper
ISBN: 978-0-566-08875-9

Ageing Populations and Changing Labour Markets
Edited by Stella Vettori
ISBN: 978-0-566-08910-7

Towards Ecological Taxation
David Russell
ISBN: 978-0-566-08979-4

Regulating Multinationals in Developing Countries
Edwin Mujih
ISBN: 978-1-4094-4463-3

Social and Environmental Reporting
Riham R. Rizk
ISBN: 978-0-566-08997-8

Human Dignity and Managerial Responsibility

Diversity, Rights, and Sustainability

Edited by

ANA MARIA DAVILA GOMEZ
University of Quebec, Canada

and

DAVID CROWTHER
De Montfort University, Leicester, UK

GOWER

© Ana Maria Davila Gomez and David Crowther 2012

All rights reserved. No part of this publication may be reproduced, stored in a retrieval system or transmitted in any form or by any means, electronic, mechanical, photocopying, recording or otherwise without the prior permission of the publisher.

Ana Maria Davila Gomez and David Crowther have asserted moral rights under the Copyright, Designs and Patents Act, 1988, to be identified as the editors of this work.

Gower Applied Business Research
Our programme provides leaders, practitioners, scholars and researchers with thought provoking, cutting edge books that combine conceptual insights, interdisciplinary rigour and practical relevance in key areas of business and management.

Published by
Gower Publishing Limited
Wey Court East
Union Road
Farnham
Surrey, GU9 7PT
England

Gower Publishing Company
Suite 420
101 Cherry Street
Burlington,
VT 05401-4405
USA

www.gowerpublishing.com

British Library Cataloguing in Publication Data
Human dignity and managerial responsibility : diversity, rights, and sustainability. – (Corporate social responsibility series)
   1. Personnel management. 2. Industrial relations. 3. Respect for persons. 4. Corporate culture. 5. Organizational change. 6. Employee rights. I. Series II. Davila Gomez, Ana Maria. III. Crowther, David.
   658.3'15 – dc22

Library of Congress Cataloging-in-Publication Data
Human dignity and managerial responsibility : diversity, rights, and sustainability / [edited] by Ana Maria Davila Gomez and David Crowther.
       p. cm. – (Corporate social responsibility)
   Includes bibliographical references and index.
   ISBN 978-1-4094-2311-9 (hbk.) – ISBN 978-1-4094-2312-6 (ebook)
 1. Management – Moral and ethical aspects. 2. Business ethics. 3. Social responsibility of business. 4. Diversity in the workplace. 5. Industrial sociology. I. Davila Gomez, Ana Maria. II. Crowther, David.

   HF5387.H8574 2011
   174'.4–dc23

2011025602

ISBN 9781409423119 (hbk)
ISBN 9781409423126 (ebk)

Printed and bound in Great Britain by the MPG Books Group, UK

Contents

List of Figures and Tables	vii
Biographies of Editors	ix
Biographies of Contributors	xi

Introduction: Managerial Responsibility for Human Dignity 1
               Ana-Maria Davila-Gomez and David Crowther

PART I   UNDERSTANDING THE ISSUES

1   Self-Discovery of the *Becoming Being* and Some Managerial Implications   13
    Ana-Maria Davila-Gomez and David Crowther

2   Management, Virtues and Human Dignity: Towards a
    Better Future for the "Whole"   27
    Ana-Maria Davila-Gomez and Sandra Socorro Lotero Patiño

3   Economic Accountability, Regulatory Reform and Ethical
    Management: Towards a New Language of Largesse   41
    Julia J.A. Shaw and Hillary J. Shaw

4   Caring, Sharing and Collective Solidarity in Management   57
    Ana-Maria Davila-Gomez and David Crowther

PART II   THE EFFECTS OF CHANGE

5   Local Governance and Social Movements in Québec:
    The Perverse Effects of Corporate Culture   75
    Denyse Côté and Étienne Simard

6   Knowledge Workers and Creativity Class: From Hopes and
    Ideals to Day-to-Day Reality   97
    Silvia Ponce

7   Technological Change in Organizations: From Managing
    Resistance to Integrating Employee Creativity   127
    Sylvie Grosjean and Luc Bonneville

PART III   EFFECTING CHANGE

8	The Management and Acceptance of Diversity *Natalia Dankova*	147
9	Enhancing Human Dignity through Philosophical Education *Sergio Castrillón*	159
10	Managing Human Dignity and Corporate Performance *Pierre-Paul Morin*	181

PART IV   CONCLUSIONS

| 11 | Governance, Dignity and Responsibility: Towards a Symbiosis
David Crowther and Ana-Maria Davila-Gomez | 195 |

Index 213

List of Figures and Tables

Figures

I.1	The triple bottom line	5
6.1	Task design characteristics	118
6.2	The inner and outer dimensions of dignity	120

Tables

6.1	Workers' stereotypes and their production contexts	100
6.2	Services types and workers' stereotypes	102
6.3	Knowledge worker definitions	106
6.4	The research design	111
6.5	Cases and their context	112
7.1	A few lexicographical definitions of the term resistance	131
7.2	Sources of resistance and suggested behaviours (responses)	133

Biographies of Editors

David Crowther is Professor of Corporate Social Responsibility and Head of the Centre for Research into Organisational Governance at De Montfort University, UK. He is also Chair of the Social Responsibility Research Network (www.socialresponsiblity.biz), editor of *Social Responsibility Journal* and Director of The Durability Institute. He has published more than 30 books and has also contributed 350 articles to academic, business and professional journals and to edited book collections. He has also spoken widely at conferences and seminars and acted as a consultant to a wide range of government, professional and commercial organizations. His research is into corporate governance and corporate social responsibility with a particular emphasis on the relationship between governance, social, environmental and financial performance.

Ana-Maria Davila-Gomez is an associate professor in the Department of Administrative Sciences at the University of Quebec (Université du Québec en Outaouais) in Canada, where she teaches Management, Organizational Change, and Interculturality. Her current researches include managers' challenges towards more socially responsible organizations, as well as human virtues and responsiveness from management education. She holds a PhD from the École des hautes etudes commerciales de Montréal, Canada, and an MBA and an Industrial Engineer degree from the Universidad del Valle, Colombia. For several years, she worked at various private and public organizations in Colombia (e.g., governmental service, telecommunications, and manufacturing) supporting and implementing Information Technology (IT) and Business Process Reengineering projects.

Biographies of Contributors

Luc Bonneville is an associate professor at the University of Ottawa (Department of Communication) and researcher at the Interdisciplinary Research Group in Organizational Communication (IRGOC). Luc Bonneville works on computerization of healthcare organizations, more precisely in an organizational communication perspective. He also works on the logics of implementation of information-communication technologies (ICTs) in the healthcare organizations, on the interactions between physicians, nurses, and so on, and patients in a technological environment.

Sergio Castrillón holds a PhD in Administration from HEC-Montréal. His doctoral thesis constitutes an original research about the philosophical foundations of management education from the perspective of senior professors. He combines critical perspectives with an in-depth reflection about wisdom, which is fully pertinent for the challenges that management education faces within contemporary societies. Professor Castrillón also holds a Masters degree in Intercultural Management from ICHEC Brussels Management School, and a Masters in Political Sciences from Antioquia University. He is a professor in EAFIT University, teaching at the undergraduate and postgraduate levels. His areas of interest are focused in management education, business and society, and organizations' responsibility.

Denyse Côté is a sociologist, political scientist, and community organizer; she is also Professor at the Départment of social work and social sciences of the Université du Québec en Outaouais and Director of ORÉGAND (Observatoire sur le développement régional et l'analyse différenciée selon les sexes). Her research interests concern social change and social innovation in the public and private spheres: in families, in local communities, by social movements, and in gender relations. She has been involved in a number of innovative third-sector projects as a community organizer, activist, and expert.

Natalia Dankova is a professor at the Université du Québec en Outaouais, Canada, in Language Studies. She completed her doctorate in language sciences in 1997, in Paris. She has worked in the fields of language teaching (French as a second or foreign language, Italian, Russian at the workplace) and research-wise she has focused in psycholinguistics and applied phonetics. She currently teaches linguistics, history of the French language and second language acquisition and applied phonetics. Natalia Dankova remains active in the field of francization of immigrants by offering assistance to teachers of French as a second language, and advising and supporting immigrants throughout their transition. Natalia Dankova publishes scientific papers concerning the second language acquisition, psycholinguistics, variation in French, spoken Esperanto and integration of immigrants in Canada.

Sylvie Grosjean is an associate professor in the Department of Communication at the University of Ottawa, Canada. She develops a pragmatic approach of the communication in organizations and her recent researches focus on the organizing properties of communication. Her current research interests include the coordination of actions in work teams (emergency situations, computer mediated communication), the role of technological artefacts (information system, workflow, and so on) and documents (reports, digital documents, and so on) on the team's cooperation and/or coordination and the mobilization of knowledge in organizations (process of organizational remembering). She is member of the Interdisciplinary Research Group in Organizational Communication (IRGOC) at the University of Ottawa. She is the co-editor of two French books *Repenser la communication dans les organizations* (2007) and *Introduction aux méthodes de recherche en communication* (2007).

Pierre-Paul Morin is a civil engineer and holds an MBA from the University of Miami as well as a doctoral degree in Project Management from the Université d'Aix-Marseille. His thesis was on human resource and change management in projects. He had a 25-year career as a CEO of consulting firms and hi-tech companies, and is now a full-time teacher at the Université du Québec en Outaouais. His research focuses on the management of technical processes and projects.

Sandra Socorro Lotero Patiño, is an MSc student in Project Management at the University of Quebec (Université du Québec en Outaouais), Canada. She holds a postgraduate diploma in Management from the Universidad Santo Tomás de Aquino, Colombia, and also a degree in Agronomy and a diploma in Animal Production, both from the Universidad de Santa Rosa de Cabal, Colombia. Her current researches are concerned with the ethical considerations for managers of social projects. For several years she has worked in Colombia within social projects whose aim is the development of micro-businesses, through the support and implementation of project methodology. Currently, she works as an assistant researcher at the university where she studies.

Silvia Ponce is Associate Professor at HEC Montreal, Quebec, Canada. She holds a Bachelors degree in Chemistry, a Masters degree in Chemical Engineering, and a PhD in Business Administration. She has extensive experience in R&D. For more than 20 years, she conducted fundamental and applied research on polymeric materials, publishing in recognized scientific periodicals of the field. She currently teaches Operations Strategy, Management of the Technological Innovation Process, and Production and Operations Management to undergraduate and graduate students (MBA, MSc and PhD programmes). She performs research on Operations Management, more precisely on Technological Innovation, Manufacturing Networks, Operations Strategy and Knowledge-Intensive Services (outsourcing R&D and Business Intelligence Services). She has directed more than 15 theses on technology transfers and innovation comprising, among others, case studies of high-tech enterprises (telecoms, aeronautics, pharma, biotechnology, nanotechnology, nutraceuticals), quality and business practices (Six Sigma, ISO 9000 and 14001, Qualimètre, Continuous Improvement), project management, service innovation and manufacturing networks.

Hillary J. Shaw is a senior lecturer at Harper Adams University College, Newport, Shropshire, UK, since October 2006. His main area of academic interest is into the global food system, and food retailing in particular. His research areas include food access by disadvantaged consumers, food deserts, the globalization of food retailing, and the corporate social responsibility of food retailers, global and local, towards the community they operate within. Hillary was awarded a PhD on his research into the extent and classification of food deserts from the University of Leeds in 2004. He has also undertaken a research project with the School of Geography, University of Southampton, UK, on the societal and economic effects of supermarkets opening local outlets in small towns in Hampshire.

Julia J.A. Shaw began her academic career at the University of Lancaster, where she held her first full-time lectureship and completed a jurisprudential doctoral thesis on Kant's moral philosophy and its application to ethical dilemmas arising in a formal legal context. Her PhD was awarded in December 1998. Accepting a post at Aston University's Business School, she became Director of Legal Studies and published in legal ethics and legal philosophy, also in business ethics and corporate governance. Following a visiting lectureship at Nantes University in France and as external examiner at Beijing University in China, Julia now holds a post at De Montfort Business and Law School in Leicester, UK. Maintaining an active interest the theory of moral responsibility and political philosophy, her research activities are mostly in the areas of socio-legal theory and CSR.

Étienne Simard is a Masters student in regional development at the Université du Québec en Outaouais. He has worked on several research projects in the field of local and regional governance. His thesis pertains to regional corporate citizenship in Québec. He has also been a student, community and union activist, in particular on issues of public transportation, financial access to post-secondary education, and democratic governance of public institutions.

Introduction: Managerial Responsibility for Human Dignity

ANA-MARIA DAVILA-GOMEZ AND DAVID CROWTHER

Introduction

One of the most significant issues in corporate social responsibility (CSR) at the moment is that of human rights. Normally this is taken to mean a concern with exploitation in the supply chain – child labour, slavery and so on in developing countries. Human rights of course applies equally to the treatment of employees in (and outside) the workplace. It is gradually being acknowledged that this too is a vital issue which is being addressed by companies and needs to be researched by academics in order to present a more rounded understanding of CSR and all of its dimensions. Indeed the treatment of employees is also widely recognized as an important aspect of sustainability. This book is therefore timely as concern for this subject is rising as a concern for sustainability – and its implications – rises. This book is different, however, as it takes multiple perspectives on the workplace and some of the issues which are not readily addressed in this literature – such as employee perspectives and the management of diversity.

Equally many works have looked at the responsibility of managers – particularly in the light of the crisis of governance – but mostly in the context of widening responsibility to incorporate a responsibility towards stakeholders. Such stakeholders are generally interpreted as being external to the corporation – customers, society and the like – whereas employees are claimed by all organizations to be one of the most important stakeholders. This is somewhat ironic in the light of normal behaviour towards employees, particularly the less senior and less qualified people. This book therefore takes a perspective on this and argues that there is a clear connection between maintaining the dignity of the workforce and corporate performance. It does this by elucidating managerial responsibility and setting the theme within the lens of sustainability and its components.

There has been a considerable shift in the perceptions of corporate social responsibility in recent time. It seems to have become generally accepted by businesses and their managers, by governments and their agencies, and by the general public that there is considerable benefit in engaging in CSR. Consequently every organization is increasingly going to have its CSR policy which will have been translated into activity. Despite the fact that many people remain cynical about the genuineness of such corporate activity, the evidence continues to mount that corporations are actually engaging in such socially responsible activity, not least because they recognize the benefits which accrue. It seems therefore that the battle is won and everyone accepts the need for CSR activity – all that remains for discussion is how exactly to engage in such activity and how to report upon that activity. Even this has been largely addressed through such vehicles as GRI and the recently introduced ISO26000.

Nevertheless the need for social responsibility is by no means universally accepted but evidence shows that ethical and socially responsible behaviour is being engaged in successfully by a number of large corporations – and this number is increasing all the time. Additionally there is no evidence that corporations which engage in socially responsible behaviour perform, in terms of profitability and the creation of shareholder value, any worse than do any other corporations. Indeed there is a growing body of evidence[1] that socially responsible behaviour leads to increased economic performance – at least in the longer term – and consequentially greater welfare and wealth for all involved.

All of this means that a wide variety of activities have been classed as representing CSR, ranging from altruism to triple bottom line reporting, and different approaches have been adopted in different countries, in different industries and even in different but similar corporations. And recently the agenda has shifted from a concern for corporate social responsibility to a concern for sustainability and many activities have been re-designated accordingly (Aras and Crowther, 2009a). This book takes a different perspective to normal and considers this activity in the context of the effect upon the people involved.

The Brundtland Report and After ...

At the present time the term sustainability is both a ubiquitous and a controversial topic because it means different things to different people. Nevertheless there is a growing awareness that this is a vital topic at the present which has raised concern about whether it can be delivered by multinational companies in the relatively straightforward way that they promise (World Commissions on Environment and Development (WCED), 1987; Schmidheiny, 1992). The starting point must be taken as the Brundtland Report (WCED, 1987) because there is general acceptance of the contents of that Report and because the definition of sustainability in there is pertinent and widely accepted. Equally, the Brundtland Report is part of a policy landscape being explicitly debated by the nation states and their agencies, big business supra-national bodies such as the United Nations through the vehicles of the WBCSD[2] and ICC,[3] (see for example Beder, 1997; Gray and Bebbington, 2001). Its concern with the effect which action taken in the present has upon the options available in the future has directly led to glib assumptions that sustainable development is both desirable and possible and that corporation can demonstrate sustainability merely by continuing to exist into the future (Aras and Crowther, 2008a). It is important therefore to remember the Brundtland Commission's (WCED, 1987: 1) definition of sustainable development that is the most accepted by everyone and used as the standard definition of sustainable development:

> ... development that meets the needs of the present without compromising the ability of future generations to meet their own needs.

---

1   See Crowther (2002) for detailed evidence.
2   World Business Council for Sustainable Development.
3   International Chamber of Commerce.

This report makes institutional and legal recommendations for change in order to confront common global problems. More and more, there is a growing consensus that firms and governments in partnership should accept moral responsibility for social welfare and for promoting individuals' interest in economic transactions (Amba-Rao, 1993).

Significantly, however, the Brundtland report made an assumption – which has been accepted ever since – that sustainable development was both possible and desirable; and the debate since has centred on how to achieve this. Thus ever since the Bruntland Report was produced by the World Commission on Environment and Development in 1987 there has been a continual debate concerning sustainable development (Chambers, 1994; Pretty, 1995). Similarly emphasis has been placed on such things as collaboration, partnerships and stakeholder involvement (Ladkin and Bertramini, 2002; Brown, Tompkins and Adger, 2002). It has, however, been generally accepted that development is desirable and that sustainable development is possible – with a concomitant focus on how to achieve this. Quite what is meant by such sustainable development has, however, been much less clear and a starting point for any evaluation must be to consider quite what is meant by these terms.

There is a considerable degree of confusion surrounding the concept of sustainability: for the purist sustainability implies nothing more than stasis – the ability to continue in an unchanged manner – but often it is taken to imply development in a sustainable manner (Marsden, 2000; Hart and Milstein, 2003) and the terms sustainability and sustainable development are for many viewed as synonymous. For us we take the definition as being concerned with stasis (Aras and Crowther, 2008b); at the corporate level if development is possible without jeopardizing that stasis then this is a bonus rather than a constituent part of that sustainability. Moreover, sustainable development is often misinterpreted as focusing solely on environmental issues. In reality, it is a much broader concept as sustainable development policies encompass three general policy areas: *economic, environmental and social*. In support of this, several United Nations texts, most recently the 2005 World Summit Outcome Document, refer to the *"interdependent and mutually reinforcing pillars"* of *sustainable development* as *economic development, social development, and environmental protection*.

Brundtland and Sustainability

The problem with Brundtland is that its concern with the effect which action taken in the present has upon the options available in the future has directly led to glib assumptions that sustainable development is both desirable and possible and that corporation can demonstrate sustainability merely by continuing to exist into the future (Aras and Crowther, 2008c). It has also led to an acceptance of what must be described as the myths of sustainability:

- sustainability is synonymous with sustainable development; and
- a sustainable company will exist merely by recognizing environmental and social issues and incorporating them into its strategic planning.

Both are based upon an unquestioning acceptance of market economics predicated in the need for growth and are based upon the false premise of Brundtland to which we will return later. An almost unquestioned assumption is that growth remains possible (Elliott, 2005) and therefore sustainability and sustainable development are synonymous. Indeed the economic perspective of post-Cartesian ontologies predominates and growth is considered to be not just possible but also desirable (see for example Spangenberg, 2004). So it is possible therefore for Daly (1992) to argue that the economics of development is all that needs to be addressed and that this can be dealt with through the market by the clear separation of the three basic economic goals of efficient allocation, equitable distribution and sustainable scale. Hart (1997) goes further and regards the concept of sustainable development merely as a business opportunity, arguing that once a company identifies its environmental strategy then opportunities for new products and services become apparent.

Sustainability is of course fundamental to a business and its continuing existence. It is equally fundamental to the continuing existence not just of current economic activity but also of the planet itself – at least in a way which we currently understand. It is a complex process, as we have discussed. Moreover it is a process which must recognize not just the decision being made in the operational activity of the organization but also the distributional decisions which are made. Only then can an organization be considered to be sustainable.

Others have tended to assume that a sustainable company will exist merely by recognizing environmental and social issues and incorporating them into its strategic planning. According to Marrewijk and Were (2003) there is no specific definition of corporate sustainability and each organization needs to devise its own definition to suit its purpose and objectives, although they seem to assume that corporate sustainability and corporate social responsibility are synonymous and based upon voluntary activity which includes environmental and social concern.

The Descendants of Brundtland

There have been various descendants of Brundtland, including the concept of the Triple Bottom Line (Aras and Crowther, 2008d). This in turn has led to an assumption that addressing the three aspects of economic, social and environmental is all that is necessary in order to ensure not just sustainability but to also enable sustainable development. Indeed the implicit assumption is one of business as usual – add some information about environmental performance and social performance to conventional financial reporting (the economic performance) and that equates to triple bottom line reporting. And all corporations imply that they have recognized the problems, addressed the issues and thereby ensured sustainable development. This implication is generally accepted without questioning – certainly without any rigorous questioning. Let us start with an investigation of the Triple Bottom Line – the three aspects of performance.

Sustainable development policies encompass these three general policy areas: *economic, environmental and social*. Reporting upon these three aspects has become known as Triple Bottom Line reporting and this has become a common feature within the reporting or both commercial firms and other organizations.

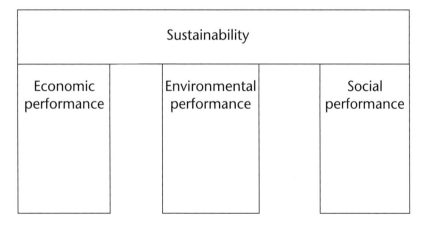

Figure I.1   The triple bottom line

It will be apparent of course that in order to achieve sustainable development[4] it is first necessary to achieve sustainability and there are a number of elements to this. What is important for sustainability is not just addressing each of these elements individually but also paying attention to maintaining the balance between them. It is the maintenance of this balance which is the most challenging – but also the most essential – aspect of managing sustainability. There are a number of elements which must be addressed but these can be grouped together into four major elements, which map exactly onto the model for evaluating sustainability outlined earlier. These four major elements of sustainability (Aras and Crowther, 2009b) therefore are:

- Maintaining economic activity, which must be the central *raison d'être* of corporate activity and the principle reason for organizing corporate activity.
- Conservation of the environment, which is essential for maintaining the options available to future generations.
- Ensuring social justice, which will include such activities as the elimination of poverty, the ensuring of human rights, the promotion of universal education and the facilitation of world peace.
- Developing spiritual and cultural values, which is where corporate and societal values align in the individual and where all of the other elements are promoted or negated; sadly at present they are mostly negated.

It is our contention that the current focus upon environmental issues – climate change, carbon footprints in particular – has led to a lessening of regard for the social issues. And what social issues are considered are based upon a concern for human rights in the supply chain. As a consequence employees and the effects within the workplace have tended to become ignored.

The concern with the supply chain of a business has assumed prominence; in other words with what is happening in other companies which that company does business with – their suppliers and the suppliers of their suppliers. In particular people are concerned

---

4   Many authors continue to assume both the possibility and desirability of sustainable development, hence our mentioning it. For us, however, the achievement of sustainability is both a necessary precondition and sufficient in itself.

with the exploitation of people in developing countries, especially the question of child labour but also such things as sweat shops.

So no longer is it acceptable for a company to say that the conditions under which their suppliers operate is outside their control and so they are not responsible. Customers have said that this is not acceptable and have called companies to account. And there have recently been a number of high-profile retail companies which have held their hands up to acknowledge problems and then taken very public steps to change this.

Interestingly the popularity of companies increases after they have admitted problems and taken steps to correct these problems. In doing this they are thereby showing both that honesty is the best practice and also that customers are reasonable. The evidence suggests that individual customers are understanding and that they do not expect perfection but do expect honesty and transparency. Moreover they also expect companies to make efforts to change their behaviour and to try to solve their CSR problems.

Companies themselves have also changed. No longer are they concerned with greenwashing – the pretence of socially responsible behaviour through artful reporting. Now companies are taking CSR much more seriously not just because they understand that it is a key to business success and can give them a strategic advantage, but also because people in those organizations care about social responsibility.

So it would be reasonable to claim that the growing importance of CSR and sustainability is being driven by individuals who care – but those individual are not just customers, they are also employees, managers, owners and investors of a company. So companies are partly reacting to external pressures and partly leading the development of responsible behaviour and reporting. These are issues reflected in the chapters of this volume.

In the first chapter Davila-Gomez and Crowther explore some concepts that we consider must be taken into account when reflecting about identities at work. These concepts are: axiology, conceived as what people value as good ways of acting; ontology as the being's experience of continuous self-discovery through perception and interpretation; and some psychoanalytical considerations. They pose a question about identity regarding how people value what their managers demand, or how they obey these demands without necessarily agreeing and preferably finding ways to avoiding additional workload, or to conserve their jobs, or how and what they cherish the most from their institutional and professional social image. Then they develop a critical reflection presenting some empirical data from some distance-learning courses, based on Information and Communication Technologies (ICT), from which we extract values and attitudes cherished by people within their interactions with their managers and colleagues. Some managerial implications are then presented.

In the second chapter Davila-Gomez and Socorro argue that worldwide reality shows us how human activity has historically procured progress and richness to some persons while generating impoverishment and neglect of human dignity to others as well as damage of the environment. Management activity, as the conductor of organizational actions, has its part in the reality we are dealing with nowadays. Responsibility is therefore an imperative for individuals in power in the decision-making process that affects communities and nature. In this sense, they argue for the need of virtues in managers in order to instil a sense of goodness and care in their behaviour, including as well human dignity to showing respect for others and nature. Therefore, they reflect about the need for a holistic approach which, to us, includes a glimpse of idealism and existentialism,

Introduction: Managerial Responsibility for Human Dignity

in order to implement countermeasures against the majority of managerial practices and theories that are based upon a positivistic and materialistic approach which, at its turn, is tied with an anthropocentric view that generates disregard for the wholeness. Finally they develop some reflections about these themes, and we present at the end some considerations for a better future.

According to Shaw and Shaw the history of business rhetoric, particularly that employed by the financial world, inevitably forms a critical contribution to the language of power, in which the history of profiteering is best conceived as a history of resistance to assuming social responsibility, an oppositional narrative. From this perspective, the financiers act recklessly and they do not relate immediately (if at all) to the consequences their own practices; rather they appear to connect only with the theory of their profession and the illusion of its unity in a single cause. Going beyond mere ethical laxity, this particular phantasm obscures and represses any question of legitimacy or responsibility in a wider sense. Such complication confers status and worth, and serves to justify for example the settlement of disproportionately large bonuses in a failing global economy. The purpose of this article is to examine the utility to business education of aesthetics, literature and the ancient ideal of the rule of law in an increasingly complex global environment. Recent financial scandals have exposed a range of vulnerabilities in the management decision-making process and, increasingly, big business is searching for ethical answers. It is suggested that there is a need to develop the necessary critical, analytical and empathic qualities of, in particular, the business student in order that our future global corporate leaders might also be moral managers.

Davila-Gomez and Crowther, in Chapter 4, consider that organizations are an intrinsic constituent of the *wholeness*; shareholders and managers must exercise *solidarity* and *sharing* when performing an organizational action. By means of a critical reflection based on Christian precepts such as *caring* and *concern*, they explore the current organizational disregard towards human, social and ecological parts of the whole. As managers are crucial in the organizational moral conduct, they inquire about the limits and possibilities of today's business education to encourage the aforementioned values. Moreover they present some possibilities for allowing the awakening of the student's consciousness towards reality and the need to change it, through, among others, sharing and solidarity within the collective and the whole.

Côté and Simard, in Chapter 5, examine how social movements are being influenced by corporate culture and how, through this influence, a tradition of social responsibility is being eroded. Local governance is now articulated in the Canadian province of Québec at the juncture of government and civil society. Local and regional levels of government have become central in this context of government decentralization. Strong endogenous social movements that were the hallmark of modern Québec society can no longer rely on a centralized (Québec) welfare state as their respondent, but rather on local and regional authorities. Confrontational politics have also practically disappeared and been replaced by "partnerships" between bureaucratic bodies and civil society. This has fostered a prevalence of corporate organizational culture in social movements. Community organizations are thus being mobilized by regional and local authorities in lieu of their bureaucratic organizations so as to implement their own priorities and agendas. Activism is rapidly dying out and social utopias and radicalism are also being regulated, albeit by the institutionalization and professionalization of community groups dependent for their economic survival on these new conditions of governance. Their analysis is based on data from three empirical research projects spanning 15 years, on participant observation of the phenomena under study as well as professional and personal participation in various community groups and associations.

During the last decades, knowledge and creativity have been giving place to a variety of new types of work. Knowledge workers and the creativity class have even been considered a "new" social class. Many authors and researchers have discussed issues concerning how to manage (or un-manage) these "special" workers. But very few (if any) have inquired about their hopes and ideals, their life-motifs and expectations in their relationships to work conditions, creativity expression and environment. In this chapter, Ponce presents and analyses a series of case-episodes, covering a wide range of knowledge-based and creative activities going from arts – painting, music and cinema – computer workers and engineers up to scientists and researchers. The cross-case analysis and the discussion of the human dignity dimension in these contexts bring to light common and underlying characteristics as well as misconceptions and managerial dysfunctions. Some propositions are developed in order to contribute in fulfilling workers hopes and expectations.

In the next chapter Dankova is concerned with such questions as what factors lead to assimilation and in what conditions can diversity be preserved. Multiculturalism manifests itself through both societal and individual multilingualism. However, the terms multilingualism and multiculturalism are most often used in reference to a society, rather than to an individual who has integrated several languages and cultures. She considers whether diversity and assimilation dependent on a collective and individual willingness can be assimilated or diversified. The chapter begins with an analysis of the dynamics of diversity and assimilation, based on the Canadian experience. Canada remains one of the few countries to advocate immigration. Its cultural and linguistic portrait changes with each wave of immigration and with the assimilation of Amerindian peoples and long-established immigrants. It continues by discussing the importance given to the cultural diversity of immigrants in the receiving society through reference to the public consultation organized by the Bouchard-Taylor Commission on *reasonable accommodations* carried out in the province of Québec in 2007–2008.

For modern society, multiculturalism has become both a problem and ambition: there is a desire to promote multiculturalism in society; however, the actions needed to accomplish this are not easy to undertake. The respect of cultural and linguistic differences is at the heart of the problems linked to human dignity and human rights. Acceptance of multilingualism by the state and by the individual contributes to civic peace and political stability, and to the successful integration of immigrants, especially in countries that promote immigration for demographic and economic reasons. Hence, she points out some managerial implications for both public and private directors of organizations in terms of multiculturalism and multilingualism. These reflections allow us to indicate some points of concern while considering multiculturalism in an international arena.

As Morin observes, human dignity is not a new concept. It was already a concern for Greek philosophers and, more recently, was confirmed as a legal principle in the 1948 Charter of Human Rights (General Assembly of the United Nations, 1948). Lately, it has become an issue in business research and publications. Even though it has been discussed for centuries, the applications of the concept have never been simple on the one part. Also, the definition of dignity itself and its evolution through time and societies make it an even more elusive concept. Based on recent European court judgments, not only was its application questioned, but a doubt on its relevancy was even raised. The principle of mutual responsibility was also introduced, opening a completely new perspective on the subject. Positivist and constructivist paradigms each shed a very different light on dignity. The ethics of utilitarianism, deontology and existentialism are also useful to better understand how dignity is interpreted in the specific context of business decisions. In this chapter he looks into these as well as the ideas of individual freedom, corporate rules and the potential conflicts between the two. He also examines the conscious motivations of individuals and groups as well as the unconscious sources of their behaviours through social roles. Furthermore he explains the relationship between reaching productivity objectives and fostering human dignity principles, two apparently opposing principles. Morin does this using the links between the strategic planning process and the conscious understanding of the corporate context, values and beliefs.

Crowther and Davila-Gomez argue that recent corporate behaviour has exposed multiple misdeeds which have in turn demonstrated many failures in governance which need to be addressed. Although much attention has been paid to these governance failures, there still remain, however, a surprisingly large number of pertinent issues which have barely been mentioned – and have certainly not been explored in detail – despite the fact that they need to be addressed in order to create an environment in which a similar set of circumstances will not reoccur and cause the next crisis. One such issue – an extremely important issue – is the relationship between risk and rewards. Elementary economic theory teaches us that enterprise is concerned with taking risk and that rewards accrues to those taking risk if they are successful. Risk of course means that success is uncertain and that failure is also a possible outcome. So taking risks does not always lead to gaining rewards. It therefore follows that the higher the level of risk which is taken the higher the level of rewards for success that should accrue because the chance of failure equally rises. Finance theory was developed in order to quantify the relationship between success and failure and make the rewards commensurate with the risk. This quantification ensured that arbitrage would occur to equalize the risk/reward relationship across various enterprises in a freely operating market system. These are things that we all learn as part of an introductory economics course. This risk – reward relationship is a necessary part of economic activity and so a necessary part of business life. Its severing has led to irresponsible behaviour and arguably to a loss of dignity – certainly on the part of those who have suffered from the corporate excess. This chapter provides an finale to this volume by seeking to reconnect these issues and to show that if all people are treated with dignity then not only is corporate behaviour inevitable responsible but also the crisis of governance will not recur.

References

Amba-Rao S. C. (1993); Multinational corporate social responsibility, ethics, interactions and third world governments: An agenda for the 1990s; *Journal of Business Ethics*, 12, 553–572.

Aras G and Crowther D. (2008a); Corporate sustainability reporting: a study in disingenuity?; *Journal of Business Ethics*, 87 (supp 1), 279–288.

Aras G. and Crowther D. (2008b); Governance and sustainability: An investigation into the relationship between corporate governance and corporate sustainability; *Management Decision*, 46 (3), 433–448.

Aras G. and Crowther D. (2008c); The social obligation of corporations; *Journal of Knowledge Globalization*, 1 (1), 43–59.

Aras G. and Crowther D. (2008d); Evaluating sustainability: A need for standards; *International Journal of Social and Environmental Accounting*, 2 (1), 19–35.

Aras G. and Crowther D. (2009a); The durable corporation in a time of financial and economic crisis; *Economics and Management*, 14, 211–217.

Aras G. and Crowther D. (2009b); *The Durable Corporation: Strategies for sustainable development*; Farnham; Gower.

Beder S. (1997); *Global Spin: The Corporate Assault on Environmentalism*; London; Green Books.

Brown K., Tompkins E. L. and Adger W. N. (2002); *Making Waves: Integrating coastal conservation and development*; London; Earthscan.

Chambers R. (1994); The origins and practice of participatory rural appraisal; *World Development*, 22 (7), 953–969.

Crowther D. (2002); *A Social Critique of Corporate Reporting*; Aldershot; Ashgate.

Daly H. E. (1992); Allocation, distribution, and scale: Towards an economics that is efficient, just, and sustainable; *Ecological Economics*, 6 (3), 185–193.

Elliott S. R. (2005); Sustainability: An economic perspective; *Resources Conservations and Recycling*, 44, 263–277.

Gray R. and Bebbington J. (2001); *Accounting for the Environment*; London; Sage.

Hart S. L. (1997); Beyond greening: Strategies for a sustainable world; *Harvard Business Review*, Jan/Feb 1997, 75 (1), 66–76.

Hart S. L. and Milstein M. B. (2003); Creating sustainable value; *Academy of Management Executive*, 17 (2), 56–67.

Ladkin A. and Bertramini A. M. (2002); Collaborative tourism planning: A case study of Cusco, Peru; *Current Issues in Tourism*, 5 (2), 71–93.

Marrewijk M. van and Werre M. (2003); Multiple levels of corporate sustainability; *Journal of Business Ethics*, 44 (2/3), 107–119.

Marsden C. (2000); The new corporate citizenship of big business: part of the solution to sustainability; *Business and Society Review*, 105 (1), 9–25.

Schmidheiny S. (1992); *Changing Course*; New York; MIT Press.

Spangenberg J. H. (2004); Reconciling sustainability and growth: Criteria, indicators, policies; *Sustainable Development*, 12, 74–86.

World Commission on Environment and Development (WCED) (1987); *Our Common Future* (The Brundtland Report); Oxford; Oxford University Press.

PART **I**

Understanding the Issues

It is not very long ago that corporate social responsibility was a new concept and very few people knew what it was. Certainly it was new to businesses and only a very few made any attempt to practise any aspect of it – indeed it was regarded as an extra cost for businesses who needed to be persuaded that they should become involved. But things have changed very quickly. Now almost everyone has heard of the concept of CSR and almost every business has a policy and a strategy for implementing aspects of CSR because they understand that the business benefits are enormous. And this is true for everywhere in the world. In this book we will examine the growth of the phenomenon of CSR and the benefits; and we will use examples from all over the world to illustrate that it is truly a global concept. We will develop our understanding of CSR in the context of its use in business and in society while at the same time developing our understanding of the theoretical underpinnings.

Most people initially think that they know what CSR is and how to behave responsibly – and everyone claims to be able to recognize socially responsible or irresponsible behaviour without necessarily being able to define it. So there is general agreement that CSR is about a company's concern for such things as community involvement, socially responsible products and processes, concern for the environment and socially responsible employee relations (Aras and Crowther, 2008). According to the European Commission (EC) CSR is about undertaking voluntary activity which demonstrates a concern for stakeholders. But it is here that a firm runs into problems – how to balance up the conflicting needs and expectations of various stakeholder groups while still being concerned with shareholders; how to practice sustainability; how to report this activity to those interested; how to decide if one activity more socially responsible that another. The situation is complex and conflicting. In this book therefore we are concerned with different aspects of CSR, both with theorizing and with implementing CSR in practice.

All of this concern for CSR has, however, focused primarily upon certain aspects of what is essentially a very broad topic. Currently it is undoubted that environmental issues – primarily concerning climate change and resource depletion – predominate the discourse. The effect of this is that the three pillars of sustainability identified by Brundtland have become unbalanced and social issues have become perceived as less important. When they are considered it tends to be in the context of human rights and the treatment (and probable exploitation) of workers along the supply chain. Thus there is a need to redress this concern and bring about a more equitable concern. Thus this section provides an introduction to some of the issues which are important but ignored.

References

Aras G. and Crowther D. (2008); The social obligation of corporations; *Journal of Knowledge Globalization*, 1 (1), 43–59.

CHAPTER 1

Self-Discovery of the Becoming Being *and* Some Managerial Implications

ANA-MARIA DAVILA-GOMEZ AND DAVID CROWTHER

Introduction

Many would not dispute that managers acting through and for an organization have a human responsibility in the sense of contributing to the continual development of the people working with them. Hereby, we are concerned with the manager's influence on the individual's interpretation of reality, seeking to present how sometimes there is conditioning, other times pressure, or simply put, free choice for the individual. As experiencing reality may cause satisfaction or discontent in individuals (see Pelzer, 2005; Carr, 1998), there is a need for mangers to act with greater concern towards others, which implies, taking into account others' meanings and not only those of shareholders. As pointed out by Verstraeten (1998), business administration entails also a sense of morals and ethics.

Thus, our paper explores some additional concepts that we consider must be taken into account when reflecting about identities at work. We discuss the way in which values are socially identified as good ways of acting (see Rokeach, 1973). An individual's identification with a set of values reflects the validity he grants to axiology, and consequently, her or his own reality (the being, the person – see Husserl, 1859–1938). As such, while identity includes the individual's experiences, her or his introspection and the continuous being of the individual, there is a call for the consideration of ontology.

Hence, it is imperative to include the interpretation process of the self (Perls, 1975) as well as some psychoanalytical considerations, and finally, their interconnections with axiology and ontology. In this sense, it is important that managers take into account the previous considerations in order to acknowledge the reality of their organizations, and not only the reality that the positivist managerial approach states (see for example the positivist-functionalist approach in Porter, 1998). Contrary to the above, we argue that organizations are called to be more responsible towards a wide range of stakeholders others than exclusively shareholders (see Crowther and Rayman-Bacchus, 2004). In this sense, to question the purposes behind organizational action is required in order to procure changes (see Alvesson and Willmott, 1996).

For the above, firstly, we present and discuss the aforementioned concepts that we claim are necessary. Secondly, we present our empirical data of some ICT based distance-learning courses, relating here the pertinence of the concepts that we introduce. At the end, we present our final remarks and conclusions. We choose to base our empirical data on an organizational process that includes Information Technology (IT) because of the complexity that it offers. As shown by Schwarz and Watson (2005), an individual who participates in an IT change may be confronted with multiple identities within the groups, depending on where the identities belong (formal or informal), the managerial style of her or his director, and the different phases of the IT project, among others. Moreover, Brocklehurst (2001) indicates that an IT introduction entails a deeper change in the nature of procedures and power relationships among the individuals, which questions and redefines identities at work. In this sense, Chia and King (1998) indicate that as organizations are in a continuous transformation, moreover when changes include novelties, organizational thought and theory need to pass to ontology of becoming. As such, in our view, the organizational becoming influences also the continuous self-discovery of the being (the individual's).

Complementarily, we consider that IT may be seen by some individuals as a means of productivity, but to others, and it is the case for education (see Davies and Crowther, 1995; Crowther, 2003), it is seen as a means of democratization and expansion of services (see Guri-Rosenblit, 1999). In this way, two different interpretations of an IT-related matter may be the cause of a variety of senses and meanings that depend on the purpose of their use. At the same time, as we treat identities at work, we explore how with our concepts (interpretation, axiology, ontology, intention, and so on) different perceptions and values are interpreted as an individual's ideal of work, or if it is the case, satisfactions or impediments to their integral life (inside and outside the organization).

Axiology and Values

Values are one of the most explored topics while conducting researches concerned by identities in organizations. In a sense, values are conceived as the precepts, a sort of norms of conduct, that a group, community, or congregation cherish as good for its collective (see d'Iribarne). In philosophy, this conception means axiology (see Morfaux and Lefranc, 2005).

At the same time, the specific values of a group allow to stand out the differences just as much as the similarities when comparing it with other groups (see d'Iribarne, 2002). Inside organizations, many kinds of groups are constituted; some are arranged in a formal way – for example, departments, units – and others emerge naturally – for example, colleagues who become friends and extend their relationships outside work. For the first kind, formally arranged groups, there is enough management theory supporting their conformation, such as the structuration of work – for example, knowledge management, (see Davenport and Prusak, 1998). We argue that, first of all, this follows the classical precepts of bureaucracy (see Weber, 1864–1920) which allows the establishment of hierarchy, norms, and procedures, and secondly, this continues to answer to Taylor's scientific prerogative of productivity in which people, resources, and time are allocated to activities that allow the maximization of performance in every possible way (see Taylor, 1856–1915).

For the second kind of constituted groups, the informal, there are other types of social structures that emerge, not always as a result of strategic planning, but mostly as an abstract socially accepted way of doing things. For these groups, Organization Theory recognizes the influence of Giddens' (1984) works, as well as the sociological component of human and group's interactions (see Crozier and Friedberg, 1977). To these emergent and natural organizational phenomena, some give the name of "organizational culture" (see d'Iribarne, 2002) as a specific way in which the organization, as a whole proceeds internally and externally with some characteristic values, habits, and customs. Hereby, while associating a human characteristic to an impersonal entity (the organizational image), we allow the organization to have an identity given the fact that we are putting inside of it, norms and ways of doing things while following group values. The question here is that there is in fact a culture that may represent, to some extent, the behaviour of an organization as a whole – as an entity. This is, however, the result of not only one group, but instead of many formal and informal groups, which at their turn, constitute an agglomeration of behaviours and values that people, individually, cherish.

Self-Identification and Others' Expectations

The latter is also valid when we enter the field of the individual's identification in a group, and in a broader scope, to the explicit and formalized organizational values. As we know, it is through the formalized process of strategic planning that vision, mission, and organizational values are established (see Porter, 1998). While this follows a positivistic approach, the purposes of those in power are taken into account and, therefore, the established often values do not reflect the values shared by other groups inside the organization, nor what individuals inside groups cherish. As such, people without power inside a hierarchy find themselves following norms and values at work that do not necessarily have any meaning to them. Consequently, many people do not find a meaning for what they do at work other than an economic reward that allows them to excel in other arenas of their integral life (for example, family, hobbies, and so on). Sometimes people accept others' expectations without questioning themselves because either it may represent an opportunity for career success, or it allows them to be protected against their superior's abuse of authority (that is, what Collinson (2003) defines as *Conformist selves* in search of security). Therefore, we argue that there are also those who may not share the imposed values; however, following them represents the opportunity to be promoted in the hierarchy, therefore, presenting a way to fulfil their professional careers, regardless of the organizational mission.

Based upon a psychoanalytical approach, Carr (1998) indicates that the acceptance of individuals for following the organizational values, or assigned activities, is sometimes conscious and other times unconscious. In some cases, a not totally conscious motive of the action of an individual is answering its super-ego's external world of expectations. By the same token, and as explained by Crowther and Davila-Gomez (2006), a past desire to please the phantom figure of a strict parent who demands success, triggers a manager to excel in a world of global competitiveness. Following Freud (1856–1939), this represents an identification.[1] This indicates that the identification of individuals with

---

1   This is what has been described by Crowther (2002) as the drive for individuation.

their work may be understood in various aspects. One aspect represents the occasion for an individual to excel as a professional; another aspect includes the opportunity to find means for fulfilment in other arenas (for example, family), while for other individuals it is simply an authentic shared value with the organization's mission, and finally, from any of these aspects, there may be a hidden motive of which the individual is not always totally conscious about.

On the other hand, dissent, conflict and behavioural problems in organizations may be seen as a response from people to some repressive managerial methods, given that direct protestation is not always permissible. Here, a complementary avenue to express feelings and opinions is found. As an authoritarian threatening figure (see Merleau-Ponty, 1975) a superior may appear as a controlling phantom figure of a parent for someone, or as a challenging endeavour of change for others. As repression and emotions foster inside the organization, the manifestations of anger in individuals are evident; as Pelzer points out:

> *Research indicates that we become angry when our self-concept or public image is under attack; when we face physical and verbal aggression; when our plans are interrupted; when we are unfairly treated; when we face incompetence, both because of ignorance or egocentric motives; when we face a relationship threat; and when a situation evokes generalised learned responses. Indeed even when there is no apparent anger-provoking event, anger may be aroused when people experience discomfort or depression. (Pelzer 2005:115)*

As explained by Freud (1856–1939) and Klein and Riviere (1964), what a being understands and interprets as the action capabilities of another being towards him or her, is intrinsically linked with childhood experiences. In some cases, these experiences may have been very unpleasant and, therefore, many of them are hidden in the unconscious, which later obliges the person to construct defensive barriers to avoid similar situations that may reproduce that pain.[2] As those experiences lay in the unconscious, employees may see the manager's behaviours and attitudes as supportive, threatening or challenging. It goes the same for managers, who could see a possible rebellion in an individual who does not follow the explicit rules – the strategic values – or who questions the proposed strategic plan of the firm. Nevertheless, the manager may see in a challenging individual quite the opposite: a human being who merits a promotion and who has a promising career, because, among others, some of the demanded skills for managers are risk, tenacity and commitment. Either view is possible for the same person, depending upon the viewpoint of the manager, because of the expectations and interpretations created through her or his unconscious.

Therefore, as power relationships are present in the reality of the organizations, it is important to elucidate what is cherished and considered as good by the individuals regarding the behaviour of others; mostly, those who have more power, for us, directors and managers. The way in which socially accepted values (either explicit or not) are also identified by individuals as the other individual's way of acting, is essential for a manager,

---

[2] This results in an inner conflict which has been interpreted by Bettelheim (1976) as part of the search for meaning to life through the reintegration of the conscious and the unconscious (Bettelehim, 1984). It has been described (Fromm, 1974) as a battle between the opposing instincts of life and death or between the idealist and materialist strivings of the individual (Fromm, 1980). For some people this can be reflected in a drive towards conformity as a means of escaping from the isolation of the self (Fromm, 1957). In extreme circumstances this can result in a person resorting to madness by attempting to hold what Laing (1961) describes as an untenable position. They can also result in paranoid behaviour through the dominance of feelings of guilt (Klein, 1932) or in psychosis (Lawrence, 1995).

not only to obtaining collaboration (as sold by the positivist theory of organizational behaviour – for example, Kolb, Rubin and McIntyre (1984) – or conductive change management – for example, Kotter (1996)) but mostly for contributing to a common development of the collective in a sense of wholeness (see Marcel, 1965). Hereby, referring to this way of acting, as individual's attitudes, and in the sense of finding some good attitudes, we enter the domain of human qualities that we relate with what Socrates highlighted as virtues (see the *Meno* dialogue in Plato, 428–347 BC). Consequently, a virtuous manager may procure satisfaction and fulfilment for his employees, or at least, less dissent or discomfort than the majority of other managers. Thus, it is important to explore what individuals cherish as good values and what might managers do in order to facilitate personal fulfilment to others.

Ontology, Meanings and Satisfaction

As the individual may be conscious or not about her or his identification or acceptance with the organizational cause, and with the work assigned within, it is important to explore how this happens, and if possible, and to a certain extent, how this is linked directly with a self-acceptance of discomfort. As such, we enter the field of ontology, given that whatever makes sense to a person is directly related with whatever she or he is experiencing or whatever constitutes her or his being. As ontology refers to the science of the being, not in a static manner, but mostly in the dynamic process of *becoming being* (in a sort of a continuous experience), the organizational experience influences the being experience and vice versa.

Husserl (1859–1938) gives the name of phenomenology to this process of reflexivity, in which perception through the senses complements with the inner psyche life of the individual in order to obtain an abstraction of reality, which has some external objective components, as well as some internal and subjective components. According to Husserl, through perception and subjectivity, the individual establishes a subjective truth of a reality, and that, by means of introspection, while the experience of reality is occurring. Here, an a priori knowledge modifies actual and on-coming knowledge. For any action, perception occurs and a meaning is given to this occurrence as an imminent constituent of the interpretation; therefore, the action inside that reality contains intentions. As such, and as sustained not only by Husserl but also by Schelling (1775–1854), truth about a reality may be different for various persons, depending on their own experiences and their unique life, because, among other things, the interpretative schemas of each individual are in a continuous co-construction through subjective reasoning and others' expectations, as well as alternative explanatory avenues.

Schelling values the subjective activity of the being in the sense of intuition of the external objective world. To him, it is freedom which allows a person to exercise her or his reflective capabilities, to achieve the ideal of a reality (an idea), and also of the self. As freedom enables the *being* to continuously *become being*, it constitutes also a choice, and as such, it represents willingness to do so. In our view, it is this will, and this free choice that occurs in every instant when a person is interpreting the meaning of actions. In the case of managers, this implies that an interpretation process takes place when they are making decisions and acting. Therefore, managers can evaluate the possible consequences of decisions and actions.

Hence, the individual's free will to act contains the capacity of being responsible towards others. We claim the need for a signification of actions (that is, satisfaction and self-realization). In the same way in which shareholders and directors increase their capital by means of organizations' actions, norms and procedures, which gives them in a way some satisfaction and meaning, there is also a need to demand the right that people working in organizations find within a meaning, a signification, and as an ideal, a complementary part of their entire fulfilment as a being.

In this sense, identity for managers should not only be oriented with organizational strategic values, but also with other stakeholders' needs and realities. As such, identity and self-identification towards something or towards the needs and values of someone or even of a group, is a question of choice, of will.

Empirical Data: ICT, Distance Learning and Continuous Redefinition of Identities

To address the aforementioned reflections in a practical case, we present here a meta-analysis of empirical data coming from the following sources: a recent study of ICT distance learning, the biographical experiences of the authors as academics, and other research in the domain of distance learning that constitute our documentary sources. From the first source, we take into account a qualitative study that we conducted in two postgraduate management programmes offered in the distance learning modality with the ICT support (one in Quebec, Canada, and the other one in Mexico).[3] From our biographical experience, we have considered the development of various courses we have taught in England and in Latin America, as well as some remarks and comments that we have obtained while interacting with other professors that have also developed distance-learning courses or programmes. Finally, for the documentary sources, we take mostly what is presented in various websites of business programmes using distance learning,[4] and organizations for international development aids encouraging distance learning.[5]

To develop a meta-analysis that includes the complexity of the three empirical sources, we followed an interpretative approach in the sense of the hermeneutics (see Gusdorf, 1988). As follows, we present three cases: (i) the complex role of individuals who act simultaneously as professors and project managers, (ii) the administrative staff assistants who must act as conciliators, and (iii) the professional expert in IT or pedagogy.

---

3   In a non-published research note, a preliminary analysis of some empirical data was presented at the 22nd Standing Conference on Organizational Symbolism – SCOS 2004 (under the title of "Sensemaking of Information Technology Solutions: The Need to Integrate the Actor's action-meaning – Individuals, Community and Organizations") in order to gain feedback and academic insight before submitting it for peer-review publication. Therefore, in the paper we develop here, we made an in-depth critical reflection of the whole empirical data, introducing also additional concepts and data coming from other empirical fields.

4   We consulted various important distance-learning programmes in business administration in North America, Latin America and the UK, such as Athabasca University (Canada, http://www.mba.athabascau.ca/Titan/aucimwebsite.nsf/frmHome?OpenForm), TéléUniversité (Canada, http://www.teluq.uquebec.ca/), Open Business School (UK, http://www.open.ac.uk/oubs/), Harvard Business School – Executive Education (USA, http://www.exed.hbs.edu/products/tel/index.html), Penn State (USA, http://www.worldcampus.psu.edu/iMBA.shtml), and *Universidad Virtual del Tecnológico de Monterrey* (Mexico, http://www.ruv.itesm.mx/portal/principal/oe/). We consulted the websites in July 2006 for the last time.

5   Among others, we consulted the website of Unesco – Education and ICTs (http://portal.unesco.org/education/en/ev.php-URL_ID=18613&URL_DO=DO_TOPIC&URL_SECTION=201.html) which refers distance-learning projects and initiatives worldwide (some of them in business education). We consulted the website in July 2006 for the last time.

Polyvalent Identity: Professor or Project Manager?

When distance learning appears as a diversification activity in a university that educates in a traditional way (where the presence of students and professors is required), professors, already under contract in the organization are asked to collaborate with the new method of delivery. A project of distance-learning courses (or programme) is launched, and normally, someone who is an expert in IT, manages it. However, as time goes by and educational decisions need to be made, the institutional direction realizes that it is better for the project if its management is changed. Consequently, a professor becomes project manager, and very often, this person is someone who has had a previous experience in managing a department or in other kind of institutional projects, all of them, where the aim was the axiological social value of education. As this new project includes not only an educational component (democratization), but also the goal to achieve productivity by means of IT (therefore more students representing more money, market expansion – the marketization of higher education referred to by Crowther (2003) – including international sites, and so on), some professors ask themselves if all the energy invested in implementing the project is worth the effort in their personal lives. As such, in the sense of maintaining a security at work (Collinson, 2003), some professors seek also to prove to their university director their value as managers, adding to their already well-earned reputation as educators.

Sometimes, professors assigned as project managers do not have all the technological expertise required, and they see themselves intervening with IT departments, or other business units of their own institution, in order to obtain support to take better decisions within the project; in other occasions, in order to obtain help when something does not work appropriately. An incremental workload is put in the professor's shoulders,[6] because she or he does not stop being a professor who teaches and investigates as well in her or his academic discipline.

Furthermore, professors as managers should confront many times institutional strategic plans, propose new avenues, and also, deal with their superior's humour and personality. This is critical in the case where an educational project includes also other institutions and therefore inter-organizational dynamics. For some professors who have gone through this experience, often the senior managers have put on their shoulders a huge responsibility without the required liberty and tools to make decisions or to advance in the project. As we have observed, sometimes the self-reflection that a professor makes occurs after the action has already taken place, because, at the moment when the action was occurring (for example, the implementation of an ICT learning course) for many people, at that moment, it was more important to perform well, meeting a deadline, in order to keep their jobs; it represented a safety issue.

Whatever the case, some professors find, in the previous experiences, the occasion to prove themselves as managers, and in doing so, they test the axiological validity of the concepts they normally teach in their management courses. For some professors, project

---

6   Thus, higher education has experienced the emergence of distance-learning modules based on the new ICT, with developments apparently being driven largely by the desire to increase teaching efficiency. In general, courseware developed using this technology has been based on the traditional model of learning which is concerned with the interaction between teacher and learner, and in which the teaching strategy is dependent upon students' needs and preferred learning styles (Crowther and Davies, 1996a,b; Davies and Crowther, 1995). Technology has generally been regarded as having a subordinate role in this process.

experiences enrich their knowledge to the extent of showing them how organizational dynamics (departments, professions, hierarchies, collaborators) are more complex than what they appear to be in theory. Some professors use these experiences as a case study of organizational change, while others recognize that productivity pressures that arise from IT implementations invade also other spaces of their life (privacy, family time, leisure time, and so on). Professors need to allocate more time to comprehend their newly transformed duties. As some professors indicated, this experience shows them also the reality, in which many of the manager's complaints and their assistant's needs are not always listened to, by their superiors (directors or shareholders). Therefore, professors who experience a feeling of isolation or a feeling of being ignored, acknowledge that these kinds of feelings may appear in any organizational situation.

On the other hand, when a programme or a course is completely implemented to be given in the distance learning mode, there is always a need to teach it differently. It is as if conceptualization, planning and organization processes have done their part, and the action begins; the project as such has finished. In this new way of doing things, there is a need to improvise, even if a professor is very organized and a technical and pedagogical staff is available to support him or her. Following Bengtsson (2006), we identify that through a Life-World approach, the continuous pedagogical practice that entails the phenomenological experience of being a professor, enables innovation, accommodation and integration of new activities that are intrinsic to reality.

Some professors find that while teaching by distance learning they are losing the human contact with their students, because many interactions are no longer synchronous or face-to-face. Others find, as well, that teaching a course to 150 students simultaneously (which would represent a desirable productivity aim) eliminates for them the possibility of interacting more directly with the professor, given the fact that there is not enough time to talk (or to write emails on a personal basis, rather than collectively) to each one of the students. Some professors feel that the potentiality and impact of their courses has diminished because of the lost opportunity to attend, directly, the students' questions.

On the contrary, some professors identify that distance learning is not a mere question of productivity, and that similar results to those obtained in a course requiring actual presence are always possible with ICT aids. As such, some professors cherish a lot the possibility of a teleconference with synchronic interaction, which to some extent is possible if the satellite posts are interconnected to allow telephonic conversations in order to solve doubts. In this scenario, the size of a course cohort is not necessarily so big, and a more adequate surveillance of the students is possible. The problem with this technology is that it is very expensive; therefore, educational institutions favour asynchronic interactions (email, web pages, written mail, and so on).

Complementary to the preference of synchronous or asynchronous interaction, as we have observed, there is the consideration that while some societies value more the possibility of interacting face to face, others prefer a less intense form of personalized interaction. As such, we have seen that in most of the Latin American countries, the majority of students and professors prefer to interact by means of teleconferences through a simulated face-to-face interaction, whereas most of the students and professors of Anglo-Saxon countries value the asynchronic possibility because it offers them the possibility to control and organize their time, to gain and to give independence from and to everyone, respectively. Nevertheless, every case has its exceptions, and it is here when we recognize that even if there are some axiological general values for a community, the opportunity for an individual's different way of thinking is always pertinent, and as such, the ontology allows self-preferences even if they are different from the group to which someone belongs.

As shown, the normal activities that a professor was used to performing are now transformed. A polyvalence of duties is asked and improvisation and creation help to accommodate the professor for the new ways of acting. In the process of change, identities are questioned in the sense that professors experience fear of not being up to the expectations and consequently unable to perform as asked with the new IT; nevertheless, satisfaction is also experienced, after difficulties and problems are dealt with and the project and the course are nicely delivered. Ontological reflexivity is exercised because of the continuous questioning of the validity of the actions, projects and purposes. Professors, as any other human being, have also other social ties (family, community), therefore, their aim is not just their professional career but also the time they are able to spend outside the organization. In a sense, all the implications and situations that professors experience through distance learning constitute a learning opportunity that helps them to realize the importance of some human and social aspects that are mostly neglected in the traditional positivistic orientation of the dominant organization theory.

Conciliation and Mediation Agents

Alongside the professor's experiences there is also what other individuals feel and perceive. Many interactions, assignments and students' duties happen in a cyber world that professors do not control entirely. On the one hand, in the case of a course of 150 students, as it is impossible for the professor to be able to interact directly with each student in a continuous manner, there is a need for having some personnel support. On the other hand, even in the case of a course of 30 students where a direct interaction is more possible, there is, however, the need to send written material to students, to collect their responses and work, to actualize Web pages, to survey good IT functioning, to inform students about institutional policies, assignment dates and transcripts, among others. A completely new set of logistical activities emerge.

This complexity of the educational function is then alleviated to some extent by means of employees acting as *coordinators* or *tutors* that help professors and the university in their duty. In these new posts, a coordinator may serve simultaneously, various professors in different logistical activities, and a tutor may do the teaching assistance by sending corrections and interacting with students on behalf of various professors. Coordinators and tutors allowed themselves to indicate to us what they value the most in their interaction with professors who are acting as project managers. They told us that every professor is different, and even if two professors teach the same course, the experience with each one is not the same, even if in some cases the material is standard. Professors are seen by many employees as sort of an "elite" in the organization (that is, as explained by Alvesson and Robertson (2006) regarding power and control of situations). In that sense, we observed how many coordinators and tutors decided to serve professors almost without a major questioning of the professor's power, because, among others, professors represent the axiological social image of the organization's mission. Professors are those who finally deliver the service of education. This acceptance of power represents a social norm that is not explicit in the written organizational values; however, it is acknowledged as an informal reality.

On the other hand, even if the authority of the professor is not necessarily questioned, there is, however, a proposition of alternatives that coordinators make to professors in order to improve their interactional approach with students or other administrative instances of the university. As indicated by Dillenbourg (1999), through interaction, a negotiation of meanings and interests is needed while collaborating in groups. As interactions increase in time, coordinators and tutors learn to know, identify and differentiate their managers – the professors. The interaction that each professor demands is different. Each professor has her or his own pedagogy and a unique approach to interacting with students. As well, each professor has her or his own personality and, therefore, different attitudes and qualities while interacting. Even if we talk about distance learning, much of the interactions between professors and coordinators or tutors are face-to-face and synchronic, therefore, perceptions and interpretations in individuals take place in the very instant when they are occurring.

Consequently, in order to maintain good relationships with everybody, to solve any concerns, to answer sometimes violent emails, to alleviate the students' fears of failure, coordinators and tutors told us that they have to develop a sense of empathy, tolerance, and openness towards the different styles they have to handle. They need to identify personalities and what other individuals value as good. They see themselves as conciliators between professors and students, professors and the university administration, students and the university administration.

What is very interesting in this matter is the fact that these attitudes are not explicit in any written code of conduct or in any axiological statement. They do not make part of the strategic values of the organization. This is something that, in a separate way, almost every coordinator identifies as a requirement to perform well in its job. In our opinion, it is an informal set of values, an axiology that goes beyond norms, an axiology that answers the very essence of its meaning: well serve the community – students, professors and the institution. Consequently, when we ask coordinators and tutors about their inner motives to perform their posts, they identify almost instantaneously the social service with which they collaborate: education as a priority for a nation's development, and also they identified a human moral duty of helping others to negotiate, to calm differences. Equally, when we asked them about how do they perceive their work is affecting them, many told us that they experienced a sense of satisfaction every time that a problem is solved through their help, and also when they see their collaboration represented in a course that is modified, improved, or simply when they see a student graduate. In addition, they feel very satisfied when a professor – one of their managers – recognizes the help and effort invested in their tasks.

Complementarily, some of the tutors and coordinators are also students in the distance learning modality, and they told us that this allows them to organize better their time with other activities (family, community). Additional to the multiple managers-professors they have, they work under a hierarchical supervisor, who often is also a professor entrusted with an administrative function. In the same way employees struggle with their director, coordinators experience also the same type of struggle with professors when the latter act as project managers. A coordinator may feel that his supervisor is open, stubborn, imposing, authoritarian, even a conciliator, or a humanistic director. As such, coordinators have formal (department director) and informal managers (professors), and they need to balance well the relationships with all of them in order to not neglect any of them. Naturally, conflicts arise and inter-departmental or inter-hierarchical disputes occur.

As with any employee, coordinators suffer from the lack of support of their directors as well as feeling abandoned in the midst of their job. Therefore, what they cherish the most in their directors' attitudes is when they demonstrate with acts that they are concerned by the problems of others. For us, in this identification, those who conciliate and help others to solve problems expect of others to act likewise. Ontology of goodness and social awareness is then developed in coordinators as part of their experience of being.

Professionalism and Career Ideals

As we have observed, and as it has been confirmed by various employees, even though pedagogical and technical experts recognize the social value of the institution for which they work, they seem, however, to be more satisfied by the accomplishment of their own professional activity. Technical careers enable people to be satisfied while offering to the organization some alternative ways of increasing productivity. These persons have a high sense of creativity and cherish the opportunity of collaborating and solving problems through inventive and resourcefulness. They help professors to improve their didactical material, to increase their computers' speed in order to have a better response time while interacting with other people, and to propose new pedagogical activities that will improve interrelationships with students.

They criticize, however, how some professors or people in administrative posts do not recognize some of the potentialities these techniques have to offer for organizational improvement. They are also concerned by the way in which some employees, at any hierarchical level, show lack of interest in technical progress. As well as coordinators needing recognition, pedagogical and technical experts indicate that they prefer to work with professors (who also act now as project managers) who act as good leaders in teams, which includes listening and furnishing material and monetary resources to implement the improvements. Equally, they also have a director of their own department, from whom they expect good treatment and support. As the majority of the activities that experts carry out are related to projects, few of them see their work as an increase in their workload, except when one person is participating in so many projects that she or he needs a little support from his colleagues. Hereby, they cherish the fact that their directors are open and vigilant to distribute evenly the workload and that each one of them receives a fair amount and nature of the projects that are assigned among them.

In their social experience, these experts work daily with people of other departments, learn a lot of other activities, and value teamwork with humanistic leadership. This axiology helps them to contextualize the impact of their job for the benefit of the organization as a whole. This gives them satisfaction. They appreciate the social objective of their organization, and in their ontology, they experience a continual professionalization that never ends because of the constant complexity of the problems they need to face, the new solutions, the innovation and the external world of technical actualization.

Concluding Remarks: Managers' Self-Discovery and Openness to Otherness

Our data confirms what Llewellyn (2004) refers to as a redefinition of identities while implementing change. However, as our data indicates, identity and values in an individual go beyond the group to where they belong. Regardless of the profession, job, or hierarchical position, the values that many people cherish the most are those in which the collective is represented. Education, integrity, dedication, care and concern for others are well introspected as axiological ideals. Complementarily, for almost every one, in order for an organization, a team, or a project, to contribute well to the development of the collective, managers should demonstrate attitudes and qualities of assertiveness, openness, listening and caring. As coordinators indicated, empathy, conciliation and openness are possible not only for people in a hierarchical structure, but also for anyone at any level. As such, even if coordinators occupy a powerless post, they have, however, the power to conduct well and mediate efficiently all the activities.

For the manager, there is a need to gain confidence. As our empirical data shows, this is possible when managers' attitudes demonstrate comprehension, openness and sensibility to others' problems, conflicts and interests. As many people told us, this is a process that takes time, in which demonstration through experiences, in fact, shows how a person behaves. More than promises or good statements (explicit organizational values), people judge and interpret the value of others mostly by their actions. Even if value statements and conduct codes are necessary in order to establish social rules, they are not enough. There is a need for behaviour exemplarity. An axiology that contains values that people introspect as valid is more accepted. People perceive and interpret continuously the validity of values that are imposed as code of conduct, and when these do not make sense, people may accept them but mostly by means of resignation, because ontologically, these just resemble the values that their inner self really cherishes.

Complementarily, in the knowledge of others, first impressions are very delicate, because others' interpretation of our reality begins with the perceptions they have regarding us. The idea, the truth that we construct about others, as well as our own comprehension of our self-identity, is a result of continuous interactions. The perception someone has about our attitudes and social values enter to question every new experience that threatens the solidity of concepts before introspected. For a better understanding of employees' interactions among themselves and with managers, it is imperative to develop an openness to the different ways of interpretation, and the relative truth that comes within.

Hence, managers are also human, and they have to be very tactful in their relationships with others given the fragility of the human aspect. Even a non-premeditated intention of causing distress to others might present if the self is dominated by unconscious motives or super-ego expectations (those of parents, directors or society). However, as we claim, even though we may be unconscious of some of our motives, in the moral sense, we have a consciousness that tells us what is right or wrong (that is, what Davila-Gomez (2005) and Solomon (1998) argue as imperative for managers to conduct ethically). Therefore, it is important for managers to acknowledge their inner self. In doing so, self-reflection about their unconscious motives may allow them to conduct an introspective examination of their past in order to elucidate the inner motives of their intentions behind their actions, and therefore if necessary, be enabled to change attitudes towards others, and also, to reconsider organizational decisions and directors' orders.

The discovery of the inner-self represents an ontology of self-appreciation and self-identification in which the individual continuously rediscovers and complements himself while experiencing his *becoming being*. As a key to start questioning the purposes that lie behind organizational actions – and also the nature of shareholders' values – and ultimately shareholders' strategies, for the *becoming being*, there is first the need to exercise a self-reflection to unveil her or his own meanings.

References

Alvesson, M. and Robertson, M. (2006) "The Best and the Brightest: The Construction, Significance and Effects of Elite Identities in Consulting Firms", *Organization* 13(2): 195–224.

Alvesson, M. and Willmot, H. (1996) *Making Sense of Management: A Critical Introduction*. London: Sage.

Bengtsson, J. (2006) "The Many Identities of Pedagogics as Challenge: Towards an Ontology of Pedagogical Research as Pedagogical Practice", *Educational Philosophy and Theory* 38(2): 115–128.

Bettelheim, B. (1984) *Freud and Man's Soul*. New York: Vintage.

Bettelheim, B. (1976) *The Uses of Enchantment*. London: Penguin.

Brocklehurst, M. (2001) "Power, Identity and New Technology Homework: Implications for 'New Forms' of Organizing", *Organization Studies* 22(3): 445–466.

Carr, A. (1998) "Identity, Compliance and Dissent in Organizations: A Psychoanalytic Perspective", *Organization* 5(1): 81–99.

Chia, R. and King, I. (1998) "The Organization Structuring of Novelty", *Organization* 5(4): 461–478.

Collinson, D.L. (2003) "Identities and Insecurities: Selves at Work", *Organization* 10(3): 527–547.

Crowther, D. (2003) "Social Responsibility and the Marketisation of Higher Education", *Staff and Educational Development International*, India 7(1): 23–40.

Crowther, D. (2002) "Psychoanalysis and Auditing", S. Clegg (ed.) *Paradoxical New Directions in Management and Organization Theory*, pp. 227–246. Amsterdam: J. Benjamins.

Crowther, D. and Davila-Gomez, A.M. (2006) "Is Lying the Best Way of Telling the Truth", *Social Responsibility Journal* 1(3 and 4): 128–141.

Crowther, D. and Rayman-Bacchus, L. (2004) "The Future of Corporate Social Responsibility", in D. Crowther and L. Rayman-Bacchus (eds) *Perspectives on Corporate Social Responsibility*, pp. 229–249. Aldershot: Ashgate.

Crowther, D. and Davies, M.L. (1996a) "Multimedia, Mesmerism and Teaching Strategy", *CALECO 95 Conference Proceedings* (September), Bristol, pp. 11–17.

Crowther, D. and Davies, M.L. (1996b) "Case Studies in Teaching Accounting – The Way Forward Using Multimedia as a Delivery Vehicle", *7th CTI-AFM Conference Proceedings* (April), Brighton, pp. 12–19.

Crozier, M. and Friedberg, E. (1977) *L'acteur et le système: les contraintes de l'action collective*. Paris: Seuil.

Davenport, T.H. and Prusak, L. (1998) *Working Knowledge: How Organizations Manage What They Know*. Boston: Harvard Business School Press.

Davies, M.L. and Crowther, D. (1995) "The Benefits of Using Multimedia in Higher Education: Myths and Realities", *Active Learning* 3: 3–6.

Davila-Gomez, A.M. (2005) "Beyond Business Ethics: Managers' Ethical Challenges Concerning Community and Employees", in D. Crowther and R. Jatana (eds) *Representations of Social Responsibility* Vol. 1, pp. 74–104. Hyderabad, India: ICFAI University Press.

Dillenbourg, P. (1999) "Introduction: What Do You Mean By 'Collaborative Learning'?", in P. Dillenbourg (ed.) *Collaborative Learning – Cognitive and Computational Approaches*, pp. 1–19. Oxford: Pergamon.

d'Iribarne, P. (2002) *Cultures et mondialisation: gérer par-delà les frontières*/[sous la direction de] Philippe d'Iribarne; avec Alain Henry [et al.]. Paris: Seuil.

Freud, S. (1856–1939) *Nouvelles conférences sur la psychanalyse*. France: Gallimard, coll. Idées, 1984.

Fromm, E. (1980) *Beyond the Chains of Illusion*. London: Abacus.

Fromm, E. (1974) *The Anatomy of Human Destructiveness*. London: Penguin.

Fromm, E. (1957) *The Art of Loving*. London: Unwin.

Giddens, A. (1984) *The Constitution of Society: Outline of the Theory of Structuration*. Cambridge: Polity Press.

Guri-Rosenblit, S. (1999) *Distance and Campus Universities: Tensions and Interactions: A Comparative Study of Five Countries*. Oxford: Pergamon Press and International Association of Universities.

Gusdorf, G. (1988) *Les origines de l'herméneutique*. Paris: Éditions Payot.

Husserl, E. (1859–1938) *The Idea of Phenomenology*. Dordrecht/Boston/London: Kluwer Academic Publishers, 1999.

Klein, M. (1932) *The Psychoanalysis of Children*. London: Hogarth.

Klein, M. and Riviere, J. (eds) (1964) *Love, Hate and Reparation*. New York: W.W. Norton and Company.

Kolb, D.A., Rubin, I.M. and McIntyre, J.M. (1984) *Organizational Psychology: an Experiential Approach to Organizational Behavior*, 4th edn. Englewood Cliffs.: Prentice-Hall.

Kotter, J.P. (1996) *Leading Change*. Boston: Harvard Business School Press.

Laing, R.D. (1961) *Self and Others*. London: Tavistock.

Lawrence, W.G. (1995) "The Seductiveness of Totalitarian States of Mind", *Journal of Health Care Chaplaincy* October: 11–22.

Llewellyn, N. (2004) "In Search of Modernization: The Negotiation of Social Identity in Organizational Reform", *Organization Studies* 25(6): 947–968.

Marcel, G. (1965) *Homo Viator*. United States of America: Harper Torchbooks.

Merleau-Ponty, M. (1975) *Les relations avec autrui chez l'enfant*. Paris: Centre de documentation Paris V.

Morfaux, L.M. and Lefranc, J. (2005) *Nouveau vocabulaire de la philosophie et des sciences humaines*. Paris: Armand Collin.

Pelzer, P. (2005) "The Hostility Triad: The Contribution of Negative Emotions to Organizational (Un-)Wellness", *Culture and Organization* 11(2): 111–123.

Perls, F.S. (1975) "Theory and Technique of Personality Integration", in J.O. Stevens (ed.) *Gestalt Is*. Moab, Utah: Real People Press.

Plato (428–347 BC) Socrates' *Meno* dialogue, in J.M. Cooper and D.S. Hutchison (eds) Plato *Complete Works*, pp. 870–608. Indianapolis/Cambridge: Tacket Publishing Company, 1997.

Porter, M.E. (1998) *On Competition*. Boston: Harvard Business School Publishing.

Rokeach, M. (1973) *The Nature of Human Values*. New York: Free Press.

Schelling, F.W.J. (1775–1854) *System of Transcendental Idealism (1800)*. Charlottesville: University Press of Virginia, 1978.

Schwarz, G. and Watson, B.M. (2005) "The Influence of Perceptions of Social Identity on Information Technology-Enabled Change", *Group and Organization Management* 30(3): 289–318.

Solomon, R. (1998) "The Moral Psychology of Business: Care and Compassion in the Corporation", *Business Ethics Quarterly* 8(3): 515–533.

Taylor, F.W. (1856–1915) *Scientific Management, Comprising Shop Management – The Principles of Scientific Management [and] Testimony Before the Special House Committee*. New York: Harper, 1947.

Verstraeten, J. (1998) "From Business Ethics to the Vocation of Business Leaders to Humanize the World of Business", *Business Ethics: A European Review* 7(2): 111–124.

Weber, M. (1864–1920) *The Theory of Social and Economic Organization*. Glencoe: Free Press, 1947.

CHAPTER 2

Management, Virtues and Human Dignity: Towards a Better Future for the "Whole"

ANA-MARIA DAVILA-GOMEZ AND
SANDRA SOCORRO LOTERO PATIÑO

Introduction

In a world of a global economy, organizations increasingly are driven by the competitive nature of financial performance and market expansion, which are, in many cases, the primary goals (see Crowther and Rayman-Bacchus, 2004; Chanlat, 2002). Hereby, managers are constantly pressured by shareholders' demands for increasing share-value through productivity. This worldwide organizational reality increasingly impoverishes the majority of the world's population and continuously generates ecological damage (see United Nations, 2006). Hence, we see how many actions are perpetrated towards the dignity of some human actors in organizations (for example, employees), as well as members of the collective (or collectives) in which organizations operate. Some examples of abuses are the mere fact of a way of management that follows a utilitarian approach, in which employees are considered as resources (human resources) for increasing productivity and not necessarily as human beings with an integral spectrum of emotions, family life and societal concern. Equally, inside the worldwide competitive dynamic in which organizations operate, people outside organizations are seen as commercial targets (customers) and not necessarily as citizens or members of a community whose lives (in terms of progress, environmental quality, spare time, collective projects, among others) are influenced by the results of organizational actions.

On the contrary, if we practise management in organizations following a critical and constructive approach, we may be able to identify that the organization's finality should also be concerned with the continual co-construction of society and its collectives, therefore, improvement (and not impoverishment) needs to be addressed (Davila-Gomez and Crowther, 2008, 2006). Thus, we consider that human beings need to be acknowledged in their integrity, and as such respected in their dignity. Inside an existential perspective, and following the moral precepts of wholeness (see Marcel, 1965; Kierkegaard, 1813– 1855), we identify that organizations, as any other party of the whole, influence with their actions the other parties of the whole. Hence, managers, as constituents of the whole, need to act and to make decisions ethically, which for us implies a sense of virtue. We conceive virtues in a human being as the ability to express his or her integrity while conducting in a responsible way towards the wholeness (that is, what Socrates argues as the goodness of the soul that a human being reflects in his or her action – see *Socrates' Dialogues* in Plato (428–348 BC) and what Hume (1711–1776a) identifies as sentiments, dispositions to act with benevolence and generosity).

In this chapter, we explore the meaning of virtues,[1] serving us some bibliographical review regarding the philosophical concepts aforementioned and their link with management,[2] to finally be able to elaborate some suggestions for a more responsible management practice that respects human dignity.

Individual's Responsibility

We start in this point addressing our concerns by reflecting about how human dignity and virtues are needed in management. To us, virtues in managers help to address the necessity of a broader exercise of justice and responsibility in organizations.

The stakeholder approach (see Freeman, 1984) states that organizations need to take into account the interest of the various groups of the collective. Furthermore, the modern approaches of social responsibility and corporate governance claim the exercise of transparency in organizations.

Nevertheless, our observations indicate that sometimes there is a lack of transparency regarding the consideration of stakeholders. In various cases, this participation, when it is not mandatory for the government of the country where the organization operates, is left to the willingness and good sense of managers or shareholders of the organization. As such, we identify that organizations by themselves are the result of human actions, and as such, those who talk and participate are human beings. However, our literature review indicates that in the dominant management theory (positivist and neo-liberalist) there is a tendency to identify the organization as an entity which thinks and acts by itself. That is why, when following a positivistic approach, it is not always so difficult for a manager, or a shareholder, who has failed in the eyes of stakeholders, to find an exit to the problematical situation in which his or her organization might be. If the organization is considered the entity, then, in practical terms, the human being, the manager, might not necessarily be acknowledged as directly responsible. Some recent events exemplifying the unethical behaviours and lack of responsibility during the last two decades (that is, the cases of Enron, Arthur Anderson, AIG, *la Caisse de Placements du Québec* – Pension Funds of the Quebec Province in Canada, among others) show how in the midst of critical times of an organization, some top management executives are either absent, fleeing from trouble or simply declared ill when it comes time to face the community, which is concerned by the responsibility of the organizational actions that the aforementioned managers were conducting. As pointed out by McMahon (1995)

---

1 The authors acknowledge and thank the valuable suggestions of Carlos E. Prieto for the completion and contents of this article, as well as the aid of the research assistance of Geneviève Guilemète, Gislaine Moraes and Simona Dutchevici.

2 Some of the data we utilized in this article comes from the theoretical review of a research we are conducting about the place of virtues in management education (research that has been subventionated by the *Fonds de recherche sur la société et la culture* – FQRSC, Québec, Canada).

while discussing the validity of the ontological and moral status of organizations, the individual's moral responsibility should not disappear.

Controversially, these kinds of events help us as a society to awaken our critical questioning about the righteousness of the social contracts already operating, in which a society allows an organization to exist and operate, but at the same time, not defining clearly the role played by the individuals leading the organization. These controversies allow us to grow as a more just society as these events call for new legislation because of the moral questioning of motives, purposes and also meanings and signification of actions. The sad part of this process is that we may ask if we need the crisis to strike us hard in order to evolve as a society. Or, should we, as individuals of a society start questioning occurrences, habits and regulations before watching new events unfold with negative consequences for individuals of the collective? Because, even if we learn eventually not to commit the same kind of mistakes, some of them could have been prevented if some of us, as members of our society, would have questioned the right things at the right moment, or even if others among us as managers or directors of organizations would have conducted ourselves more ethically, not only in the sense of respecting deontology codes, but mainly in the sense of developing a moral conscience about what is right and what is wrong. Should we wait until the way in which we proceed generates more occurrences regarding human indignity (that is, workers with the uncertainties regarding their pension funds, governments where the citizen's voice is not necessarily taken into account, among others)?

As the previous points indicate, it is much more common to talk about organizational social responsibility than managerial responsibility. And as the controversial occurrences in society unfold, the concept of social responsibility is not necessarily exclusive for private organizations that are pursuing the steady increase of the share value as capitalism dictates; it is also inclusive of public institutions as they assure the continuity and sustainability of the collective for the future. In order to achieve organizational responsibility, managers must be held accountable for their actions.

This implies the necessity of considering the nature of human responsiveness towards others (what for DeKoninck (2005) means human dignity). We talk here about the condition of the human dignity of a being (a manager or a shareholder who owns the majority of shares) who entails per se the responsibility of being good and noble towards the aims to which the other individuals (either separately or by collective aggregation) entrust in him or her. Our researches, and also the inequities of the human reality worldwide (see United Nation, 2008), indicate that in addition to norms, rules and governmental regulations for organizational behaviour, there is a need to address the responsibility of powerful individuals; those who direct the course of organizations (managers and shareholders). In this sense, we claim the need for the development of a social conscience (see Davila-Gomez, 2008) in the individual. For this, we address the conceptions of human dignity and virtues in the next points.

Virtues, Reason and Human Dignity

Inside the discipline of management we can cite the presence of not only practitioners, but also academics and other individuals who live with the consequences of managerial acts. Hereby, we refer to employees of organizations, members of various communities, where organizations operate, and also individuals at the level of governmental institutions that have the mission to regulate the well-being of society.

In order for managers to operate ethically, and to take into account the point of view of a broader spectrum of stakeholders, they require a special kind of intrinsic value. Our questioning brings us to the concept of virtues.

Our literature review indicates that in the discipline of management, the concept of "modern virtue ethics" has been developed in the last two decades with a broader attention. While consulting some of the authors working on this specific area (that is, Moore, 2008, 2005; Bastons, 2007) we realize that they base themselves most of the time on the former works of Solomon (1992) and MacIntary (2007),[3] who, at their turn, rely in the Aristotelian ethics of action which demands reasoning and intellect, in the search for causality of actions. In this sense, the action of the individual reflects the virtues of that individual, and it requires codes of ethics and rules. Thereby, deontology is crucial.

To Solomon (1992), the applicability of virtues in business comes from "the essential sociability of the virtues that is not only good for business (congeniality, honesty) but essential to the very life of business (trust, dependability)" (p. 192). To Solomon, following Aristotle's ideas, virtue refers to "an exemplary way of getting along with other people, a way of manifesting in one's own thoughts, feelings, and actions the ideals and aims of the entire community" (p. 192). Furthermore, we understand that to Solomon, the place of virtue in an individual and its importance to a "business virtue" implies questioning about how it contributes to the social harmony of the organization and how it affects the integrity of individuals. He underlines the importance to business of the virtues of congeniality, honesty, loyalty, generosity, fairness, trust and toughness.

Agreeing with the previous Solomon's precepts (therefore Aristotle's ideas), we question, however, the fact that he states that virtues are different depending on the cultural context in which an organization operates. Our disagreement comes with the factual reality of globalization in which the way of treating a human being in any part of the world should be the same (respecting his or her dignity) regardless of the differences in a country's legislation. In this sense, to us, virtues are more universal concepts applicable to the behaviour of individuals, not only mere social rules in which the entity organization should operate. In general, our argument is that an organizational collective action is the result of the behaviour of individuals.

In general, modern authors recall, among others, the traditional well-known four cardinal Greek virtues such as temperance, courage, justice and fortitude. We also know that Aristotelian thought is on the basis of materialism – or what some authors call realism (as it was also anchored by the thought of Saint Thomas Aquinas and more recently by Descartes and Kant). In this line of thought, realism is more tangible and descriptive to absorb and comprehend phenomena by the human mind. For instance, to us, when MacIntyre (2007) elaborates a genealogy on the definition of the concept of virtues, he relies mostly on this position of realism (following Aristotle's ideas), in which reason leads to the understanding of phenomena. To him, as we comprehend it, idealism or other more soul-oriented criteria such as intuition, sentiments or passions are not necessarily the best support to rely on for taking decisions and conduct actions.

Additionally, following the genealogy of realism, we identify that it follows an anthropocentric view while reasoning about the human complexity, as, for instance,

---

[3] Which first edition dates from 1981.

Kant (1724–1804) (who is also at the base of many modern thought theories) states that men are the ends and that all the other things that exist are the means. In this sense, the environment is not an end per se, therefore, following this line of thought, the possibility of attaining some of the aims of social responsibility is little.

We recognize, however, that in the sense of Kant's idea of "men are ends" there is a valuable element when he considers human dignity within human interactions. In this sense, dignity refers to equity and respect among men, as Kant considers men as equal in their rights. For this, human dignity needs to be respected in any organization action. In this order of ideas, the virtues of justice and temperance, for an organization, or more precisely, for a manager inside an organization, should entail the respect of norms and governmental regulations that are prescribed beforehand to organizations in order to conduct with fairness and equity any action towards any human being making part of the stakeholder's group.

Nevertheless, even if regulations exist, we know that some human individual's behaviour may be in contradiction with what socially is established as justifiable, hence, corruption (see Everett, Neu and Rahamn, 2006) takes place at governmental levels as well as inside organizations. Following Aristotelian thought (see Aristotle, 384–322 BC), it should be reason (including norms, and rules) that leads to taking better ethical decisions; however, this way of proceeding does not always drive us to do the right moral thing (see Koehn (1998), who analyses in this sense not only the result of the organizational action but mostly the action of the individual). For instance, organizations operating overseas should be responsible for the population on the other country, as for instance, paying social security, fair salaries and other social advantages, if we take into account and respect the international precepts that aim to demand foreign investors to help in the development of the community where the organization is operating. We know already that regardless of these humanitarian aims, this is not always the case, as fairness and justice (the target virtues) do not always reflect organizational actions abroad. The United Nations (2008) present some statistics of how human development is not increasing in some developing countries regardless of foreign investments and financial aids. We could see some of the causes regarding this issue in the fact that every country has its own regulations, sometimes less favourable in terms of human dignity and equity when compared with other countries.

Additionally, our literature review indicates that various authors that treat the inclusion of the aforementioned virtues in organizations, will confer the organization the power to be virtuous by itself as an entity (that is, Solomon, 1992; MacIntyre, 2007; Moore, 2008; Caza, Barker and Cameron, 2004, among others). For instance, Kaptein (2008) presents a corporate ethical virtues model that includes clarity, congruency of supervisors, congruency of management, feasibility, supportability, transparency, discussability, and sanctionability. Even if we agree with the need to have virtuous actions coming from the organization's activities, as a collective of individuals, we cannot forget our premise in which there will not be a collective result (that is, a virtuous organization) unless the individuals' behaviours within the organization are virtuous in their own right. All of the above, in reference with what is considered as just and moral by a concept of human dignity and not only solely by a concept of deontology of norms, shows that norms are distinct in each country's legislation (as for example, on some intrinsic rules of conduct in various professions, norms forbidding women to join the workforce, children allowed to work at a very young age, and so on).

Human Dignity and the Danger of Anthropocentrism

Recognizing the valuable insights offered by a scientific approach such as realism, that we discussed in the previous point, we are nevertheless concerned about the way in which we could add the issues regarding the environment. Inside an anthropocentric approach is the environment only a means to an end which is the survival of men? How do we conceptualize here the aim of sustainable development which is claimed nowadays by worldwide organizations (that is, the United Nations) and by some academic arenas? Should it be a question of the survival of humankind, a question of stewardship or a question of harmony with the wholeness of the planet?

One of the roots of the detachment between humans and nature, to us, is the separation between the collective results (that is, an organization as an entity) and the environment, where the latter one is considered as less valuable than human survival. Human history teaches us that the behaviour of humankind has been mostly anthropocentric (or at least for the last two millennia in the western cultures). With this, we, as humankind, have agreed, repeatedly in our history, with the separation of the soul and science. The separation of religion and scientific action indicates that nowadays it is common that an individual's fidelity to the rites and norms of his or her religion is not necessarily corresponding to the virtue of his or her behaviour. As stated by Shaftesbury (1671–1713):

We have known people who, having the appearance of great zeal in religion, have yet wanted even the common affections of humanity and shown themselves extremely degenerate and corrupt. Other, again, who have paid little regard to religion and been considered as mere atheists, have yet been observed to practice the rules of morality and act in many cases with such good meaning and affection towards mankind as might seem to force an acknowledgement of their being virtuous. (p. 163)

Our experience and researches[4] show that this tradition has been mainly thought to us since medieval ages at schools and universities (that is, business and management schools). Moreover, regardless of the fact that Eastern cultures have a great richness in aspects concerning spirituality teachings (that is, what Bhatta, 2004, presents as qualities needed in leaders – such as kindness, generosity, truthfulness, purity of thought, proper behaviour, self-control and gratitude), our literature review indicates that even for the case of eastern authors in management, there is a tendency to address mostly the question of financial growth and competitiveness, favouring these kinds of issues in the same line of thought as realism and materialism discussed formerly.

This same anthropocentrism is present even in various discourses of social responsibility. In this sense, Crowther (2008) indicates that in the practice of the stakeholders' approach, there is a void concerning the attention given to the environment as it does not speak the language of humans by itself, and because of this, a group of human individuals must talk on its behalf (that is, Greenpeace).

In other words, the paradox between anthropocentrism and scientism is that it has been science that acknowledged recently that the universe (the one known to date by humankind) has existed for around 13.7 billion years (see NASA, 2003). In the same order of ideas, our planet (Earth) has existed for about 4.5 billion years (see NASA, 2009),

---

4   Idem 2, Davila-Gomez (2003), among others.

and within the various life forms, humankind (and its predecessors) have been dated (archeologically) at about 6 million years old. To put facts into perspective, let us suppose that the planet was one day old. In this scenario, humankind would have existed in the planet during the last minute. Thus, the universe as vast as it is, and the Earth, have existed long before our kind. This leads us to realize that if we think that humans are the only ends, there is something missing in the acknowledgment of reality.

The traditions of thought regarding materialism and realism referred to above indicate that it is very common for individuals exercising managerial functions worldwide to behave in an individualistic manner (that is, personal careers, own organizational success) and not always consider their role in the collective. If we want people to get involved in organizational actions, for our own sake and for future generations, we need to broaden our views of the human action and survival inside the interconnection of all things in the wholeness; a leap further from the dominant thought of materialism and realism has to be achieved.

Therefore, it is crucial to conceive virtues that might help to awaken an environmental consciousness.

Virtues, Sentiments and Wholeness

The previous points indicate that inside materialism and realism there is a dominance of reason prevailing over sentiments. In the same sense, we understand also that according to Marcel (1964), the excess of rationalism in our modern world makes it sometimes so easy to forget the imperatives of human dignity.

Equally, as discussed by Hume (1711–1776a,b), when we allow our mind to be governed solely by our reason, the sentiments of being good to oneself and to others may vanish as we consider just tangible results and we are not worried about otherness; commonly, reason only helps us to identify the benefits that a particular behaviour offers to us and does not necessarily drive us to question ourselves about the motives, the nature, and the consequences of our decision. This is what we explored also as the danger of anthropocentrism and individualism.

In short, as stated by Marcel (1965) in one of his works:

> *But it must be noticed that the attitude of those who in the name of reason take up their position against hope is in all points comparable with that of the people who claim to avoid risks. In both cases what they want to avoid is disappointment. (Marcel, p. 55)*

Our reflections indicate that a glimpse of idealism is needed in management, and this, to us, in the sense explored by Socrates (in Plato, 428–348 BC) about the ideal that humanity may carry out for their own well-being, or in the sense of what Rousseau (1712–1778) discusses when he was questioning the righteousness of the established social contracts (laws) that sometimes allow injustice and unfairness to happen in the civic life. Additionally, if we want individuals to take into account not only the reasonability of actions (that is, causes and best decisions for the sake of organizations), but also the depth and nature of motives behind those actions, we consider that an existentialist approach is also required if we are asking ourselves, as humankind making part of the wholeness, about our purposes, motives and roles. The latter questioning is what we understand as the exercise of reflexivity (see Kierkegaard, 1813–1855; Alvesson and Sköldberg, 2000) which we consider as more open than solely reason. Reflexivity demands from our part evaluation and criticism of reality, of our role, of our own involvement, and why not, of our connection with the wholeness. To us, reflexivity addresses the concern for the "beauty" of our actions; beauty claimed by Socrates in the sense of goodness.

Therefore, despite recognizing and supporting the Aristotelian perspective of virtues, we decided, however, to complement our analysis by relying upon the definition of virtues coming from philosophers who dedicated a special attention to what we may call the meaning of actions in human beings, as we also want to address the need for developing social and environmental consciences in individuals in order to conduct actions that respect the human dignity. We adhere to the propositions of Socrates for whom (see Virtues, Menon and Alcibiades Dialogues – in Plato 428–348 BC) virtues are the qualities of the person that allow him or her to function with goodness and righteousness.

By the same token, we identify that Hume (1711–1776a) talks about virtues as sentiments, as something that comes from passion and not from reason. As such, virtues need to be at the root of the ontological principle of the individual in order to allow him or her to conduct with fairness and care for others, and integrity of oneself. Hume presents the need for the virtues of benevolence, generosity, humility and truth, among others. Additionally, according to Marcel (1964), virtues refer also to those traits of a person that allow him or her to think about the consequences of their actions, therefore considering the future. We pretend to link these purposes with the necessity of a more holistic approach, that based upon human reflexivity (as one way of contributing to the social and environmental conscience in individuals) awakens also awareness in minds and as such, sensitivity and sentiments of wholeness. By reflection and by experience, virtues, considered as sentiments, help to seek a better future.

Following Minteer and Manning (1999) we identify that the virtue of "openness" allows diverse stakeholders regarding an ecological matter to interact inside the practice of democracy of a community to discuss about the validity and nature of ethical thinking and policy formulation. To them, the discussion about meanings and challenges of possible alternatives surrounding an ecological matter allows citizens to grow in the sense of expressing themselves and understanding the positions of others.

We consider that this kind of exercise, which is invaluable for public matters concerning the care for the environment, is also crucial for private organizations that make an ecological impact in a community, as a result of their activities. It is also valuable for other kinds of governmental institutions in which citizens are not only members of the affected community, but also in various cases, employees of the institution. In this sense, communication and dialogue (in the sense of Socrates' view – see Plato, 428–348 BC) offer an excellent environment for contributing to the development of mutual understanding between different stakeholders. As such, if the environment per se does not talk our human language, it does not mean that we do not have to take it into account in the analysis and reflections of our human interventions. Hence, a call for the practice of the virtue of temperance is very important, as it allows the individual in charge (the manager, either in the private or the public sectors) to well manage the activities of mutual understanding as well to grow in the matter of comprehension of others, and to act as the moderator of dialogues with civilian participation, seeking to obtain at the end agreements to actions between different stakeholders with different interests. Temperance also helps the individual to well-manage him or herself, as well as to stimulate the growth of the individual's inner self. The virtues of benevolence and generosity presented by Hume (1711–1776a), are also very helpful here, given that by means of the procedures aforementioned, a manager may become conscious of other people's needs (or nature) that he or she did not acknowledged before. Therefore, virtues (as sentiments in Hume's sense) such as comprehension, and compassion will develop in managers, while he or she lives the ongoing experience of the exercise of his or her functions and responsibilities.

By the same token, Boiral (2007) explains that in order for an organization to evolve in the exercise of taking into account the impacts of its activity towards the environment, top managers should be informed about the environmental issue at stake as well as the employees of the organization. Hence, communications and workshops may generate proactive actions coming from both the directors and the employees.

We see how the concept of sensitivity for awareness and understanding is crucial in the development of virtues in individuals. We, as managers should go outside our organizational black box (our brick offices) and by observation, by curiosity, by experience, unveil the nature, motives and senses of environmental issues at stake. This is also valid for social and human issues concerned with the organizational activity. Managers need to be more proactive for the goodness of the wholeness, and not only proactive for increasing share value. As we already have discussed, the limited proactive concern with material productivity has its roots in the dominant realistic and materialistic thought of focusing existence towards benefits for humankind. Moreover, as we have also discussed previously, even within an anthropocentric view, we may also be unfair towards some individuals, as distribution of wealth is not always equitable inside nations, or as we presented it while exploring human dignity, equality is not recognized in practice regardless the fact that many countries in the world already apply regulations aiming for equality.

That is why we must contribute to the development of virtues in the sense of benevolence (following Hume), goodness (as aimed by Socrates) and sensitivity in managers, who are, or will be (if we consider management students) either directors with a salary and bonuses, or even shareholders that own the majority of a company. We also include managers working in public institutions, as they have the right to vote in crucial organizational decisions. Hence, personal responsibility is also oriented to procure a better future when society, or other circumstances of life, have put us in a position of power (vote, decision, education) and command of institutions and individuals.

The Virtue of Hope and the Aim of a Better Future

The imperative of opening to a perspective of wholeness includes, to us, the need for virtues in the individual that allows the consideration of issues related to others (that is, society, community) and nature. We are all responsible for a better future. We need to work for it, believe in its possibility; in short, we need to have hope. We need to introspect in our psyche conviction and belief in those kinds of issues. As stated by Marcel (1965):

> *We see from this why it is legitimate to consider hope as a virtue; the truth is that all virtue is the particularization of a certain interior force, and that to live in hope is to obtain from oneself that one should remain faithful in the hour of darkness to that which in its origin was perhaps only an inspiration, an exaltation, a transport. But there is no doubt that this faithfulness cannot be put into practice except by virtue of a cooperation, whose principles will always*

remain a mystery, between the goodwill which is after all the only positive contribution of which we are capable and certain prompting whose centre remains beyond our reach, in those realms where values are divine gifts. (Marcel, p. 63)

Therefore, "hope" as a virtue, implies to work in cooperation with the willingness of each one of us, and it can be instrumentalized while constructing a better reality, a more desirable future, which is an ongoing experience in continuous movement, for not only the individual entitled with power, but also to those living the consequences of organizational decisions and actions, as well as nature and the environment that also coexist with us upon the ideal of wholeness. As we cannot control nor impose the willingness of goodness in others, we must rely on the continuous development of the individual's inner self. Through cooperation, we can just promote the development of virtues as sentiments through reflexivity. In this sense, human dignity, to us, implies the respect of the possibility of hope.

While thinking about a better future, for instance, there is a need to think not only about the organization as an economical entity, but also as a social actor that at its turn is the result from the actions of various individuals who posse conviction, values and the power of transforming the present reality to a better one. In this sense, Dunphy (2009), while treating the role of organizations and managers in the future, states that we, as co-creators of this future, need to leave apart our fears and work with a spirituality that recognizes the need for sustainability and nature in its whole.

Thus, sensitivity (as sentiments), if not yet developed in an individual, should be one of the traits of character to develop, mostly in managers who are increasingly more implicated in globalization dynamics. We consider that there are various ways of reinforcing this sensitivity. Some individuals are formed to these considerations of respect towards nature and equity towards others during childhood, either by their parents or by some remarkable schoolteachers. Others, whom are not necessarily educated respecting these kinds of values, may gain conscience through life either by biographical experience or by openness to introspection and to reflect about what is happening in the world they inhabit. In this sense, existentialism takes place when individuals by themselves ask about their role and purpose in life. However, an individual who acknowledges a reality that requires to be modified may not necessarily agree to adapt his or her behaviour in order to work constructively for a good settlement in terms of justice and respect of others and nature. It remains a personal decision, a moral choice. We consider that even in that case, decisions and the individual's room for manoeuvre may count with broader spectra of information coming from previous experiences from which the individual can rely on as support. This whole situation may be easier when some of the experiences that have occurred have been positive for the individual, or if he or she conducts a process of reflexivity about the nature and meaning of the lived experiences. However, as explored before, the virtues of temperance and fortitude help an individual to reflect about the meaning and learned lessons of past experiences, even if they are not always very pleasant.

By the same token, we identify that the practical attainment of personal responsibility not only comes from the execution and respect of the socially accepted norms (that is, governmental regulation). To us, it goes even further in the sense that, critically, for managers of either public or private organizations, there is a civil responsibility entailed in their function, which claims to see beyond what is commonly socially accepted as foreseeable. In this sense, we rely in what Shaftesbury (1671–1713) states:

But though a right distribution of justice in a government be so essential a cause of virtue, we must observe in this case that it is example which chiefly influences mankind and forms the character and disposition of a people. For a virtuous administration is in a manner necessarily accompanied with virtue in the magistrate. Otherwise it could be of little effect and of no long duration. But where it is sincere and well established, there virtue and the laws must necessarily be respected and beloved. (Shaftesbury, p. 187)

We talk here in a recurrent manner about foresight and forethought. Possessing these abilities implies for the individual the opportunity to exercise the ancient Greek virtues of fortitude, as well as of courage to face situations that might be not easy to resolve. As such, courage is crucial to a manager who is facing with his or her power the possibility of contributing with his or her actions for a better future for him or herself, for others and for nature. Therefore, our claim for idealism expressed in a previous point is crucial. While exerting the virtue of courage, managers have the ideal of a better future. They have hope. This courage implies being strong to face adversity and difficulties, to want to go beyond what normally is already known as commonly socially understandable, to imagine innovative solutions oriented to proposing solutions to diverse spectra of interests coming from diverse stakeholders.

Thus, in the line of thought of existentialism we presented in previous points, reflexivity about the profound purposes of actions, and its consequences for others and nature, helps individuals to unveil how, for instance, even if an action that does not impact directly the individual (that is, his or her own carrier, family, organization) it may, however, in some cases, have disastrous consequences for others. Sometimes, gaining sensitivity implies putting ourselves in somebody else's position; somebody who will suffer the consequences. It is possible as well to imagine the future of the environment after our actions, or imagine the sentiments of distress, joy or hatred that our future generations might experience as a result of our present actions or its lack thereof. Sometimes, in order to awaken our conscience, it is better to imagine our own blood, our loved ones, as all of us still may have a little of anthropocentric individualism in our minds.

In these terms, introspection, as discussed before, aided by reflexivity, helps to gain sensitivity, to open our eyes to the reality of other individuals. We are exploring alternative ways to acknowledge the wholeness, but mostly, consolidate the awareness as an internal sentiment. We argue that the idea of wholeness is mostly experienced while interacting with others and nature. For instance, as discussed in the previous point, if we talk about the need to exercise more communally the stakeholder approach, openness to listening to other points of view helps with mutual understanding. Moreover, as explained by Marcel (1964) and DeKoninck (2005) (mostly when addressing the concern for human dignity), as humankind, we progress socially and humanly in the world, peace with nature, in a common effort from all of us.

Conclusion

A better future implies personal responsibility. Managers, as actors and guides of decisions of the present and the future, have the moral obligation of well-behaving by acting with thoughtfulness regarding others and nature. A holistic approach inside the introspective continuous development of individuals is required. Virtues and human dignity help individuals to apprehend the sentiment of procuring benevolence, care and empathy towards the concerns of others and towards nature. Responsiveness implies not only the imperative to reflect about the consequences of our actions, but also the nature, sense and motives of those actions, as well as the preoccupation for our experience as human beings and our contribution and connection with the wholeness. In this sense, a detachment from an anthropocentric vision of existence helps individuals to acknowledge and to become aware of their own existence. A glimpse of idealism and existentialism helps in the development of virtues allowing humans to function with dignity towards themselves, others and nature, which implies, according us, to behave with respect, justice, empathy, benevolence and hope.

References

Alvesson, M. and Sköldberg, K. (2000), *Reflexive Methodology: New Vistas for Qualitative Research*, Sage, London.

Aristotle (384–322 BC), *Ethique à Nicomaque*, trad. J. Tricot, Librairie Philosophique J. Vrin, Paris, 1959.

Bastons, M. (2007), "The Role of Virtues in the Framing of Decisions", *Journal of Business Ethics*, 78, pp. 389–400.

Bhatta, C.P. (2004), "Effective Leadership: Human Values Perspective", in A. Das Gupta (ed.), *Human Values in Management*, Ashgate, Aldershot, pp. 223–240.

Boiral, O. (2007), *Environnement et gestion: de la prévention à la mobilisation*, Presses de l'Université Laval, Québec.

Caza, A., Barker, B. and Cameron, K. (2004), "Ethics and Ethos: The Buffering and Amplifying Effects of Ethical Behaviour and Virtuousness", *Journal of Business Ethics*, 52 (2), pp. 169–178.

Chanlat, J-F. (2002), "Le défi social du management: l'apport des sciences sociales", in M. Kalila (coord.), *Les défis du management*, pp. 59–82, Ed. Liaisons, Paris.

Crowther, D. (2008), "Stakeholder Perspectives on Social Responsibility", in D. Crowther and N. Capaldi (eds) *The Ashgate Research Companion to Corporate Social Responsibility*, pp. 47–63, Ashgate, Aldershot.

Crowther, D. and Rayman-Bacchus, L. (2004), "The Future of Corporate Social Responsibility," in D. Crowther and L. Rayman-Bacchus (eds) *Perspectives on Corporate Social Responsibility*, pp. 229–249, Ashgate, Aldershot.

Davila-Gomez, A.M. (2008), "Inquiring about Social Conscience", in D. Crowther and N. Capaldi (eds), *The Ashgate Research Companion to Corporate Social Responsibility*, pp. 221–229, Ashgate, Aldershot.

Davila-Gomez, A.M. (2003), *Hacia un management humanista desde la educación a distancia: intersubjetividad y desarrollo de cualidades humanas – un caso de Québec y otro de México*, Thèse (PhD), École des hautes études commerciales, Montréal.

Davila-Gomez, A.M. and Crowther, D. (2007), "Psychological Violence at Work: Where does the Human Dignity Lie?", in A.M. Davila-Gomez and D. Crowther (eds) *Ethics, Psyche and Social Responsibility*, pp. 15–33, Ashgate, Aldershot.

Davila-Gomez, A.M. and Crowther, D. (2006), "Reaching the true nature of organizations: human and social finalities" *Social Responsibility Journal*, 2 (1), May, pp. 104–111.

De Koninck, T. (2005), "Archéologie de la notion de dignité humaine", in T. De Koninck and G. Larochelle (eds), *La dignité humaine – philosophie, droit, politique, économie, médicine*, pp. 13–50, Presses universites de France, Paris.

Dunphy, D. (2009), "In Search of the Future: notes for Spiritual Adventurers", in D. Bubna-Litic (ed.), *Spirituality and Corporate Social Responsibility*, pp. 153–175, Gower, Farnham.

Everett, J., Neu, D. and Rahaman, A.S. (2006), "The Global Fight against Corruption: A Foucaultian, Virtues-Ethics Framing", *Journal of Business Ethics*, 65, pp. 1–12.

Freeman, R. (1984), *Strategic Management: a Stakeholder Approach*, Pitman, Boston.

Hume, D. (1711–1776a), *A Treatise of Human Nature*, Vol. 1 and Vol. 2, Dent and Sons, London, 1934.

Hume D. (1711–1776b), *An Enquiry Concerning the Principles of Morals*, Open Court, La Salle, 1966.

Kant, E. (1724–1804), *Critique of Pure Reason*, Dent, London, 1964.

Kaptein, M. (2008), "Developing and Testing a Measure for the Ethical Culture of Organizations: The Corporate Ethical Virtues Model", *Journal of Organizational Behavior*, 29, pp. 923–947.

Kierkegaard, S. (1813–1855), *For Self-examination and Judge for Yourselves!* – 1851, 1974, Oxford University Press, London, Princeton University Press.

Koehn, D. (1998), "Virtue Ethics, The Firm, and Moral Psychology", *Business Ethics Quarterly*, 8 (3), pp. 497–513.

MacIntyre, A. (2007), *After Virtue – A Study in Moral Theory*, 3rd edition, c. 1981, University of Notre Dame Press, Notre Dame, Indiana.

Marcel, G. (1965), *Homo Viator*, Harper Torchbooks, United States of America.

Marcel, G. (1964), *La Dignité Humaine et ses assises existentielles*, Aubier, Paris.

McMahon, C. (1995), "The Ontological and Moral Status of Organizations", *Business Ethics Quarterly*, 5 (3), pp. 541–554.

Minteer, B.A. and Manning, R.E. (1999), "Pragmatism in Environmental Ethics: Democracy, Pluralism, and the Management of Nature", *Environmental Ethics*, 21 (2), pp. 191–207.

Moore, G. (2008), "Re-Imagining the Morality of Management: A Modern Virtue Ethics Approach", *Business Ethics Quarterly*, 18 (4), pp. 483–511.

Moore, G. (2005), "Humanizing Business: A Modern Virtue Ethics Approach", *Business Ethics Quarterly*, 15 (2), pp. 237–255.

NASA (2009), *How Old is the Universe?*, http://map.gsfc.nasa.gov/universe/uni_age.html, consulted July 2009.

NASA (2003), *New Image of Infant Universe Reveals Era of First Stars, Age of Cosmos, and More*, http://www.nasa.gov/centers/goddard/news/topstory/2003/0206mapresults.html, consulted July 2009.

Plato (428–348 BC), *Socrates' Dialogues*, in J.M. Cooper and D.S. Hutchison (eds) *Plato, Complete Works*, Tacket Publishing Company, Indianapolis/Cambridge, 1997.

Rousseau, J.J. (1712–1778), "Discourse on the Origins and Foundations of Inequality among Men," in J.J., Rousseau, *The First and Second Discourses*, St Martin's Press, New York, 1964.

Shaftesbury, (Anthony Ashley Cooper, Earl of Shaftesbury – 1671–1713), "An Inquiry Concerning Virtue of Merit", in Shaftesbury, *Characteristics of Men, Manners, Opinions, Times*, pp. 163–230, Cambridge University Press, New York, 1999.

Solomon, R. (1992), *Ethics and Excellence – Cooperation and Integrity in Business*, Oxford University Press, Oxford.

United Nations (2008), *World Economic and Social Survey – Overcoming Economic Insecurity*, http://www.un.org/esa/policy/wess/, consulted July 2009.

United Nations (2006), *World Economic and Social Survey – Diverging Growth and Development*, http://www.un.org/esa/policy/wess/past-issues.htm, consulted July 2009.

CHAPTER 3
Economic Accountability, Regulatory Reform and Ethical Management: Towards a New Language of Largesse

JULIA J.A. SHAW AND HILLARY J. SHAW

Introduction

In this late modern era – driven by globalization, mass communication technologies and the corporate agenda – the basic values of life have been reordered and the individual has effectively been reduced to a mere abstraction. The effective dismantling of the welfare state, once a safeguard against unrestrained capitalism, has abandoned individuals to the mercy of the market. The free market has been handed a global geo-political arena within which to move labour, production and capital at will in order to maximize profit; whilst the quest for standardization, centralization and automation has created a society with greatly diminished social capital, in which people have little political influence and are discontented in their state of separation from the dominant (and largely self-determining) economic and legislative power bases. The growth of surveillance technology used against ordinary citizens together with the expansion of regulatory state powers, for example, continues to pose a significant threat to basic human rights. Contrast this incursion on civil liberties with the laissez-faire approach adopted towards privileged corporate citizens who operate in a largely unregulated environment. The banking sector is one such case, where the burgeoning fiscal crisis has exposed the ethical laxity of our financial institutions. The continuing settlement of disproportionately large bonuses in a failing global economy is just one illustration of a management culture which is unwilling to assume responsibility for the disastrous consequences of its own practices, and within which any question of legitimacy is obscured or repressed.

The richly remunerated and privileged modern power elite appear to be not only indifferent to the consequences of their actions but are too often immune from punishment. It is this reimagining and recalibration of the fundamental concepts of democracy, transparency, accountability, fairness and justice which has exacerbated the imbalance of power, fostered feelings of alienation and contributed to the destabilization of society. It is suggested that in order to fill the accountability vacuum, it is first necessary to consciously take into account and even prioritize the fundamental ideal of human dignity and the flourishing of all human actors on a daily basis. To this end, in this chapter we discuss various examples of poor governance (organizational and governmental) that indicate in the current economic, and wider societal, climate of mistrust and extreme circumspection, that a new set of safeguards need to be implemented. Furthermore, managers must be seen to be making moral decisions on a sound ethical basis, towards effecting a positive social impact beyond merely serving the economy and their own desires.

Reimagining the Remit of Managerial Responsibility in an Age of Disenchantment

In answer to Freud's question "What does business want?", the foremost concern of the modern organization continues to be to replicate itself rather than to pursue meaningful engagement with a wider range of stakeholders. As evidenced recently within the financial sector, the modern manager displays a large level of self-interest, seemingly unimpeded by any moral consideration. This attitude was summarized by Adam Smith in *Wealth of Nations*, "It is not from the benevolence of the butcher, the brewer, or the baker that we expect our dinner, but from their regard to their own interest. We address ourselves, not to their humanity but to their self-love ..." (1910:13). Although Smith acknowledges the desirability of moral codes of behaviour in social and political matters in later writings (1975:191), in his seminal work, he has no need for any moral explanation as to why the baker wishes to sell his bread and the customer wants to buy it. His theory is underpinned by the idea that, guided by "an invisible hand", the pursuit of self-interest alongside an appropriate institutional infrastructure would produce a wider distribution of social goods more efficiently than alternative systems and this has been favourably regarded by his successors. Reports of recent spectacular business failures which have adopted such mechanistic value-free management practices, for example, Enron, WorldCom and Lehman Brothers in addition to institutional lapses, for example, Andersen and Merrill Lynch, have revealed what would appear to be a chasm between theory and practice. Although there are exceptions, this general disengagement with the requirements of wider society and the environment manifests itself more clearly in times of economic recession, when state funding for social purposes is also reduced.

Whilst it is inarguably essential that managers are committed to the economic health of their organizations and the *cash nexus*,[1] in an era of increasing privatization and the assumption by private agencies of hitherto public services, an overarching commitment to the promotion of social welfare, civic well-being and the wider aims of civilization (where possible and appropriate) is imperative. Such a commitment would not only be advantageous in terms of communal gains and comply with, for example, the UK government's drive to create a "Big Society"; but also by increasing the company's public profile as a caring and responsive business alert to the requirements of social capital is, in this media-led world, good for public relations and likely to increase their economic

---

[1] A phase used by Thomas Carlyle to describe the relation of individuals to one another mediated only by means of a seemingly "neutral" transaction.

capital. Due to the retreat of the state in providing essential social services, for example in the UK, the division between the public and private spheres has become blurred which has produced local and national inequalities, affected individual freedoms and increased existing tensions within identity politics. Vital public goods including health, education, housing, transport, employment rights and labour conditions are all, to a lesser or greater extent, subject to private control (and therefore market forces) and in many instances the new private agencies are failing to provide necessary public services, or at least to an acceptable minimum standard. This has resulted not only in the frustration of public expectations but there has also been a consequent rise in the violation of basic human rights, to the extent that the private domain has rightly become an area of public unease (Shaw and Shaw, 2010:469–471). As the logic of the neo-liberal framework has shifted attention from state organizational responsibility to corporate social responsibility and good governance, the question of the proper remit of the business and business manager is now an urgent concern.

Although the last decade has seen various corporate social responsibility (CSR) initiatives and at least a commitment to the letter of CSR, by the inclusion of company mission statements and annual competitions for the "greenest" business, social responsibility and ethical management is still understood in narrowly-defined terms. Other considerations, such as efficiency, are a core part of the management training curriculum; the Executive MBA run by the University of Texas School of Management in the US emphasizes "efficiency, effectiveness and economy" in its business modules. However, the vast increase in the speed and quantity of information we encounter from a variety of sources means we receive more "messages" every day than medieval man encountered in his entire lifetime, yet we are encouraged to accomplish even more in less time, effectively denied the important possibility of contemplation. Even with the assistance of software solutions to integrate the flow of information and hypothetically realize more time for reflection, this is rarely the case. Concentrating on technological innovations, therefore, does nothing to improve the experience of the manager who, whilst remaining an expert in his or her department and specialization, is reduced to the role of a dehumanized servile functionary. The sheer volume and diversity of information produced in this digital era is constantly increasing and overwhelms; with a range of decisions to be made, there is little time allocated in which to consider or properly formulate plans of action with regard to a wider set of often complex societal engagements. For Adorno, this modern phenomena comprises an "iron law" in that, however useful it might be to have as much information as possible at one's disposal, in such quantities it will never "touch the essential and degenerate into thought" (Adorno, 1991:84). At a certain speed, it is impossible to see what is happening, and what is happening is unrecognizable, blurred by momentum, and this would result in what Socrates described as an "unexamined life [which] is not worth living" (West, 1979:41) For Socrates the point of living is to examine one's soul and aspire to attain knowledge and insight in order to challenge received wisdom and replace it with one's own; such exploration and understanding was believed to lead to a deeper comprehension of the world and the individual's connection to society.

Socrates was concerned about virtue in the *Apology*, particularly in the way in which we treat other people, our ethical conduct. In the modern world, management – particularly in the provision of services – has become increasingly remote from the client in the belief that their responsibility does not extend beyond the cash nexus.

Call centres are an example of this mindset in practice, whereby British clients with problems relating to, for example, their power supplier or phone service provider are increasingly subjected to a range of technical hurdles (for example, multi-step automated phone instructions) and poor customer care (for example, not receiving appropriate advice, dealing with different operatives who have no personal knowledge of the case). The idea of after-sales care and general customer service is rarely uppermost in the mind of the sales manager, and there is a tendency towards adopting a dualistic approach. For example, most literature for managers still seems to support the belief that the technical and mechanistic elements represent the extent of their appropriate realm of concern and any moral-ethical considerations, where they arise, lie outside this ambit. For the most part, the moral-ethical dimension is retrospective and left to the lawyers.

This lack of concern by the corporate business (especially when delivering a public good or service) for the individual in society is exacerbated by the fact that we live in an age of "spin", bluff, hype, chutzpah, front and bottle, where facts are airbrushed or even distorted in the cause of "excellence", "quality" and other empty-headed nouns which serve to present a spruce image and sell products. For example, by subtle alteration of "the truth" by a clever web of spin, Enron entered into a series of complex relationships, including Andersen (one of the "Big 5" auditing firms), in order to inflate its profits and remove $billions of debt from its balance sheets. Consequently, following Enron's demise in December 2001, thousands of employees found themselves not only unemployed but divested of their life savings and pension plans as they had been encouraged to invest in the company and were "rewarded" by directors in (worthless) company shares. No redundancy provisions had been considered and no contingency plans were in place to, for example, minimize the financial effects on employees in terms of lost earnings, difficulty in finding another job and psychological stress. This also had a knock-on impact on the wider community in terms of the local welfare system having to cope with larger numbers of benefits claimants (where applicable) and the increasing demand for medical treatment in respect of stress-related conditions. The trickledown effect on the local economy, for example, raising the spectre of negative multipliers resulting in falling sales experienced by local shopkeepers (particularly smaller retailers), service providers and the local economy generally. The shockwave generated by this, one of the first of a spate of such scandals, was so considerable because as a household name, it was automatically assumed that whatever Enron did it would be legally, if not morally, sanctioned. It was not contemplated that serious financial transactions would be rather subjected to techniques employed by barrow-boys, marketers and the tabloid media. The question arises as to how the scope of managerial responsibility might be extended to include ethical obligations and stimulate a desire by managers to critically examine their beliefs and values, so as to determine the course of right action towards an appropriately broad set of stakeholders.

Against the prevailing management culture that values individual success at the expense of the common good, it is proposed that university business schools can achieve much more by including ethical, critical and social perspectives in addition to a broader range of reading resources across all modules to improve the emotional literacy of managers. In 1929, *The Aims of Education* was written in order to emphasize the role of universities in imparting knowledge but more importantly for developing the free play of the imagination. Although responsible for educating the leaders and future managers of the world, the author Whitehead believed that the cultivation of imagination was materially transformative, and managers need to be able to generate creativity and alternative possibilities – beyond the narrow realm of transferrable skills, business models and bottom lines. To paraphrase John Stuart Mill, "men are men before they are [businessmen] and if you make them capable and sensible men, they will make themselves capable and sensible [businessmen] … what professional men should carry away with them from a University is not professional knowledge, but that which should direct the use of their professional knowledge, by bringing the light of general culture to illuminate the technicalities of a special pursuit" (1867:255). This means that society benefits from educating future managers who are responsive to, and curious about, the world outside the confines of their own narrow specialism. Business education would, therefore, be neither instrumentalist nor utilitarian and would go far beyond merely "illuminating the technicalities"; it would rather inculcate within the modern manager an affinity for spirited leadership with the capacity to engage with all aspects and actors connected to the corporate enterprise:

> *the atmosphere of excitement, arising from imaginative consideration, transforms knowledge. A fact is no longer a bare fact: it is invested with all its possibilities It is no longer a burden on the memory: it is energising as the poet of our dreams, and as the architect of our purposes. Imagination is not to be divorced from the facts: it is a way of illuminating the facts. It works by eliciting the general principles that apply to the facts, as they exist, and then by an intellectual survey of alternative possibilities that are consistent with those principles. (Whitehead,1929:139,140)*

In real terms this would amount to an awakening of the corporate manager's conscience and right from the beginning of the educational process, making sure that assessing the benefits and the contemplation and avoidance of harm to the broadest set of societal actors is of paramount importance. This normative approach requires nothing less than a genuine commitment to ethical, caring and responsible behaviour and a firm commitment to the "spirit" of ethical organizational behaviour, based on promotion of best practice, towards the good of all. This echoes Kant's moral theory; although a transcendental idealist, he was also interested in how reason might inform everyday life. Kant's ethical theory is driven by the idea of individual human capacity, the capacity for moral reason. His *Critique of Practical Reason* is of particular relevance as it introduces the "categorical imperative" which constitutes an ethical principle, comparable with the biblical maxim and "golden rule", do unto others as you would be done unto. As a binding duty, it confers the obligation to treat others as "ends", not "means" in themselves, recognizing that this is the right of all members of a kingdom of equals. According to Dávila-Gómez and Crowther, there is a pressing "need to develop solidarity, empathy and willingness in search for togetherness [which] becomes a moral imperative for organizational life given that organizational actions are driving humanity's reality" (2007:29). It is suggested, therefore, that not only is conscionable and responsible management compatible with the pursuit of profitability, it is also an ethical requirement synonymous with the realization of the civic, emotional and spiritual good of all humankind. The following sections will discuss case studies which critically analyse a set of recent management failures and suggest alternative regulatory measures which are, at the same time, practical and fulfil a moral imperative.

From China to the Credit Crunch: Origins of the House Price Bubble

The end of 2010 continues to see financial repercussions from the Credit Crunch, which began in 2007. The spectacle of the relatively newly independent country of Ireland reluctantly accepting "bail-out" funds from the EU and IMF, which it perceives as a humiliating loss of sovereignty, is only eclipsed by the ongoing riots in Greece, as the populace protests against austerity cuts in the government budget. At least so far in Ireland only financial lives have been ruined by mortgage foreclosures and monetary cutbacks; in Greece real lives have been lost as buildings burn.

In Britain, the blame for lost money, lost homes, lost lives, has been laid squarely at the door of the banks, for their so-called "reckless lending", especially in the subprime mortgage market, promoting a bubble market in housing, followed by an abrupt unwillingness to lend, thus putting a squeeze on house prices and the economy generally. At some point any overinflated bubble market will reach a tipping point, known as the "Minsky Moment". This event is named after a twentieth century Keynesian US economist, Hyman Minsky; it is when market stability suddenly gives way to chaos and even panic. The "Minsky Moment" in the US housing market, when investors are forced to make a fire sale of assets in an already falling market to cover their debts, occurred in 2006, in response to a sustained rise in US interest rates throughout 2005. However it can be argued that the seeds of the Credit Crunch were sown much earlier than this; a crucial event occurring in 2001 when China joined the World Trade Organization (WTO). Insufficient and ineffective regulation of the banks by government has also been pinpointed as a cause of the Credit Crunch; naturally there are now calls for closer regulation of bank mortgage lending, an end to "liar loans", a more responsible attitude to lending in the sub-prime sector. Ironically it is the banks' very caution in mortgage lending, in demanding higher deposits, thereby contributing to the depression in house prices, that now attracts opprobrium in a way that the far more carefree lending of the early 2000s never did. However, it can also be argued that renewed regulation of the banks by government alone is insufficient, and may not prevent another future asset bubble and burst; because all parties acted rationally, at the time, a wider regulatory initiative at multiple levels, is necessary to attain stability in world finances.

China joined the WTO in December 2001, a hugely symbolic step in a process that arguably began in 1960 when the split between China and the USSR became open and irreversible, and was followed by a slow growth in both political and commercial contacts between China and the West, notably (West) Germany, as well as the USA (Sieren, 2007:xi–xiv). China is vast; it accounts for a fifth of the world's population. "Let China sleep, for when she wakes, she will shake the world", Napoleon is credited with saying, some two centuries ago (Boyle, 2004). China's GDP is rapidly catching up with even the USA's; between 1952 and 2005 its per capita GDP at Purchasing Power Parity (PPP) rose from 2.7 per cent of the USA to 15.7 per cent, and its total GDP (PPP) rose from 9.5 per cent of USA to 64.0 per cent (Brandt et al., 2008:2). The bulk of this catching up, by either measure, has occurred since 1990. With Chinese manufacturing costs at a fraction of those prevailing within the OECD countries, China's manufacturers and America's consumers both acted entirely rationally in building a huge trade imbalance for China against the USA throughout the 2000s. Meanwhile many western economies de-regulated their banking sectors, another rational move to free up what was seen as the main engine of growth as the manufacturing sector shrank in these countries.

China's accession to the WTO occurred three months after another landmark world event, the Twin Tower attacks in New York on 11 September 2001 (9/11). The 9/11 attacks severely damaged consumer confidence in the USA; to repair this confidence President Bush famously stated "We can't let the terrorists stop us from shopping" (Norris, 2005). To reinforce President Bush's message, the US Federal Reserve reduced nominal interest rates, which had been on a downwards trend anyway because of the lower inflation resulting from inter alia the availability of cheaper Chinese-manufactured goods to US consumers. Between 2000 and 2004 the three-month US interest rate fell from over 6 per cent to just 1 per cent (*The Economist*, 1983–2010a). US inflation remained subdued over this period at around 2–3 per cent, aided by a flat world oil price, US$ 27.60 in 2000 and US$ 28.15 in 2003 (OPEC). Similar trends were observable in western European economies. Again, economic policymakers, and the consumer population, acted entirely rationally.

Meanwhile, China's annual GDP growth, already an impressive 8 per cent in 2000, accelerated to nearly 12 per cent by end 2007 (*The Economist*, ibid.). China was buying increasing amounts of raw materials on the world markets, and rational market forces responded with price rises; between 2003 and 2008 the world oil price rose from US$ 28 to a peak of US$ 145. China was metamorphosing from a world engine of deflation into a generator of inflation. Spikes in oil, food, metals, and other commodity prices were exacerbated by speculation within the financial sector; again a rational development within a sector whose job description could almost be said to be to make money out of shifts in prices. Meanwhile the US Federal Reserve, concerned about the increasing US trade deficit and also looming inflation, rationally decided to increase interest rates. Between 2004 and 2007 US three-month rates rose from 1 per cent to over 5 per cent. Significantly the US 10-year rate, which had fallen to 4 per cent in 2003, only rose to just under 5 per cent, meaning the US yield curve turned negative in summer 2006. Long-term interest rates are usually above short-term rates because of higher risk, and a reversal of this relationship, known as a negative yield curve, signifies that traders are expecting a fall in interest rates in the longer term. In other words, they are expecting an economic slowdown, and in 2007 their expectations came true as the Credit Crunch began.

Bubbleconomics: The Difficulty of Regulating Boom and Bust

Lower real (that is, minus inflation) interest rates will, in non-recessionary times, stimulate economic growth as more low-yield investment projects are rendered viable. Lower nominal interest rates may go with lower consumer price inflation but these same lower rates produce higher asset price inflation. Shares prices may rise as economic investment and construction activity booms. Consumers feel they can borrow more, and the most significant arena where this borrowing rises is to fund what is the biggest asset purchase most consumers will ever make: a house. Rising house prices have their own stimulating effect on an already-growing economy, much as the radiant heat from a fire can cause other nearby materials to ignite and give off more heat. House owners like the feel of their main asset growing in value, and may remortgage to fund spending elsewhere. They feel secure that, even if consumer price inflation is low, the percentage debt against their house is being eroded by asset price inflation. Many US and UK house owners found that the nominal annual rise in their main asset exceeded their annual salary, and these homeowners began to see their homes as a "cash machine". This may be economically irrational but is psychologically rational, because if all your neighbours are buying 4 × 4s and holidaying in Dubai, you don't want to keep your old Ford Fiesta and holiday in Spain – especially if you too can easily upgrade. Like President Bush, "we can't let future distant economic unsustainabilities stop us from shopping", incidentally generating more VAT revenue for the taxman.

Governments then have a rational interest in allowing house prices to rise; this reason is called "taxation". Property-related taxes are one of the more politically painless ways to raise tax monies. Unlike VAT, the wealthy pay the most; unlike income tax the low to middle paid don't feel so squeezed, and taxes such as stamp duty seem a small part of the total transaction on a house purchase. Death duties, or inheritance taxes, are an even more lucrative and relatively painless tax; the higher the market valuation of a deceased's main asset, the higher the tax take. The UK rate is currently 40 per cent, but only applied to the portion of an estate's value that exceeds £325,000 (Directgov, 2010). With the asking price of a 4-bed semi-detached house in the ordinary middle-class suburb of Barnet, north London, being over £400,000 even in 2010, the tax take on an estate here can easily be worth several years' worth of income tax for a Barnet resident. Even more lucrative for the government is the "tax", effectively at 100 per cent, imposed on a homeowner who has to go into long-term residential care and possesses a substantial asset which they can be forced to sell to fund at least the first few years of this care.

The financial sector also creams off what is effectively unearned rents from a rising housing market; commissions rise, the volume of commission may also grow as the housing market becomes more frenetic, and remortgaging creates more commissions still. To nobly desist from this market whilst everyone else is plunging in will merely attract unfavourable comparisons; at least from the managers above, at worst from bank shareholders who will question why such a lucrative source of commission income is being passed over. Ideally one wants to get out, but only just in time; this converts the whole housing market into a pyramid scheme, playing roulette with people's living standards, and is scarcely ethical.

For all parties involved, from home owners, bankers, and estate agents to house builders, shopkeepers, and government, nobody has a rational reason to want the house price escalator to stop. Only first-time buyers seem to lose out, and they are generally young and fewer in number than home owners and less likely to vote anyway. Renters may also lose but they too are fewer in number and possibly more concerned with joining this escalator than in voting to halt it. As house prices continually rise beyond consumer price inflation, beyond wage inflation, a few dark clouds appear on the economic horizon. As far back as 2001 the Affordable Housing Scrutiny Committee of the Greater London Authority stated "each of these key groups [of workers in jobs in health services, schools, transport, and, policing] is associated with a clearly identified recruitment and retention problem [caused by lack of housing that is affordable to these workers], which is severely undermining service delivery" (Hillier, 2001). But in an age of globalization and free movement of labour, lower-grade workers can always be brought in from elsewhere, and many will put up with temporary cramped and very cheap accommodation, because their family and children remain in cheaper world locales. In Marxist terms, we have outsourced the reproduction of the labour force, and the benefit is that indigenous asset prices can continue to grow beyond what is sustainable for lower-grade worker's families.

So the housing bubble continues to grow, because for almost everyone it is rational to want it to continue to grow.

In this respect the recent European and North American housing market has been rather similar to the enterprises of a certain John Law, a Scottish financier born in Edinburgh in 1671; his career is described in the book *Extraordinary Popular Delusions and the Madness of Crowds* (Mackay, 1995:1–45). Amongst the many bubbles and financial schemes described in this book, from the Tulip(o)mania of 1637 to the South Sea Bubble of 1720, perhaps the Mississippi Scheme of John Law is closest to the UK housing market situation just before the 2007 Credit Crunch. John Law convinced naive and un-geographically-knowledged investors that the Mississippi region contained vast riches, that even gold was to be mined there. Rather like commission-hungry UK estate agents promising unending house price rises to new purchasers, John Law promised the impossible annual return of no less than 40 per cent upon the shares bought in his Mississippi scheme. And for a while such returns were actually realized, even exceeded, simply by the upwards price momentum established by the demand for these shares. There are other strange echoes of our housing crunch; the Rue de Quincampoix, in which Law's shares were traded, was narrow, and accidents frequently occurred (ibid.:14–15), just as in the 2000s the escalating housing market also produced its negative economic side effects. Just as in the 2000s, when ancillary trades such as builders and estate agents flourished on the back of the boom, so with the Mississippi Scheme, a hunchback reportedly became rich by renting his back out as an open air writing desk. Even the actual house rents in the Rue de Quincampoix soared by 1,700 per cent. The major difference between then and now was that the political establishment of John Law's day did not approve of his inflationary schemes.

Minsky, the US economist referred to earlier, divided the formation of an asset bubble into three stages; all of these are starkly clear when we consider the US or UK housing markets of the 2000s (*The Economist*, 2009). In stage one, an asset (owner-occupied or buy-to-let housing) is sought after, but investors only take on debt that they can both service the interest on and repay the capital over time; a repayment mortgage. In stage two, investors take on such a level of debt that they can only afford the interest repayments; an interest-only mortgage. In the UK in 2007 there was an intermediate stage between one and two where the normal life of a mortgage (25 years) was being extended to 50 years, and there were even proposals for 100-year mortgages, as in the Japanese housing bubble two decades earlier. A UK mortgage website (Mortgage Guide, 2007) beguilingly stated:

> *It is likely that interest rates are likely to keep rising in the UK because of persistently high house price inflation and high levels of borrowing. However this could leave many homeowners, especially first time buyers, in danger of failing to keep up with mortgage payments. And therefore are in danger of having their home repossessed. Some people argue 50 year old mortgages are bad because it means you will be paying mortgage payments when you are retired. However a 50 year old mortgage is much better than the alternative of not being able to buy or keep up with the mortgage payments.*

Minsky, who died in 1996, would have been fascinated. The third stage is when investors take on loans that they cannot even afford to service the current interest on, unless either their income rises or the asset they have borrowed to buy rises sufficiently in price for them to resell it and pay back the lender with the difference. These are the mortgages made to the sub-prime market in the US, or the "stated income" loans, or so-called "liar loans" made in the UK, often to self-employed applicants with no certifiable regular level of income. Again, some level of sub-prime/stated income loans is rational, because otherwise self-employed people would be shut out of a rising market, as would some less affluent mortgagees for whom owning a home might be their route out of near-poverty. And if one lender exited this market in the mid-2000s, others would simply enter and reap the gains.

Spanish philosopher, George Santayana, stated "Those who cannot remember the past are condemned to repeat it" (Partington A, 1992:555). In psychological terms people tend to be "present-biased" (*The Economist*, 2010b); they discount past and future events heavily. A small cost is avoided now even if the penalty for so avoiding will almost certainly be a much larger amount payable in the not so distant future (Duflo et al., 2009). The recorded history of Tulip(o)mania or the South Sea Bubble has not prevented history repeating itself, and it is doubtful if many mortgage lenders know the full story of such past bubbles. That is why there are calls for (re-)regulating the banking sector, concerning lending policies which might give rise to another future painful asset bubble. However, as demonstrated earlier, the mortgage lending sector was no more or less rational, or greedy, than any of the other many agencies and individuals implicated in the housing boom, its economic origins, and the subsequent Credit Crunch. Therefore the next section calls for a wider scheme of regulation, across many levels of the world economy from supranational organizations to individual lending.

"It's regulation Jim, but not as we know it": Nudging from Above

Bubbles once started have a momentum of their own although they may have very different origins. John Law's Mississippi Scheme bubble was arguably started by one individual, and Tulip(o)mania started when the entire middle classes of Amsterdam decided they wanted this plant (Mackay, 1995:89). The blame for starting the current Credit Crunch has been laid, by Britain, upon the banking sector; the USA has blamed China for artificially depressing the value of the Renminbi. *The Economist* (2010c) states:

> the original sin lies with [the Irish Government]. It paid too little attention to its gung-ho banks and asset markets. A property bubble blew up and Ireland became dangerously dependent on the revenues that flowed from it. The country's financial regulators were incompetent at best, cronies at worst.

A key feature of the Credit Crunch has been that of financial contagion, the global spread of risk, a history of multiple international causes. Such financial developments are often beyond the knowledge of Dublin house buyers, or those in the UK or USA, just as the true mineral resources of the Mississippi Valley were beyond the knowledge of French investors on the Rue de Quincampoix.

Ireland has demonstrated the reluctance of countries, even those linked by membership of the European Union, to give up any financial sovereignty, the right to set domestic interest levels and tax rates for example. From a tax perspective, a frothy housing market is similar to other socially undesirable but fiscally lucrative goods such as cigarettes; governments may claim to want to curb such goods but are rather glad such curbs are ineffective (Shaw J.J.A., 2010:668). Neither would it be desirable to prevent investors from making poor investment decisions, if they so wish; the great advantage of the free market is that money can be lost here, or unexpected gains may materialize, with wider societal benefits. However, free markets work best when information flows freely; it is desirable for risky investors to know the risks they are being exposed to. Banks have a legal duty first to their shareholders, and if an investment seems rational at the time, should they reduce shareholder profits by warning off such an investment because of possible future problems?

Such dilemmas of dual duties of care suggest that prevention of future bubbles such as the Credit Crunch can only be achieved with regulation at an international level. The UK has the Financial Services Authority (FSA), overseeing the activities of financial services companies. What may be needed is a Financial *Sustainability* Agency, set up not at national but at supra-national level. This agency would bring to the world of finance and banking the sort of sustainable principles proposed on an environmental level by the Brundtland Report (Aras and Crowther, 2009:26–28). Since Brussels is emerging not only as capital of the European Union but also as the "regulatory capital of the world" and leader in CSR initiatives (Shaw, H.J., 2010:197), this city could host such a body. The Financial Sustainability Agency would watch, not all world commodity and property prices, but certain key indicators where individuals might be at risk. House prices in developed countries could be on its watch list, along with key commodities such as wheat, where financial speculation at a time of potential shortages or price spikes has exacerbated food shortages and insecurity for many. It might be appropriate to fund this Financial Sustainability Agency by a "Tobin Tax" on relevant commodity transactions, such as wheat purchases or re-mortgages, that is, a low-level tax intended to deter frenetic market speculation rather than more "normal" market trades.

An emerging bubble can be detected either by an abnormal increase in trading volumes in that commodity (hence the Tobin Tax, to dampen this), or by price rises above the general level of inflation. Such price rises, especially if occurring in the short term, suggest a rise above the commodity's "intrinsic value". This intrinsic value can be hard to define, but if, say, there is an excess-RPI price rise over four consecutive quarters, especially an accelerating excess-RPI rise as in many European or US housing markets, it is likely that a bubble is emerging. The role of the Financial Sustainability Agency in warning of emerging bubbles would be no more than advisory, but it could nevertheless exert powerful moral suasion through its dissemination of information to governments, news agencies, and banks. By publicly advising democratic governments, for example, it lays that government open to censure from the opposition if the government chose to let the bubble develop, for short-term fiscal gain, followed by the foreclosure misery now evident from Dallas to Dublin.

The idea of a "nudge", rather than outright coercion, to achieve an economic or welfare goal is becoming more popular. In the UK, David Cameron has recently set up a so-called "nudge unit" to persuade British citizens to pursue a healthier lifestyle, without feeling forced into doing so. Nudge tactics, such as warnings on asset bubbles, would also work this way on governments potentially greedy for short-term tax gains. Through incentivization, through democratic pressure "nudged" from above, the goal would be to replace greed in politics with accountability, and to persuade banks to take the longer term view rather than being avaricious for short-term bubble profits, with the last buyers taking the biggest losses.

Replacing the Language of Greed with the Discourse of Generosity

The history of business rhetoric, particularly that employed by the financial world, inevitably forms a critical contribution to the language of power; in which the history of profiteering is best conceived as a history of resistance to assuming social responsibility, an oppositional narrative. From this perspective, the financiers act recklessly and they do not relate immediately (if at all) to the consequences of their own practices, rather they appear to connect only with the theory of their profession and the illusion of its unity in a single cause. Going beyond mere ethical laxity, this particular phantasm obscures and represses any question of legitimacy or responsibility in a wider sense. Such complication confers status and worth, and serves to justify, for example, the settlement of disproportionately large bonuses in a failing global economy. In this context the linguistic tool of repetition is significant in that it repeats an unreal history rather than attaches to real events as they occur; "repetition is in its essence symbolic; symbols or simulacra are the letter of repetition itself" (Deleuze, 1993: 17). The history of injustices, perpetrated by the lax manager, remains occluded in the mask of repetition and hidden within the imaginary system or body of (self-) regulation. Fact and fiction then become indistinguishable aided by an ahistorical silence and discontinuity which too often constitute the world of business and specifically the arguably reified financial order.

The often self-enclosed and self-referential world of business undermines the notion of an organization as a living organism, comprising human beings, which needs at its centre the proposition of a life-oriented goal, one which has its origin from within – alongside the profit motive, because "each entity ... contains the reason for its existence within itself; all parts react on one another" and for, not by, each other (Goethe, 2008:52). For Goethe there is beauty in the connection of the thinking subject and his objective nature, when substance and idea, matter and spirit, permeate each other; it creates a tangible sense of oneness with all the constituent parts of the universe. Goethe was an artist and he expresses the essential unity of the subjective and objective principles, of nature and mind, in aesthetic terms; believing that for every individual, his/her relationship to the world rests on the spirituality of nature and the naturalness of spirit. This "spirituality" is universally available and must be located within physical reality, against a mechanistic approach, and lends meaning to one's acceptance of, and behaviour in, the world. For Goethe the life of the individual is but a heartbeat in the all-embracing life of Nature, and spiritual unity is possible therefore because individuals are purported to be identical from the outset, as divergent rays of the collective human soul. For this reason each person has an equal moral value and the right to be treated with respect and dignity in acknowledgement of their oneness of essence and purpose; "To discover your way within the infinite, you need to distinguish and then unite" (Goethe, 2008:56).

Against the principle of a reciprocal society and the principle of accountability, the recent set of revelations relating to mismanagement within the banking sector has produced much anger from ordinary people who have been told to "tighten their belts" in these times of austerity. It is argued that such organizations, the financial institution being but one of many, fail to engage with wider society at their peril since in any society the authority of those wielding power depends ultimately upon the sovereignty of the general will; in which case the existence conditions for management practices are interpreted as consisting of layers of consensual social practices. These are perpetuated by countless individual acts of compliance and acceptance by private citizens and public officials, as part of the business organization, which are both interdependent and mutually reinforcing. According to Rousseau, the ruling institutions, organizations and their operations which govern society must accommodate certain aspirations which enable the social order to be realized – otherwise people will not agree to be obedient, because if they did give such a guarantee in advance then "by that very act it dissolves itself and loses what makes it a people" (1968:42). In this case, the business organization needs to train its managers to apply innovative research methods and theoretical inquiry towards the goals of an actual and potential societal benefit beyond the considerations of the balance sheet. This is perhaps not a completely controversial aspiration, because as mentioned earlier, CSR measures have been adopted successfully by some organizations; however, a major obstacle lies in the division of society into three broad categories. In general terms, the first group comprises the impoverished, browbeaten and poorly-educated working classes; the second group is composed of the institutes of governance, privileged interest groups and large corporations who seek to oppress the former category and control the third group; which comprises the well-educated, informed professionals whose role, in part, is to progress the development of society by considering the welfare of the disadvantaged. This alleged inherent power imbalance presents a challenge. Although it is desirable for the enlightened professional group (whose numbers contain business school academics) to attempt to achieve a compromise between any unreflective populists (who are vehemently opposed to the free market) and the self-serving power elite (whose numbers include powerful corporate actors), it is a difficult equation but one which must be addressed as society enters an indefinite period of economic and societal instability.

Various theorists have sought to effect a compromise by offering insight into the natural synergies produced by organizations. In 1948, American mathematician Wiener wrote about "circular causation" in his book *Cybernetics* which discussed the possibility of self-regulating systems engaging in dynamic interaction with their environment in the sense of both altering it and being altered by it. This was an attempt to understand how goal-oriented actions might be generated without consciousness; albeit with appropriate safeguards in place in recognition that human beings are too often greedy, corrupt and inadequate. Self-organization is a fundamental characteristic of most businesses and, within this environment, an agglomeration of individuals is largely responsible for any outcome, and rarely accountable outside the company gates – in the absence of formal or statutory scrutiny. This is, Wiener proposed, a form of business cybernetics which might be appropriately adopted and employed to encourage holistic engagement and acknowledgement of an interdependence with those outside the ordinary contemplation of an organization. It is possible that such an approach would give companies the real possibility of emerging as strategic influences and leaders in the area of social responsibility. A feminist perspective on recent corporate disasters may produce the conclusion that the global financial services firm Lehman Brothers would have stayed away from controversy if only they had been Lehman Sisters. There are many different perspectives which can be applied to management studies at university level and vocational training which locate the business operation within the context of civil society, and these seek to replace the "greed is good" mantra of fictional character Gordon Gekko from the seminal 1987 film *Wall Street* with a new mantra, namely "generosity is better".

Conclusion

The recent housing crisis is just the latest in a long series of speculative bubbles, all of which inevitably burst with painful and often widespread consequences. The current financial system does not seem to learn from history, to the extent that any wider discussion of the underlying premises of the financial model is impeded, if not actively discouraged, by the financial institutions themselves. The insistence on a narrow focus is likened to a "sharpening [of] the mind by narrowing it" (Holmes 1921:164,165). In fact one could ask, who should learn from history, since the global interconnectedness of the world economies means that modern bubbles may have multiple consequences and originate at many levels, from the individual to the global. Moreover it is in the interest of certain agencies not to learn from history, because they gain from at least the early stages of a bubble. However, eventually a bubble may turn out to be not just a zero sum game, where wealth is arbitrarily redistributed but little or none is created; as the housing experience in Ireland and the US has shown, a housing bubble can be a negative sum game, as repossessed housing is often damaged or even destroyed, either by its last occupants or post-repossession by vandals or squatters.

It is suggested in this chapter that a separate agency, purely advisory, with no possible vested interest in emergent bubbles, is necessary to achieve by nudging or persuasion what the current system of largely self-regulated or government-regulated bodies cannot achieve. This advisory agency would still preserve the creative dynamism of the free market; it could actually enhance this dynamism by preventing the negative sum outcomes that financial instabilities often produce. This role of advising rather than coercing might even be a future model for other intractable and multi-level global problems such as the economic uncertainties caused by global warming or chronic poverty. It is further proposed that by consciously seeking to provide an insight into the complexities of societal problems, in a manner which eludes mainstream actors who tend to prioritize the technicality and positivistic construction of the business model, it is possible to reconnect with the multifaceted wider audience who comprise the presently disenchanted world of humankind; towards the realization of a fairer, safer and more enlightened society of equal participants.

References

Adorno, T. (1991) *The Culture Industry*. Routledge, London.
Aras, G. and D. Crowther (2009) *The Durable Corporation*. Gower, Farnham.
Boyle, C. (2004) *Insurance Journal*. Accessed November 2010 at http://www.insurancejournal.com/magazines/east/2004/07/19/features/44587.htm.
Brandt, L. and T. Rawski (2008) *China's Great Economic Transformation*. Cambridge University Press, Cambridge, UK.
Dávila-Gómez, A.M. and D.E.A. Crowther (1997) *Ethics, Psyche and Social Responsibility*. Ashgate, Aldershot.
Deleuze, G. (1995) *Difference and Repetition*. Columbia University Press, US.
Directgov. Accessed November 2010 at http://www.direct.gov.uk/en/MoneyTaxAndBenefits/Taxes/BeginnersGuideToTax/InheritanceTaxEstatesAndTrusts/UnderstandingInheritanceTax/DG_179347.

Duflo, E, M. Kremer and J. Robinson (2009) *Nudging Farmers to Use Fertilizer: Theory and Experimental Evidence from Kenya*. National Bureau of Economic Research Working Paper 15131, July 2009, Massachusetts, USA.

Economist (2009) *Minsky's Moment*. 4 April 2009.

Economist (1983–2010a) financial figures published weekly – inside back cover.

Economist (2010b) *New Year Irresolution*. 2 January 2010.

Economist (2010c) *Saving the Euro*. 20 November 2010.

Goethe, J.W.V. (2008) *Goethe's Faust: Parts I and II*. Faber and Faber, London.

Hillier, M. (2001) *Final Report of the Affordable Housing Scrutiny Committee*. February 2001, published by the Greater London Authority.

Holmes, O.W. (quoting Edmund Burke) (1921) *Collected Legal Papers*. Harcourt, Brace and Co, New York.

Kant, I. (1997) *Critique of Practical Reason*. Cambridge University Press, Cambridge.

Mackay, C. (1995) *Extraordinary Popular Delusions and the Madness of Crowds*. Wordsworth Editions Ltd, Ware.

Mill, J.S. (1867) Inaugural Address at Saint Andrews. In *Classic and Contemporary Readings in the Philosophy of Education*, ed. S. Cahn. McGraw-Hill Company, New York.

Mortgage Guide (2007). Accessed November 2010 at http://www.mortgageguideuk.co.uk/50year mortgage.html.

Norris, T. (2005) Consuming Signs, Consuming the Polis: Hannah Arendt and Jean Baudrillard on Consumer Society and the Eclipse of the Real. In 2(2) *International Journal of Baudrillard Studies*.

OPEC website. Accessed November 2010 at http://www.opec.org/opec_web/en/data_graphs/40.htm.

Partington, A. (1992) *The Oxford Dictionary of Quotations*. Oxford University Press.

Rousseau, J.J. (1968) *The Social Contract*. Penguin Classics, London.

Shaw, H.J. (2010) The Regulatory and Legal Framework of Corporate Governance. In *A Handbook of Corporate Governance and Social Responsibility*, eds. G. Aras and D. Crowther. Gower, Farnham.

Shaw, J.J.A. (2010) A Case Study on The Tobacco Industry, Social Responsibility and Regulation. In *A Handbook of Corporate Governance and Social Responsibility*, eds. G. Aras and Crowther D. Gower, Farnham.

Shaw, J.J.A. and H.J. Shaw (2010) Business Education and Aesthetics and the Rule of Law Cultivating the Moral Manager, 6(3) *Social Responsibility Journal*.

Sieren, F. (2007) *The China Code*. Palgrave, Basingstoke.

Smith, A. (1910) *An Inquiry into the Nature and Causes of the Wealth of Nations, Vol. I*. Dent, London.

Smith, A. (1975) *The Theory of Moral Sentiments*, eds. D. Raphael and A. Macfie. Clarendon Press, Oxford.

West, T.G. (1979) *Plato's Apology of Socrates: An Interpretation*. Cornell University Press, New York.

Whitehead, A.N. (1929) *The Aims of Education and Other Essays*. Macmillan, New York.

Wiener, N. (1948) *Cybernetics: Or Control and Communication in the Animal and the Machine*. MIT Press, Massachusetts.

CHAPTER 4

Caring, Sharing and Collective Solidarity in Management

ANA-MARIA DAVILA-GOMEZ AND DAVID CROWTHER

A Reality that Needs to Change

We start from the postulate that managers are not only responsible for the organization's operation, but also for the moral obligation to contribute towards the continual development of their members and the surrounding community. An organization making part of a social and ecological system has to behave ethically and correspondingly with the other parts of the system. At a metaphysical level (Shelling, 1775–1854), we identify that the organization makes part of a planetary whole, as well as a part of the universe; in adopting this position, we are of course concurring with the Gaia Hypothesis[1] developed by Lovelock (1979). As Davila-Gomez and Crowther (2006) remind us, the true nature of organizations includes human and social finalities. Moreover, as stated by Boiral (2005) and Crowther (2002), ecological considerations are essential in the organization's practice.

Consequently, the reality of most of the organization's everyday actions that seek only the owners' profitability, with disregard for other stakeholders' interests, carries an imbalance in the cohesion and the wholeness of the system. Furthermore, as organizations are increasingly acting in a competitive global market, society as such becomes a worldwide concern. Inside this current complexity regarding an organization's way of operating, not only headquarters, employees, and the community surrounding the organization are at stake, but also communities overseas that are affected by off-shoring and outsourcing operations. What was previously conceived as the excess of power abuse of some industries in some countries, and which could be remedied to some extent through national legislation, is now many times out of control because

---

1 In 1979 Lovelock produced his Gaia hypothesis in which he posited a different model of the planet Earth; in his model the whole of the ecosphere, and all living matter therein, was co-dependent upon its various facets and formed a complete system. According to this hypothesis, this complete system, and all components of the system, was interdependent and equally necessary for maintaining the Earth as a planet capable of sustaining life. This Gaia hypothesis was a radical departure from classical liberal theory, which maintained that each entity was independent and could therefore concentrate upon seeking satisfaction for its own wants, without regard to other entities. This classical liberal view of the world forms the basis of economic organization, provides a justification for the existence of firms as organs of economic activity and provides the rationale behind the model of corporate behaviour adopted by society. The Gaia hypothesis however implied that interdependence, and a consequent recognition of the effect of ones actions upon others, was a facet of life. This consequently necessitates a different interpretation of organizational accountability in terms of individual and organizational behaviour.

of not having enough and appropriate international protective labour agreements or responsibility norms.

See for instance how the United Nations has been working for more than 40 years trying to legislate about that topic through multilateral discussions and negotiations. As a simple example that illustrates the repercussion on the very essence of a community caused by the above, we refer to how, since 1973, the legislation about the minimum accepted age for working was established at 18 years[2] (see International Labour Organization, 2000). As a norm, it has to be respected; however, some of its articles stipulate that this age may be reduced to 14 years, answering the pledge of some countries, that argue the need to increase their workforce in order to achieve economic development, and assuring that child labour will not be cruel and will not interfere with the child's education. However, reality indicates that these promises are not always kept and what lies behind is the possibility to meet a deadline with a very cheap labour force, leading to major profit for the owners. This way of accepting inequity inside organizations, reflects in some sense the intrinsic acceptance that some people have to sacrifice themselves in order to save others. Sadly, what lies behind this is the sacrifice of children and adolescents coming from underprivileged social strata, who must work instead of going to school. The whole situation is aggravated by the foreign capital invested in developing countries, especially at the end of the project when all profits return to the country of origin, leaving behind totally depleted local resources. What is the legacy here for incoming generations? Unfortunately, the social agreement that a country's economic development demands, for those less fortunate, is the acceptance of misfortune, and for those already wealthy, the possibility to increase their coffers.[3] The same situation occurs when some of the capital investment belongs to local shareholders, who receive profit redistribution as well. As such, inside a developing country, the elite improve their economic situation to the detriment of the majority of the population.

Many countries have always suffered from a lack of legislation that protects their citizens; nevertheless, the problem seems to have a major impact under globalization. A company that respects the rules of a developed country (for example, when legislation protects the employees from abuses in some way), may, however, go to operate some of its processes overseas, where other countries' legislation is not so protective, or simply because the wage labour is cheaper. This happens mostly in developing countries with economies that register a considerably lower average income than an average income from the developed country (see United Nations, 2006).

From a business' strategic perspective, the implementation of overseas operations requires technical, financial and marketing planning. Our research and bibliographical review[4] indicate to us that what is widely accepted as shareholders' interest is very well covered by managerial theoretical frameworks (for example, international commerce,

---

2   One of the first countries to require exemption from this rule was of course the USA – on the basis that 16 is sufficiently old to become a soldier and to kill people!

3   This is not a new situation of course. Arguably, the whole foundation of the Industrial Revolution is on the capital accumulation brought about by the exploitation of the European colonies in various parts of the world.

4   With the aid of Crowther and Green (2004), Calas and Smircich (1999), Parker (1999), Chia (1997, 1996), Burrel (1996), Séguin-Bédard and Chanlat (1983), Burrel and Morgan (1979), we extract the main orientations of different theories of organization. Afterwards, we consulted the approaches of various authors whose orientation include some of our concerns. Equally, in order to explore in-depth how the concepts of sharing and solidarity are addressed in management, we consulted various academic databases (e.g., ProQuest, Science Direct, ABI/Inform Global, among others) that access various journals such as *Organization Studies*, *Culture and Organization*, *Academy of Management Journal*,

outsourcing, re-engineering, and joint venture, among others) whereas other actors and issues are mostly neglected from much of Organization Theory and considered by many as mere ideological utopias. Hence, in management, the concepts of sharing and solidarity are not often referred to, in the sense of the wholeness we claim.

Even if one day it were possible to legislate about international "fair" labour accords or international commerce norms, there is something more essential that needs to be addressed. We talk here about the integrity of those who legislate (mainly at governmental instances – either national or supranational), and those behind the action, those with economic power: owners and managers, those who decide, those whose capital will be increased or diminished depending on legislation or on their firm's activities.

There is a need for owners and directors to act otherwise, to care about others rather than exclusively care about themselves.

Christian Teachings: Caring within the Wholeness

With the above, a central question arises: is it necessary to foresee all the possible abuses and as a response, to structure norms and laws in order to protect the powerless against the abuses of the powerful? Or, what else could be done complementary to legislation?

We argue that an organization's responsibility goes beyond norms and legislation. Recognizing the necessity of norms, because otherwise our reality would be more denigrating than it actually is, we identify that it is also a question of the individual's responsibility. We talk here about the free choices and actions that individuals in power make while exercising their liberty. What does the individual decide? Who is he or she affecting with the consequences of his or her actions and how? We talk here about *concern* for others.

Inside a positivist and utilitarian perspective of the firm's operation, the need for concern towards individuals other than shareholders is something left behind and treated mostly by academics who have a background in social sciences (for example, psychology, sociology, philosophy, anthropology). Thus, many practitioners might think that while talking about concern for others, we refer to a dogmatic religious imposition in the sense of practising charity as an asset to gain eternal peace. Nonetheless, we reclaim the need for concern as an act of caring, as a value, as a virtue (that is, what Verstraeten (1998) demands as moral duties, and willingness to behave humanely in organizations). According to Socrates (in the Meno dialogue – see Plato (399–384 BC)), a virtue represents the practical action of the soul, therefore the essence of the being. Good actions towards the external world, including others, indicate ethical choices and moral concern.

While talking about caring, we follow what Marcel (1949) and Kierkegaard (1813–1855) referred to, as the reality of losing religion. According to them, this losing, rather than a question of knowing and reciting religious precepts, treats mostly what human beings need in order to live a fulfilling life in accordance to the wholeness, which for them means to act according to beliefs such as, what it is conceived as good for oneself should also provide goodness for others. In this sense, if with my action I am inflicting pain to someone else, I am also procuring it to myself given that the other makes part of the whole as well as I do. The whole has an essence, and any part of it *shares* its essence with the other parts.

Business Strategy Review, Business Ethics Quarterly, Business Ethics: A European Review, Strategy, Management Learning, Journal of Organizational Behaviour Management Quarterly, among others.

This is the first meaning of the concept of *sharing* we reclaim in business. Sharing, more than exclusively a monetary distribution of profits between capital owners implies also to share these profits, and the goodness of the organization's activities, directly with those who contribute to its achievement. However, as we know, capital owners avoid their responsibility of sharing given that they consider that their social debt is already paid by means of taxes, and consequently, the nation's wealth redistribution is an exclusive function of the state.[5] On the contrary, in our opinion, following a wholeness orientation, sharing in a broader scope is not exclusively a function of the state; it is a normal activity of any member of the community towards all the others.

In the idea of wholeness, Marcel (1965) refers to what the German poet Rilke conceived: an interconnected total of oneness, a unity that includes not only human lives, but also nature (animals, plants and non-living things). A mutual respect for anything that exists must be shown by each one of us, because hurting or mistreating somebody or even something produces dissatisfaction and sorrow in other parts of the whole. At the same time, care for all the parts, in a sense of individual responsibility, contributes to a more balanced whole, therefore, to one's own fulfilment and satisfaction.

Moreover, Marcel (1949) indicates that even if some religious persons may act following the precepts of goodness towards other people, there is still a path to walk for the acknowledgement that existence and essence go beyond human exclusivity. Marcel denounces the anthropocentrism of many of us as an impediment for acting inside a whole equilibrium. According to him, as God is recognized by religion as the totality of the whole – to its fullest extent, the universe; in order to be responsible towards nature and the ecosystem, everything, all constituents of this whole are part of the total essence, and therefore they merit consideration, respect and caring.

The acknowledgement of this reality implies accepting the importance of equality. A factual solidarity is imperative. As indicated by Reedy (2003: 95): "solidarity belongs to the same family of ideas as mutuality, reciprocity and community". For us, a feeling of empathy, of sensibility, will help us to acknowledge that other people's existence is as important as our very own. On the one hand, regardless of social and economic strata, by essence, as a whole's essence, it is imperative for people to be concerned for other people, to care about them. On the other hand, people's rational capabilities have to be used to serve mutually beneficial purposes and reciprocity within the wholeness, rather than exclusive for individual enrichment with disregard for other's distress, or even, for a decline in the environmental quality. As nature nourishes us by providing produce for our sustenance, we have to nurture nature aiming for its conservation. And this is not only with a sense of compassion in which some remedy other's misfortune, which is indeed needed in our reality, full of inequity, but mostly in the sense of not acting while knowing beforehand that our actions will cause distress to others, or to the environment. In this sense, action with forethought is essential to succeed.

Bearing that in mind, it is apparent that managers and owners are also responsible for the suffering, goodness or pain resulting from their actions. And as such, as beings sensitive to what their choices may produce towards others and towards nature, they invest a moral component in their action. Power is not only individual egocentricity, but

---

5   The whole economic foundation of commercial activity is predicated in the Utilitarian philosophy of the separation of parts of the organization (into capital, labour, and so on) and to reward the parts on a different basis. This is used to legitimate the major portion belonging to capital on the spurious basis that it is a reward for risk.

also responsibility towards the governed systems, either personnel in an organization, citizens in a community, or the natural environment around the firm. Power entails compromise, care, and responsibility. In addition, from the point of view of management education, there is a need to contribute to the students' acknowledgement and sensibility towards otherness and wholeness.

From Philosophical Comprehension to Action

Since philosophy helps us to understand our world with the aim of helping us to achieve an individually and collectively fulfilled life, it is then necessary to look at how this concern is theorised in organizational behaviour and to what extent critical reflections concerning *caring, sharing* and *solidarity* are directly leading to practical actions. Kierkegaard (1813–1855) stated that a good Christian is not the one who knows what the theory includes, but the one who acts on it.

Looking for organizational theories that may address our concerns, and also, stimulate action, our bibliographical review[6] shows us that some authors have already denounced the egocentric praxis of most organizations. For instance, Aktouf (2001) and Alvesson and Willmott (1996), among others, criticize mostly how the ideology that lies behind an organization's actions follows a positivistic owner's view with the purpose of increasing profitability through disregarding consequences towards others: community and even supranational systems. Others authors follow in similar vein (for example, Knights and Willmott, 1999), and complement and maintain a more complete and complex understanding of the organization. Much of their value is based on the opportunity to offer new approaches for the comprehension of the organization as a whole and not as mere chain production or a market model. Indeed, as our bibliographical review indicates,[7] many of these approaches arise from a new philosophical paradigm such as postmodernism, which includes an element of post-structuralism. Post-modern theory in organization takes the precepts of the Frankfurt School of Critical Theory with thinkers and philosophers such us Horkheimer, Adorno and Marcuse, among others, who, through social reflexivity, question the validity of ideologies in praxis. Complementarily, a post-structural orientation takes, among others, the precepts of Giddens (1984), in the sense that organizations are cut into inter-related structures, the understanding of which demands more than mere mechanical and scientific considerations to operate the organizations' social and productive capacity.

With the latest approaches, cultural and sociological aspects of the organization, we are able to explain a particular organizational specificity and its connections with externality inside a whole macro-social structure. This new orientation has as well, an element of non-normative theories in which, for instance, pluralism allows the cohabitation of multiple concepts and constructs explaining a particular phenomenon, all of which coexist inside the complexity. Eclecticism takes its part for the new scientific understanding of the organization either as a social actor or as a construct of cultural and human dimension. A case of these new inclusions is the constructivist metaphysical explanation of the organization as a being or as a becoming (for example, Tsoukas and

---

6   Idem 4.
7   Idem 4.

Chia, 2002), or as a place for existential human experience (for example, Ashman and Winstanley, 2006; Agarwal and Malloy, 2000).

Following Kierkegaard's (1813–1855) ideal of virtue in action, with the aim of implementing the above, we are concerned by the way in which a manager could serve himself or herself through the previous approaches in order to include human, social and ecological considerations when he or she addressees a board of directors or a shareholders assembly when the decision-making processes starts, hence, immediate action must be taken.

For this, our bibliographical review[8] indicates that, complementary to the aforementioned, there are also new avenues that offer alternative theoretical frames that include practical models for action management. Some of these may be based on those critically oriented theories referred to previously, but they complement themselves with a praxeologic approach. Among these new approaches, we refer here to: social responsibility, and human values. For instance, within a social responsibility approach, Crowther (2002) reclaims the need to manage organizations with a genuine concern for stakeholders other than owner's, demanding as imperative the recognition of the rights of community groups, employees and also, those of environmental issues, every time that an organizational act is conducted. More specifically, for Crowther (2002) and Crowther and Rayman-Bacchus (2004), social responsibility includes the transparency and legitimacy of reports (for example, financial, Corporate Social Responsibility reports, institutional statements on the Web, in the press, and so on) and actions within the framework of a policy of openness and public accountability. In the same sense, Goodpaster, Maines and Rovang (2004) develop an applied planning framework for managers where stakeholders' relationships are detailed at a strategic level. Equally, Giri (2004) proposes a path for going from discourse to action, through a spiritual transformation of the being. Davila-Gomez (2005, 2004) and Pauchant (1995) present the need to considering meanings and ethical actions in the workplace in order to improve organizations and the collective quality of life. Similarly, Bhatta (2004) and Solomon (1998), among others, indicate that the practice of human values helps managers to act with a greater concern towards others.

With our concerns about caring and solidarity previously discussed, we identify that both a stakeholder's approach and a humanistic spiritual orientation address also some governmental issues such as regulations as well as dialogue between firms and social institutions, which, for us, implies a sense of solidarity, when every part of the whole is concerned about the other parts of the whole.

Needing to boost more caring actions in order to contribute to a better future, we present, as follows, a critical reflection about how caring within the wholeness is something, either encouraged or avoided in management education.

Management Education and the Awakening of Consciousness

Education is one of the most important instances in which future managers and owners may have the opportunity to awaken some hidden interests and to explore them. It is a good place to gain awareness of the nature of reality, to question the validity of putting later into action what they are acquiring as knowledge.

---

[8]   Idem 4.

When the new models of organizational understanding presented before are taught in business schools, they may trigger either the curiosity of the student (the future manager) or the conscious reflection of their meaning or their usefulness for practical managerial action. The great question here is: who is gaining the opportunity and the possibility to get into contact with these new questionings – with these new avenues: all future managers?

In trying to answer these questions, we take into account our previous research (for example, Davila-Gomez, 2003), some other recent texts that explore the contents and orientations of business education (for example, Arif, Smiley and Kulonda, 2005; Heil, 2000; Bickerstaffe, 1999; Broon and Lorange, 1996; Polican, 1996; Porter and McKibbin, 1988), as well as our experience as academics. From these sources, a view of a different MBA corpus indicate to us that the thematic courses including philosophy, sociology or other human sciences is something that remains, more and more, as elective option[9] – which is the same also for MSc and MA programmes. It is as if people who may benefit from these new alternative models need to be interested in them as an a priori intrinsic concern. On the contrary, the majority of BAs, MBAs or MScs provide compulsory courses such as Finance, Strategy, International Commerce, and in various occasions Human Resource Management. The few cases where courses with social and human content make part of the obligatory corpus are those where the programme adds them in its very domain – as a "major in"; for example, MSc option Social science; or MSc Environmental option, among others.[10] In this way, students who begin a general BA, MBA or MSc, when these programmes do not include a prior social and human concern, find it very difficult for them to apply voluntarily to the kind of optional courses presented above.

As such, business administration theoretical corpuses still concentrate on furnishing the future (or actual) managers with the tools that they will need to excel in a competitive world, and when it comes time for having to account for actions, financial courses will supply them with national and international accounting that follow the rules of current legislation. There are some problems here. For instance, when corporations want to increase profitability, they seek to expand their markets and increase productivity, avoiding to a greater extent any considerations regarding human, social, and ecological issues. Equally, even if there are different levels of nations' legislation, varying from controlling to liberated, accounting reports are worldwide based almost on the same model to present balances and financial data, which to us, does not show the complete true image of an organization. In fact, these reports concentrate mostly in showing the efficacy of the firm, through the increasing value of the share – an indicator of the firm's success.

Therefore, as we claim the need for solidarity and sharing in a broader scope, other constituents of the whole need to be addressed. Not everything may be controlled, measured or "impersonally" managed by means of technology. However, decisions are mostly based on financial indicators (see Cooper et al., 2001, and Crowther and Carter, 2002)[11] that fail to include the other organizational constituents we claim about.

---

9 We recognize, however, the trend for an increased concern with ethics in such courses and that therefore, as a consequence, there is now an ethical component – either as a separate module or integrated into the curriculum through other modules – in virtually all MBA courses. This does not of course detract at all from our statements here.

10 See for example the trend for Masters courses in such topics as corporate social responsibility.

11 Crowther and Carter (2002) argue that while business schools, and the academics within, continue to seek legitimation from within their own community through increasingly self-referential discourse and specialization the

This is critical for the university as a social institution, at least concerning Business Education, in the sense that a broader knowledge of the whole organization is restricted to individuals who are previously interested in those courses, instead of being a compulsory subject. Where is the ontological mission of the university that Borrero (1995) addressed? Where is nowadays the philosophical aim of Plato's academy, expanding knowledge by means of the students' contact with social realities and needs? Where is the humanistic vein of education that Pestalozzi (1746–1827) and Rousseau (1712–1778) saved from the liberal arts contained in the trivium (grammatic, rhetoric, logic) and the quadrivium (arithmetic, geometry, music-harmony, astronomy-cosmology), and ultimately the philosophy (theoretical, practical, and mechanical)? As explained by Ozmon and Craver (1999) and by the Encyclopaedia Britannica (2006), liberal arts and philosophy answered to the education needs of the elites under the guidance of the clergy during the Middle Ages. Moreover, in the practical domain of philosophy, there was a concern for morals or ethics (personal, economic and political). These corpuses constituted the basic body of knowledge of the university and were inspired from the teachings of the classical Greek philosophers who encouraged the development of the soul and the collective well-being.

As we see, inside the actual business education orientation, the general concerns of the above mentioned precepts, while essential, are nowadays relegated to an option for the student, because specialization is more important that contextualization and meaning. Where is, then, the moral aspect of education that Dewey (1975) talked about? Furthermore, what can we expected of organizational actions when the individuals, academically formed under the positivist aforementioned precepts, are likely to reproduce what are financially driven society privileges, namely increasing share value and productivity? This is one of the reasons why social changes involving improving the collective well-being take so long to produce results. As educators, we have to present other alternatives to the students different from the continuity of the "share value" financial ideal that prevail to the detriment of human development. Hereby, we align our concerns with what Reedy (2003) and Reynolds (1999) discuss about the realities of the relationship of the hierarchical student-professor power relationship as an in-class reproduction of organizational social life.

It is imperative to humanize our teaching in order to awaken feelings of caring and concern in our students. Thus, as a great endeavour for management education, it is important to target the awakening of the individual's consciousness while acting, following what Kierkegaard (1813–1855) states about becoming sober:

To become sober is: to come so close to oneself in one's understanding, one's knowing, that all one's understanding becomes action [...] Therefore we men, cunning as we always are in relation to God and godly truth, have concentrated our whole attention upon understanding and knowing; we pretend that it is here the difficulty lies, and that then the consequence naturally follows as a matter of course that we would do it. [...] All my labour with respect to knowing has no effect upon my life, upon its lusts, its passions, its selfishness; it leaves me entirely unchanged – it is my action which changes my life. [...] But still rarer than such a presentation which is the thing presented, still rarer is it than a man's understanding of a thing is his action, that the fact of his understanding what ought to be done is expressed by-oh, noble simplicity!-his doing it! No, there is nothing more deceitful than the human heart, and never

---

world of their customers is increasingly requiring generalization rather than specialization.

perhaps does it display itself more clearly than by this disproportion between our understanding and our action. (Kierkegaard, 1813–1855:130–134)

With the above, as we claim the need for managers' and owners' moral behaviour, it is imperative to have more activities of self-discovery through action in management education. In addition, this is not only exclusive to the courses treating human and social aspects, but also in almost any subject (even if it is related to finance), because, as discussed, any decision, any action of any kind, triggers consequences for the whole. Reflection on that matter helps to acknowledge and to develop a sense of accountability in the future director.

In order to procure those kinds of pedagogical activities, it is imperative in PhD programmes to encourage their application by current and future professors of managers. Thus, theoretical corpuses of any administration doctoral domain (for example, finance, strategy, organizational culture, and so on) should consider it. If we want to contribute to changes in managerial action, we also need to improve our critical teaching. Caring about our students' future is also a way of placing solidarity for the well-being of the collective, through the sharing of knowledge, experiences and also concerns to address within the whole: it is action.

Keeping in mind the above, and taking into account the reflections we made in previous points, we present as follows a deeper reflection about what is needed to be conceived as *sharing* and *solidarity* in management.

How to Share?

As indicated previously, the positivist paradigm of the firm states that, while organizations increase share value, they are able to contribute increasingly with taxes, therefore, to the wealth of a nation.[12] It is assumed that governmental instances are those charged with the redistribution of a nation's wealth. There is the assumption that people are citizens while talking about society, whereas inside the capitalist perspective, people only mean a labour force – therefore human resource – or a market target.

In this sense, for social institutions, people deserve something as reciprocity for their collaboration with creating global richness, and, for organizations, people are another resource. As such, it is inconceivable that they receive a part of the profits of the increased share value. People inside organizations lose their human condition. They are only a means by which the invested capital increases, hence, they should not receive a compensatory reward for wealth increase other than a fixed salary and a prospect of redistribution of wealth, granted by the government.

As is apparent from previous points, sharing is intrinsic to the idea of wholeness. Our bibliographical review in management[13] indicates that, most of the times, the concept of share or sharing is referred upon the meaning of "shareholder value", following the described positivistic approach. Quite the opposite, there is very little bibliography concerning the other meaning we claim (sharing with the wholeness); it is almost

---

12   Indeed Trickle Down Theory argues that ultimately everyone gains from an increase in wealth. This theory is of course nonsense and merely a legitimating device of the New Right.
13   Idem 4.

non-existent. However, increasingly, there are a vast number of texts and articles treating the concept of compassion (for example, Kanov et al., 2004; Frost, 1999; Solomon, 1998; White, 1998; Kouzes and Posner, 1992). As we referred it previously, even though compassion is necessary, there is a need for preventive action, for forethought.

To sustain our point that the actual praxis of organizations is contrary to the nature of things, a look at the *Encyclopaedia Britannica* (2006) indicates that in its nature, the concept of sharing not only implies the distribution of share, but also includes "a: to partake of, use, experience, occupy, or enjoy with others; b: to have in common". Moreover, the contrasted words for this concept are "retain" and "withhold". As such, sharing encloses naturally, the right of enjoying the share value (and the profits) with the parts of the common, to us, the wholeness, including every employee. Equally, retaining (as contrasted to sharing) the product of the wholeness by some of its parts (shareholders) implies a misbalance that produce the consequences we discussed previously (for example, inequity and injustice).

From our perspective of sharing, as daring as it may sound, in a practical example, it implies increasing salaries or other benefits proportionally to the increase in profits.[14] In fact, it is not so out of this world when we think that already some financial cooperatives and banks are converting their current-account holders to shareholders, and in some cases, for other corporations, a portion of the institution's annual profits are redistributed between current-account holders.[15] Practices of this kind need to be more frequent in more industries and firms, including international manufacturing corporations, or even in public services utilities.

Another way of sharing, and this in a more moral human dignity-sustaining orientation, is to be supportive as a manager. As Shaw (2006) and Haw (2004) remind us, there is a need for love in organizations. For us, employees need to be listened to, in order for them to be able to share their fears and even their desires to fulfil inside the organization and in society. Going beyond listening, among the managers' responsibility we discussed previously, a great deal of caring is to act in this manner, to accompany all employees in the process of helping them realize themselves as persons, and this, goes inside what we call human development in organizations which has a broader scope than a human resources management policy.

As reality indicates, in management, there is a lack of theoretical background in sharing with greater human, social and ecological concern; there is a need to develop it and to promote it from the very classrooms while applying the already described self-examination and the awakening activities. In our opinion, in order for an owner to be open to share what he or she owns by law, which is everybody's by nature, implies acknowledgment of the wholeness. It implies sensibility. It demands going beyond rationality and entering the field of the senses, the field of the meanings: the true meaning of earning profit and what it represents to the parts involved in this achievement. As such, *caring* and *solidarity* values are essential.

---

14   It is quite normal to reward the Board and senior managers in this way to recognize that they have contributed to an increase in profit. Equally, in financial institutions it is common to provide bonuses in this way. Our argument is that all employees contribute towards that profit and should therefore benefit from its growth.

15   As an example, see the case of the *Caisse Populaire Desjardins*, a financial institution in Québec (Canada) that distributes surplus earnings at the end of the fiscal year by means of Patronal allocations (see Desjardins, 2006).

Where and How May We Place Solidarity?

Based on our bibliographical review,[16] the concept of *solidarity* in management is more widely extended as subject than the concept of *sharing*, but mostly concerning the positivistic orientation and not the wholeness orientation. In fact, in the positivist paradigm, *sharing* is conceived as an inter-organizational activity in which the figure of "joint-venture" (see for example Krause, Handfield and Tyler, 2006; Mahama, 2006) allows different organizations to share mostly knowledge, markets, and some of the logistics components of the chain production. Behind these actions lies the need to reduce costs and to pay some contributions to those with the know-how to do something better and cheaper, indeed in a more productive manner, than the organization can do. In a way, the fact of counting with strategic partnerships attracts international ventures. Moreover, as a result of accounting reports showing strong businesses, attractive overseas investments are authorized by governments of developing countries upon the premise of contributing to economic development. The danger of this practice is that if *sharing* continues as we presented it before – globalization and positivism – the societal contribution is minimal and the quality of life of the individuals working in the organization is not improving significantly.

As good as this solidarity sounds for business, it does not include, however, our *solidarity* concern with the other constituents of the organization. In fact, the *Encyclopaedia Britannica* (2006) shows that solidarity is "a feeling of unity (as in interest, standards, and responsibilities) that binds members of a group together", and indicates as synonym the word "togetherness" and as a contrasted word "disorganization". As togetherness is something included in wholeness, our claim implies, then, that organizations need to share in a broader scope than what they are doing nowadays. Furthermore, as disorganization is the contrary of solidarity, the organization's reality denies a very important aspect of its essence. Our organizations are disorganized.

As our bibliographical review indicates,[17] some exceptions are made, but mostly in the case of social institutions (see for example Broussine and Miller, 2005; Reedy, 2003). As national values, it is widely accepted that social organizations, including governmental, must seek the collective's well-being, and therefore, solidarity between organizations of these kinds is needed in order to share efforts in the search for a common goal. Recognizing the importance of this aspect, we identify, however, that there is still need to reflect on solidarity inside and within organizations.

In our reality of inequities and difficulties, we conceive as very dangerous the way in which the precepts of profit-oriented operations of the firms are translated, almost blindly, into social and governmental institutions. A philosophy of positivistic administration is invading these institutions by means of leading them towards profitability (even if the profits will go to the government's coffers for later redistribution) by means of the same tools used in private sector companies such as reengineering processes, and productivity (measured and oriented towards quantitative indicators of performance).

Equally, in doing so, many public organizations worldwide contract new debt – which is extremely high in many developing countries – in order to refinance the service of the debt (formerly acquired), compromising not only the firm's cash flow, but also its normal

---

16   Idem 4.
17   Idem 4.

operations. Given that managers and directors are more concerned with and concentrated on strategy options, they also compromise the true social mission of the institution, the very reason of existence of the organization. In that way, we see for example how some health institutions fail to give full coverage to the community, or how public education fails to admit numerous potential students into their systems. As a paradox, these same institutions are receiving budget reinforcements from the state in order to upgrade their technical systems and archives, among other material components, hoping that while making the "chain operation" more productive, more services will be provided. As we see, the raison d'être comes second, because even if productivity means are put into operation, there is still a need to train more doctors, more teachers, and to improve the quality of the provided services.

Instead of managing the institutions with the solidarity of the collective in mind, we are managing them mostly thinking about cost-operation ratios, and in some cases, profitability. For instance, as an example, we refer here to the case of public service utilities that increase their price (rate) above the national consumer price index (CPI)[18] because there is a need to consolidate the company assets, even though it is known many times beforehand, that the stability of the institution's business is not at stake. In fact, some of the subsidiaries operate in other countries; however, the idea of "increasing shareholder value" is so attractive (even if this share is of public domain) that directors put in operation their knowledge background in strategy and business. These practices fail to accomplish the sense of solidarity because, even though institutions of these kinds belong to the people, to obtain the coverage of their services, is becoming more and more expensive. The average family income grows (about the same rate or lower than the CPI) and at a lower rate than the increase of the price of the utility services (a rate that frequently doubles the CPI), leading to a decline in the purchasing power of individuals, hence resulting in a general decline of their standard of living. Increasingly, people have less money to pay for their services. As citizens, we fail to enjoy the benefits of our collective share value.

Another example of social institutions being conducted with a firm's perspective of increasing share value is the case in which some employees need to be fired in order to downsize the state's bureaucracy. We see here, again, the assumption that the sacrifice of some individuals is a fair price to pay, given that, at the end, the collective will benefit. However, to us, this contradicts the very purpose of the action. There is no moral action concerned with the wholeness. It is here where we question the responsibility of directors acting in this manner. And, in an effort to try to balance more the parties of the whole, if a downsizing is required because the work done there is becoming obsolete, other possibilities of replacement have to be created or found to those who will lose their actual job. It is possible to balance the whole while repositioning and sustaining the whole, but not by inflicting distress to some of its parts for the benefit of others. For instance, human development would suggest that people coming from the closing department can be trained in new activities in order to be redeployed in other departments, or at other organizations. In this kind of initiative, managers as *caring* beings for their personnel, should generate *solidarity* between other managers of other organizations, as

---

18 As it happens with *Hydro Québec*, the public service utility that covers the province of Québec in Canada (see Radio Canada, 2006a,b).

well as between their colleagues in their own organization, in order to offer perspectives, possibilities and avenues of action to their personnel.

With the latter examples, a new problem has arisen: what is the collective benefit from managing an institution in a very successful financial way when its primary duty towards the community is failing? As we referred to in previous paragraphs, the decision for this kind of operation is the responsibility of both, the institution's directors and the government officials. It lies in the domain of the ethical choices and the consequent actions. These directors and government officials have the compromise to act responsibly towards the community that they represent. They must ensure the development of the members of the community and, therefore, act with a sense of solidarity.

Another problem with the government officials and senior executives in social institutions is that many times they are removed from their positions every time that a new political affiliation comes into power. Then, projects and initiatives change and previous ongoing efforts of social improvement are abandoned because new waves of ideas from the new directors are judged as better. However, without continuity, neither old nor new initiatives will see their project finished; in the end, winds of change will arise when the term of office of the party currently in power ends. In some of the cases, even if an initiative is planned to fit into the term of office of the political party remaining in power, sometimes governmental bureaucracy is so heavy that decisions and approvals take more time than expected.

Therefore, various social problems will remain the same until the government, represented at all levels, including all appointed directors at social institutions, accept the challenge of taking decisions and acting on them, in order to start and to finish project initiatives within the term of office. In this way, with ethical actions, changes are produced, especially when the decisions and actions emanate not only from one person, but also from many other who are interconnected in a chain of mandates, a hierarchy. This reflects collective solidarity: numerous decision-making owners working together for the well-being of the community.

As stated by Aung San Suu Kyi (1991 Nobel Prize for Peace, in an interview conducted by White, 1998), individuals must compromise with the community. Private firms must act in the same way. In our opinion, it implies a true feeling of "caring" as a natural essence, the practical action of which is served through *sharing* and *solidarity*.

References

Agarwal, J. and Malloy, D.C. (2000) "The Role of Existentialism in Ethical Business Decision-making" *Business Ethics: A European Review* Vol. 9, No. 3, July, pp. 143–154.

Alvesson, H. and Willmott, H. (1996) *Making Sense of Management: A Critical Introduction* Sage, London.

Aktouf, O. (2001) "Mondialisation et Post-mondialisation: implacables logiques de marginalisation?" *Cahier de recherche du Centre d'études en administration internationale (CETAI)* 2001–05, Sept., École des HEC de Montréal, Montréal.

Arif, M., Smiley, F.M. and Kulonda, D.J. (2005) "Business and Education as Push-pull Processes: An Alliance of Philosophy and Practice" *Education* Vol. 125, No. 4, Summer, pp. 602–614.

Ashman, I. and Winstanley, D. (2006) "Business Ethics and Existentialism" *Business Ethics: A European Review* Vol. 15, No. 3, July, pp. 218–233.

Bhatta, C.P. (2004) "Effective Leadership: Human Values Perspective" in A.D. Gupta (ed.) *Human Values in Management* Ashgate, Aldershot, pp. 223–240.

Bickerstaffe, G. (1999) *Which MBA?: A Critical Guide to the World's Best MBAs* 11th edn, Pearson Education, London.

Boiral, O. (2005) "Concilier environnement et competitive, ou la quête de l'éco-efficience" *Revue Française de gestion* Vol. 31, No. 158, pp. 163–186.

Borrero, A. (1995) "L'Université aujord'hui" *Centre de recherches pour le développement international*, Ed. Unesco, Paris.

Broon, P. and Lorange, P. (1996) "Management Education, Future of" in M. Warner (ed.) *International Encyclopaedia of Business and Management* Routledge, USA, Canada, pp. 2724–2734.

Broussine, M. and Miller, C. (2005) "Leadership, Ethical Dilemmas and 'Good' Authority in Public Service Partnership Working" *Business Ethics: A European Review* Vol. 14, No. 4 October, pp. 379–391.

Burrel, G. (1996) "Normal Science, Paradigms, Metaphors, Discourses and Genealogies of Analysis" in Clegg, S.R., Hardy, C. and Nord, W.R. (eds) *Handbook of Organization Studies* Sage, London, pp. 642–658.

Burrel, G. and Morgan, G. (1979) *Sociological Paradigms and Organizational Analysis* Heinemann, London.

Calas, M. and Smircich, L. (1999) "Past Postmodernism? Reflections and Tentative Directions" *Academy of Management Review* Vol. 24, No. 4, pp. 649–671.

Chia, R. (1997) "*Essai*: Thirty Years On: From Organizational Structures to the Organization of Thought" *Organization Studies* Vol. 18, No. 4, pp. 685–707.

Chia, R. (1996) "The Problem of Reflexivity in Organizational Research: Towards a Postmodern Science of Organization" *Organization* Vol. 3. No. 1, pp. 31–59.

Cooper, S., Crowther, D., Davies, M. and Davis, E.W. (2001) *Shareholder or Stakeholder Value? The Development of Indicators for the Control and Measurement of Performance*; CIMA; London.

Crowther, D. (2002) *A Social Critique of Corporate Reporting* Ashgate, Aldershot.

Crowther, D. and Carter, C. (2002) "Legitimitating Irrelevance: Management Education in Higher Education Institutions" *International Journal of Education Management* Vol. 16 No. 66, pp. 268–278.

Crowther, D. and Green, M. (2004) *Organisational Theory* Chartered Institute of Personnel and Development, London.

Crowther, D. and Rayman-Bacchus, L. (2004) "The Future of Corporate Social Responsibility," in D. Crowther and L. Rayman-Bacchus (eds) *Perspectives on Corporate Social Responsibility* Ashgate, Aldershot, pp. 229–249.

Davila-Gomez, A.M. and Crowther, D. (2006) "Reaching the True Nature of Organizations: Human and Social Finalities" *Social Responsibility Journal* Vol. 2, No. 1, May, pp. 104–111.

Davila-Gomez, A.M. (2005) "Beyond Business Ethics: Managers' Ethical Challenges Concerning Community and Employees" in D. Crowther and R. Jatana, (eds) *Representations of Social Responsibility* Vol. 1 ICFAI University Press, Hyderabad, India, pp. 74–104.

Davila-Gomez, A.M. (2004) "Sensemaking of Information Technology Solutions: The need to Integrate the Actor's Action-meaning – Individuals, Community and Organization" *Proceedings of the 22nd Standing Conference on Organizational Symbolism – SCOS*, Halifax, Nova Scotia, 25 pages on CD-ROM.

Davila-Gomez, A.M. (2003) *Hacia un Management Humanista desde la educación a distancia: intersubjetividad y desarrollo de cualidades humanas* Doctoral thesis, École des HEC de Montréal, Canada.

Dewey, J. (1975) *Moral Principles in Education*, copyright 1909, Southern Illinois University Press, USA

Desjardins (2006) *Patronage allocations*, http://www.desjardins.com/en/entreprises/produits_services/ristourne/index.jsp, consulted in July 2006.

Encyclopaedia Britannica (2006) "Sharing", "Solidarity", "University", "Education, history of", http://britannica.com, consulted in July 2006.

Frost, P. (1999) "Why Compassion Counts!" *Journal of Management Inquiry* Vol. 8, No. 2, June, pp. 127–133.

Giddens, A. (1984) *The Constitution of Society: Outline of the Theory of Structuration* Polity Press, Cambridge.

Giri, A.K. (2004) "Moral Consciousness and Communicative Action: From Discourse Ethics to Spiritual Transformation" in A.D. Gupta (ed.) *Human Values in Management* Ashgate, Aldershot, pp. 204–222.

Goodpaster, K.E., Maines, T.D. and Rovang, M.D. (2004) "Stakeholder Thinking: Beyond Paradox to Practicality" in A.D. Gupta (ed.) *Human Values in Management* Ashgate, Aldershot, pp. 241–263.

Haw, R. (2004) "Management by Love and Kindness and the Consequent Implications" in D. Crowther and L. Rayman-Bacchus (eds) *Perspectives on Corporate Social Responsibility* Ashgate, Aldershot, pp. 205–228.

Heil, K. (2000) "Business Education" in Maloris, J.A. (ed.) *Encyclopaedia of Business* 2nd edn, Bale Group, USA, pp. 173–175.

International Labour Organization (2000) "*C138 Minimum Age Convention, 1973*" in *Fundamental ILO conventions*, http://www.ilo.org/public/english/standards/norm/whatare/fundam/, consulted in July 2006.

Kanov, J. et al. (2004) "Compassion in Organizational Life" *The American Behavioral Scientist* Vol. 47, No. 6, February, pp. 808–827.

Kierkegaard, S. (1813–1855) *For Self-examination and Judge for Yourselves!* – 1851, 1974, Oxford University Press, London, Princeton University Press, USA.

Knights, D. and Willmott, H. (1999) *Management Lives – Power and Identity in Work Organizations* Sage, London.

Krause, D.R., Handfield, R.B., Tyler, B.B. (2007) "The Relationships Between Supplier Development, Commitment, Social Capital Accumulation and Performance Improvement" *Journal of Operations Management* Vol. 25, No. 2, pp. 528–545.

Kouzes, J. and Posner, B.Z. (1992) "Ethical Leaders: An Essay About Being in Love" *Journal of Business Ethics* Vol. 11, No. 5,6, May, pp. 479–484.

Lovelock, J. (1979) *Gaia* Oxford, Oxford University Press.

Mahama, H. (2006) "Management Control Systems, Cooperation and Performance in Strategic Supply Relationships: A Survey in the Mines" *Management Accounting Research* Vol. 17, No. 3, pp. 315–339.

Marcel, G. (1965) *Homo Viator* Harper Torchbooks, United States of America.

Marcel, G. (1949) *Being and Having* The University Press, Glasgow.

Ozmon, H. and Craver, S. (1999) *Philosophical Foundations of Education* 6th edn, Merrill, Upper Saddle River, N.J.

Pauchant, T.C. (1995) "The Healthy Organization: Reuniting the Self, the Organization, and the Natural World" in T.C. Pauchant (ed.) *In Search of Meaning: Managing for the Health of Our Organizations, Our Communities, and the Natural World* Jossey-Bass Publishers, San Francisco, CA, pp. 327–345.

Parker, M. (1999) "Capitalism, Subjectivity and Ethics: Debating Labour Process Analysis" *Organization Studies* Vol. 20, No. 1, pp. 25–45.

Pestalozzi, J.H. (1746–1827) *The Education of Man – Aphorisms*, 1951 Philosophical Library, New York 1951.
Plato (399–384 BC) *Socrates' Meno Dialogue*, in Plato, *Complete Works*, Cooper, J.M. and Hutchison, D.S. (eds) Tacket Publishing Company, Indianapolis/Cambridge, 1997, pp. 870–608.
Polican, A. (1996) "Business Schools" in Warner, M. (ed.) *International Encyclopaedia of Business and Management* Routledge, USA, Canada, pp. 507–521.
Porter, L.W. and McKibbin, E. (1988) *Management Education and Development: Drift or Thrust Into the Twenty-First Century?* McGraw-Hill, New York/Montréal.
Radio Canada (2006a) "Hydro-Québec augmente ses tarifs", in Radio Canada, *Sans Frontières*, http://www.radio-canada.ca/radio/sansfrontieres/70086.shtml, consulted in July 2006.
Radio Canada (2006b) "Hydro-Québec augmente ses tarifs", in Radio Canada, *Thématiques – Sociétés*, http://www.radio-canada.ca/radio/emissions/document.asp?docnumero=18559&numero=27, consulted in July 2006.
Reedy, P. (2003) "Together We Stand? An Investigation into the Concept of Solidarity in Management Education" *Management Learning* Vol. 34, No. 1, Mar, pp. 91–109.
Reynolds, M. (1999) "Critical Reflection and Management Education: Rehabilitating Less Hierarchical Approaches" *Journal of Management Education* Vol. 23, No. 5, October pp. 537–553.
Rousseau, J.J. (1712–1778) *Emile: Or, On Education*, 1979, Basic Books, New York.
Séguin-Bernard, F. and Chanlat, J.F. (1983) *"L'analyse des organistions – une anthologie sociologique – Tome I – Les Théories de l'organisation"* Éditions Préfonatinae inc., Québec, Canada.
Shaw, J.J.A. (2006) "Where is the Love?" *Social Responsibility Journal* Vol. 2, No. 1, pp. 112–119.
Schelling, F.W.J. (1775–1854) *System of Transcendental Idealism (1800)* University Press of Virginia, 1978, Charlottesville.
Solomon, R. (1998) "The Moral Psychology of Business: Care and Compassion in the Corporation" *Business Ethics Quarterly* Vol. 8, No. 3, pp. 515–533.
Tsoukas, H. and Chia, R. (2002) "On Organizational Becoming: Rethinking Organizational Change" *Organization Science* Vol. 13, No. 5, pp. 567–582.
United Nations (2006) *World Economic and Social Survey 2006*, http://www.un.org/esa/policy/wess/index.html, consulted in July 2006.
Verstraeten, J. (1998) "From Business Ethics to the Vocation of Business Leaders to Humanize the World of Business" *Business Ethics: A European Review* Vol. 7, No. 2, April, pp. 111–124.
White, J. (1998) "Leadership Through Compassion and Understanding – An interview With Aung San Suu Kyi" *Journal of Management Inquiry* Vol. 7, No. 4, December, pp. 286–293.

PART II
The Effects of Change

It is 25 years now since the Internet became available to a limited few people. Much has changed in those 25 years and now more than half of the people on the planet have access to the Internet and it is being debated whether or not the right of access should be considered to be a fundamental human right. The most important way in which the Internet has promoted social responsibility is through the way in which it has provided access to information for everybody. There is so much information available on the Internet that it is relatively easy to research any topic; consequently it has become possible for anyone who is sufficiently concerned to become an expert on any subject. And concerned individuals do choose to become experts on a wide range of subjects. Thus for example environmental issues are no longer the preserve of the expert – many people are concerned and are expert on such things as climate change, rainforest destruction, resources depletion or alternative sources of energy. Similarly other people have become expert on issues concerning human rights – access to education, exploitation, child labour and other issues.

And of equal import to the access to information has come the ability to disseminate that information via the Internet. It is easy to post information and to communicate with people all over the world. In many ways the Internet has enabled like-minded people to congregate together into clubs or pressure groups, and this has effectively given more power to individuals at the expense of the state, large corporations and other powerful entities. This redistribution of power in one very important way in which the Internet has promoted the cause of social responsibility.

Of particular interest therefore is the way in which access to the technology to use the Internet can redefine the corporate landscape and change the power relationship between large corporations and individuals. In this respect the changes in these power relationships can be profound and even revolutionary. The technology provides a potential challenge to legitimacy and can give individuals the ability to confront large corporations and to have their voice heard with equal volume within the discourse facilitated by cyberspace. Thus, for example, it is no longer possible for a corporation to hide its practices in other parts of the world – everywhere is visible to a searcher on the Internet. Equally it is no longer possible for a corporation to say that bad practices belong to its suppliers and are not its responsibility. Everywhere is visible and individuals are demanding accountability for all actions along the supply chain – another radical redistribution of power which has been facilitated by the Internet.

Alongside access to information has come access to education. And education is the greatest single promoter of equality. The Internet radically changes the possibility of access to education. No longer must the teacher and pupil be located together – neither geographically nor temporarily. It is perfectly possible to put material on the web which can be accessed from anywhere in the world and at any time. This gives access to education to people who were previously excluded due to their geographical location. And radical new methods of teaching are being developed as a result of this. Moreover the cost of education is reduced by these methods, which too increases possibilities of access to those who were previously excluded because of cost. This also means that repressive regimes must find other and more problematic ways of subjugating the controlling people. Social responsibility is also promoted in this way and battles are currently being waged in various parts of the world to wrestle control of the Internet and the concomitant access to information from repressive regimes or from revolutionary protestors. This places for example Google – one of the most powerful Internet-based corporations – in direct confrontation with China – one of the most powerful and repressive states.

The increasing availability of access to the Internet has instigated a discourse which means that we need to consider the present and likely future impact of this means of communication upon the construction of society and upon the lives of individual members of that society. Much of this discourse is based upon evidence that the Internet and the World Wide Web has had a significant impact upon the way in which society operates. Thus some people argue that this technology will be more liberating, participatory and interactive than previous cultural forms while others suggest that it will lead to increasing globalization of politics, culture and social systems. Postmodernist arguments suggest that the technological capability of the Internet will lead a duality of social structures. This will be manifest in increasing globalization of social structures and also increased localization of such structures. Whatever happens we can be certain that it has led to opportunities for people to exert their power, individually and collectively, and this has led to increasing concern for social responsibility.

CHAPTER 5

Local Governance and Social Movements in Québec: The Perverse Effects of Corporate Culture

DENYSE CÔTÉ AND ÉTIENNE SIMARD

Introduction

Social responsibility has always been at the heart of Québec's social and community movements. Indeed, even at the high point of its trade-union, feminist, community and nationalist movements, which occurred in the wake of the American civil rights movement, of decolonization, and of global student movements in the 1960s. The latter spawned practices of direct democracy, self-management, and popular education based on ethics of social justice. The first Québec groups emerging from these movements, alternately referred to as "citizens' committees," "grassroots organizations," or "community organizations," embodied the ideal of participatory democracy and the ethical ideal of social responsibility. While these organizations were constituted autonomously, their political struggle brought them over the years incomplete, but relatively regular public funding. With the emergence of neo-liberalism, targeted funding and government priorities based on a more "productive" and quantifiable outputs, this ethic of social responsibility vitiated and the groups lost a large part of their initial autonomy. The running of community organizations was gradually associated with managerial practices of private corporations, and this in turn produced issues similar to those now emerging in the public sector.

This chapter will shed light on the erosion of social responsibility within Québec community organizations. It will analyse how several of these community organizations adopted a new form of management modelled on private corporations. It will also illustrate the problems this entails for the development of an ethic of social responsibility within these organizations and within social movements in Québec.

Québec Community Organizations

After the Quiet Revolution,[1] a strong and variegated popular movement emerged in Québec in all spheres of social life, on a territorial basis and on specific social problems (health, housing, household debt, sexual violence, and so on). The constitutive elements of this movement – advocacy groups – offered resources, local social services, and brought together marginalized but active citizens seeking to improve their living conditions. Other community groups organized on a territorial basis rather than strictly on social class (Lamoureux and Lamoureux, 2009), subsequently joined these initial advocacy groups. They formed national federations on a sectoral basis, and later on a territorial basis, in an effort to adapt to decentralized budgetary envelopes. They offer political representation, stimulate democratic life, and systematize innovative practices (Lamoureux and Lamoureux, 2009). An example of this would be community and alternative services in mental health or in matters of sexual violence. Fighting against poor living conditions of an important segment of Québec society (Lamoureux, 1999: 12), these organizations typically oppose bureaucratic and authoritarian policies, and favour grassroots power and democracy:

> *The project of social movements, comprised of associations, trade unions and a constellation of autonomous community organizations, is pre-eminently an emancipatory, self-managing project, based on non-traditional and non-charitable [...] collective solidarities. It also represents a view that opposes a bureaucratic and authoritarian vision of the modern polity. In short, it is a democratic project that affects individuals and collectivities in their entirety. (Lamoureux, 1999: 23)*

Bearers of specific values and principles, these groups inspired the movement that advocated social responsibility within corporations:

> *[They] search for social power and [...] combat perceived helplessness through learning that what appears personal is often political. [They] create a capacity for democracy and for sustained social change. [They] can make society more adaptable and governments more accountable. Community organizing means bringing people together to combat shared problems and to increase their say about decisions that affect their lives. (Rubin and Rubin, 1992: 1, 3)*

The organizations, struggles, and methods of popular education that later shaped Québec society were largely forged by these citizens committees, local health clinics, women's health clinics, groups for disabled workers and for the unemployed, community media, groups fighting non-regulated urban renewal, groups advocating for those on social assistance, for the right to housing, and for literacy. They led to the enactment of several laws and public institutions such as the "Office de protection du consommateur" (Public Consumer Protection Bureau), the "Conseil du statut de la femme" (Council on the Status of Women), the "Loi sur l'assurance maladie" (Public Health Insurance Act), the "Régie du logement" (Housing Authority), the "Loi sur l'équité salariale" (Wage Equity Act), to name but a few. The community health clinics inspired the creation of the CLSCs (Public

---

[1] This refers to Québec's intensive period of modernization which took place after 1960. The Québec Welfare State emerged at this point.

Local Community Health Centres), the community daycares gave rise to the "Centres de la petite enfance" and to a world-renowned network of childcare services; feminist collectives spearheaded the struggle against sexual violence, creating the network of shelters for victims of sexual assault; they also fought for pay equity and for women's full access to the labour market.

Similar organizations emerged in many Western countries. However, Québec community groups have been recognized by the state for more than 25 years. On the other hand, the countries that formally recognize this social contribution of community organizations only initiated such a process a decade ago and the scope of their recognition is not as far-reaching as that of Québec (Guay and White, 2009). This can no doubt be explained by the specific situation of Québec, torn between the need to establish an internal social consensus to respond to conservative pressures emerging from English Canada and the American philanthropic tradition (Guay and White, 2009).

Indeed, the way Québec formally recognizes community groups is unique. It is embodied in a policy[2] that establishes:

> *the specificity of autonomous community organizations in relation to the social economy and the cooperative movement; [respect for] the autonomy of community organizations by disengaging from forced complementarity and partnership with the State; [the centrality of] supporting organizations' missions as the form of funding most likely to favour the emergence of innovative citizen participation in a milieu where problems are experienced first hand. (Guay and White, 2009: 20)*

This policy formally rejects the contractual type of funding generally applied in Europe, the United States, and English Canada, as well as in countries from the South. It recognizes and funds certain advocacy groups and this per se constitutes an "unprecedented situation in the world" (Guay and White, 2009).

Québec community organizations created and defended an organizational culture where transparency and direct democracy were guiding principles. However, certain tendencies and practices contrary to these have lately emerged within these organizations: "elite formation", professionalization (Lamoureux, 1999), devaluing of mobilization efforts and of popular education, in short, which have distanced these groups from their initial stakeholders. A number of community organizations now "represent and advocate on behalf of their members or clients" (Shragge, 2003: 31), while stinting on genuine mobilization efforts. Their legitimacy which was originally derived from the marginalized citizens they represented was gradually replaced by a state-conferred legitimacy.[3]

With the rise of neo-liberalism, the collapse of the Soviet Union, the redefinition of the state, and its partial retreat social issues (Klein 1995), the survival of Québec community organizations has been uncertain.

The state would no longer be the primary social provider; the market and the community were to share the responsibility. New relationships between the community and the government were in place. Community organizations were pressured into

---

2   The Québec Government's policy on the recognition of autonomous community organizations (PRSAC).

3   Begun during the Rochon Commission in 1988, this formal recognition of Québec community movement's contributions culminated in 2001 in the *Politique de reconnaissance et de financement de l'action communautaire autonome* which recognizes their "self management" and their "autonomy" without however recognizing these groups as "autonomous democratic spaces" (MEPACQ, 2004).

partnership with government, and innovative solutions were sought in order to confront the crisis (Shragge, 2003: 31).

Many community groups were able to survive thanks to their partnership with the Québec State (Côté and Simard 2010). Already reduced in the 1980s and centred on state-recognized service provision,[4] their missions have been tailored increasingly to the uncertainties of state grants, often in the form of project funding. The revenues from these project grants have been crucial for these groups that are without base funding. The price of such an uncertain public funding and of this formal recognition of their expertise has been very hefty: their internal dynamics and specific culture has been transformed. Indeed, now community groups tend to be recognized by the state for their purely "utilitarian" function:

> *This economicist notion of the role of social organizations, notably of community groups, contributes to the downsizing of their critical function and constrains them to the narrower mandate of service provision. In other words, activism yields to the management of social problems. This trajectory is evidenced in a more or less conscious acceptance of the inevitable character of social issues; such acceptance leads to a new dynamic of managing social problems, modeled on the market economy. To move from activism as a form of combating the causes underlying social problems to accepting a management role for handling these problems [...] marks a break with the ethics of social movements that drive civil society. (Lamoureux, 1999: 13–14)*

Recognized as deliverers of social services, community groups[5] have also been recognized by the state as legitimate representatives of the interests of the populations that they serve (Côté and Simard, 2010). They have been invited to sit at standing regional or provincial consultation bodies or social and economic forums in what are called processes of "concertation" (dialogue and collaboration). This legitimacy conferred by governmental and political bodies has led several community organizations to mimic the practices and culture of their counterparts and thus to relinquish the practices and culture of the social movement from which they arose. They have normalized their dependency on state funding and recognition,[6] and this, in turn, has exerted a major influence on their organizational practices and culture. Since their legitimacy no longer stems from their respective bases, and since the constraints imposed by the state are increasingly numerous, their practices in several instances have completely deviated and adopted those of the private sector. Thus, Québec's 4,000 community groups, gathered within 250 coalitions, often now exert a regulatory, rather than a mobilizing, influence in social movements. Gaining their legitimacy, their financial survival, and their partnership with government bodies, they have relinquished their original mission of popular education and ethics of transparency towards their stakeholders.

---

4   The more radical groups, which focused on methods of radical or direct action (the right to abortion, for instance) or on less socially or politically profitable issues (radical theatre, for example) quietly disappeared (Lamoureux, 1990).

5   This legitimacy led them to manage certain sectors of social intervention such as employment, social housing, community economic development, the social economy, domestic violence and sexual violence, to cite but these examples (Houle, 2006).

6   This funding is increasingly linked to sub-contracting relations within the sphere of social services.

New Public Management (NPM) and Community Organizations

New Public Management has been very influential in this transformation of community organizations' practices and culture. Against the backdrop of a crisis in public finances and of a "commodification of social relations" (Villeneuve, 2005: 7), many advanced industrial countries, OECD members in particular, have dismantled the Welfare State at different paces and with more or less virulence. This process was accompanied by a discourse peppered with ideological attacks on the redistribution of wealth: the latter, it was argued, as well as the recognition of the rights of marginalized groups, inhibited economic growth:

> *In the late twentieth and early twenty-first centuries, liberal social government came under attack for inefficiently managing government planning, regulating, and spending, and for governing too much. Neoliberal reform came to emphasize that a "society of commitments" would interfere with the growth and movement of free market solutions, hinder entrepreneurialism, drain public resources [...], and encourage certain individuals and groups to be too dependent on government at the cost of their autonomy. (Ilcan, 2009: 211)*

The process of state downsizing was achieved in accordance with the principles of New Public Management (NPM) (Giauque, 2003), based in turn on the neo-liberal idea[7] "that the public and the private sectors did not have to be organized and managed in fundamentally different ways. Indeed, that it would be better for the public services if they could be organized and managed as much like the private sector as possible" (Dawson and Dargie, 2002: 35).

In order to "replace the traditional process-based approach, which proved very difficult to evaluate and quantify, with a results-driven approach, [and in order to institute] a system of performance enhancing incentives" (Brunelle, 2005: 36), NPM offered a set of tools, "concepts and dynamics, traditionally reserved for the private sector", which it integrated into the public sector (Villeneuve, 2005: 7). The latter was thus transformed and took on new regulatory functions:

> *the organizational regulation emerging within public organizations is based on new disciplinary mechanisms, that is, on threats and shared fears of potential sanctions, as well as on shared chances where these changes create opportunities for individuals, which results in acceptance of this regulatory model and its legitimization. We call this model "liberal bureaucracy" in order to emphasize the fundamentally paradoxical nature of the process, which combines liberty and constraints, neoliberalism and bureaucracy, decentralization and concentration of power. (Giauque, 2003: 567)*

---

7   "The neoliberal orthodoxy can be represented as a generalized belief that the State and its interventions are obstacles to economic and social development. This belief may be broken down into a number of more specific propositions: that public deficits are intrinsically negative; that State regulation of the labor market produces rigidities and hinders both economic growth and job creation; that the social protection guaranteed by the Welfare State and its redistributive policies hinders economic growth; and that the State should not intervene in regulating foreign trade or international financial markets" (Clark, 2002: 771).

In Québec, community organizations had been involved in corporatist[8] relations with the Québec State before the arrival of NPM. They were gradually subjected to NPM's principles, which produced deep changes "in the labour process and in service organizations [that] are operationalized through managerial discourses [...] associated more broadly with globalization and neoliberalism" (Baines, 2004a: 6). Social responsibilities (Ilcan, 2009) were privatized and the state transferred some of these to certain community organizations that had become dependent on it.

Within NPM, governmental organizations and the non-profits they fund, are considered business units in which managers are given discretionary power to meet or exceed programme and individual goals. Accountability and efficiency, under NPM, are constructed entirely as achievement of performance targets (Baines, 2004a: 7).

The zero-deficit[9] measures introduced by the (social-democratic) government of the Parti Québecois starting in the mid-1990s, as well as the subsequent state's "re-engineering" or "modernizing" measures (Rouillard et al., 2008) brought in by the (neo-liberal) Liberal Government in 2003,[10] altered the form and the role of the Québec social state,[11] facilitating the birth of a "companion" (Klein 1995) or "neoliberal" (Bourque, Duchastel and Pineault, 1999) state. Social services were increasingly cut back, user fees were increased, and subcontracting to the private sector and to community organizations was introduced "for the good reason that it costs less; [community group] employees do not receive the salaries and social advantages that unions obtained for the workers of the public and parapublic sectors" (Piotte, 2010). This disengagement by the national state took place in the interest of the international and regional levels (Jouve 2003); this situation depends on a "ménage à trois [between] the market, the State and civil society" (Lévesque 2002). In this context, community organizations gain in recognition and position themselves in the planning process and distribution of services. They provide expertise through their involvement in governance and help legitimize the process of developing public policies (Bacqué, Rey and Sintomer, 2005), especially when

---

8   By corporatism, we mean "a system of representing interests in which the constitutive units are organized in a limited number of singular, obligatory, non-competitive categories, recognized or agreed upon – if not created – by the State and to which has been guaranteed a deliberate monopoly of representation within their respective categories in exchange for observing certain rules in selecting leaders and articulating demands and interests" (Bourque, 1995: 14). The tendency towards corporatism in Québec dates back to the period when the Church was responsible for the governance of civil society and controlled union organizations. It was a social corporatism that promoted "the harmonizing of interests between employers and workers within intermediary bodies" (Côté, Lévesque and Morneau, 207: 11). The neo-corporatism that we know today appeared subsequently, during the secularization of Québec institutions: unions and employers became "conflictual partners" within the state, working together to build a national economy, organizing themselves independently, and "calling upon the State to define an institutional framework that facilitates the negotiation of social demands and conflict regulation along the lines of Scandinavian countries" (Côté, Lévesque and Morneau, 2007: 11).

9   In 1996, the legislation on "zero-deficit" was adopted following "summits" that involved, for community group coalitions, working with the government's economic partners from the private sector. This legislation established "deficit ceilings" for each fiscal year (Belzile, 1999: 366). Its application principally targeted reductions in public services.

10   Re-engineering is defined as "the fundamental rethinking and radical redesign of business processes to achieve dramatic improvements in critical, contemporary measures of performance, such as cost, quality, service, and speed" (Hammer and Champy, 1993: 32).

11   "Thus, governments have since then increasingly loathed to intervene as planners; rather they do so in partnership with the private sector, or with the social economy sector. In this context, governments are called upon to play the catalytic role that facilitates the proliferation of agreements between economic and non-economic partners. As a result, public intervention in the economy does not disappear, but its role is transformed. In this respect, the recognition of civil society in economic development plays a central role: it ensues both from demands formulated by the economic actors and in particular by corporations, which act increasingly as stakeholders in a host of areas and cases, and from demands stemming from other social actors" (Brunelle, 2005: 30–31).

they represent a clientele (youth, the elderly, workers, women, and so on) or a particular sector (environment, culture, recreation).

As partners and subcontractors for the state, community groups seeking to benefit from public funding must therefore satisfy certain conditions modelled on NPM principles. They are required to:

> *... be less accountable to members than to a bureaucracy that has its own requirements [...]; adhere to a social planning logic based not on the requirements of deep structural changes, but on management imperatives where the control and social peace needed for the efficient running of business, are naturally present. (Lamoureux, 1999: 32)*

In this way, the public sector is opened to the market and to competition, independent service units proliferate (agencies, community organizations) and an internal market is created where contracts awarded by tender are open to the private sector (Lebel, 2009). These autonomous units can be a self-managed group of parents or of women, organized as a cooperative or as a collective, or they can be a non-profit organization,[12] created by the managers of a public service or of a private company seeking a contract in response to a request for proposals (RFP) (Lebel, 2009). At a time when recourse to RFPs and contracts has become the rule, the borders between the public and the private begin to blur. Indeed, the public sector now seems to be ruled by a principle of efficiency intrinsic to the market, rather than by the values of civic solidarity. Services are withdrawn from the public sector and entrusted to community groups conceived as responsible citizen "corporations" (Lebel, 2009), over-regulated by the state that no longer regulates the market:

> *The community practices developed in the 1990s incorporated the formal partnership arrangements discussed above into the structures of their organizations and their wider relationships [...] [G]roups shifted from a membership or social movement base to a client focus. The redefinition is inherently depoliticizing. Clients are to be served and have a less active – or no – role in either the organizations' internal processes or on wider social issues. At best, they are represented rather than mobilized. Thus, the form of political representation became lobbying by coalitions of community organizations promoting the needs of a particular population. (Shragge, 2003: 55)*

With accelerating decentralization, the state's control over community organizations became more and more targeted. It was reinforced by the application of a Québec model of regional governance and of techno-juridical regulation (Bourque, Duchastel and Pineault, 1999). This form of governance once again fuelled the "illusion of a plurality of self-governing bodies, where room for maneuver is rigorously marked out by a range of norms, which if need be, work to eliminate the extent of that autonomy" (Lamoureux, 1991: 31); in fact, such governance introduced another type of corporatism (Côté and Simard, 2010) that established itself "by adopting a clientelistic perspective" (Lamoureux, 1999: 26). It involves:

---

12 In Québec, a non-profit organization is a corporation regulated by the "Loi sur les compagnies" (Corporations Act). It is non-governmental, autonomous and voluntary, and does not share out profits (Ramboarisata and De Serre, 2007:11).

> *a process in which an occupational group, which has succeeded in establishing its members' monopoly over the definition of a particular population's needs and over the ways to satisfy them, takes charge of the production of a category of goods and services. (Paquet, 1989: 100)*

In the regions of Québec, hitherto devoid of political structures, a political level was designed in such a way as to facilitate the implementation of the neo-liberal agenda. Underpinned "by a set of representations, forming a veritable ideology, discernible in the recesses of contemporary governance discourse" (Chevalier, 2003: 206), regional governance contributed directly to the "normalization of neo-liberalism", a process which would "be realized more easily if the actors managed to use the most important elements of the local political culture" for their own purposes (Boudreau and Keil, 2006: 98).

The Transformation of Community Groups' Internal Practices

The Québec government recognizes autonomous community action and funds it as such. It recognizes its specificity in all its facets:

> *democratic action, expertise on various complex issues, well-trained personnel and inadequate working conditions compared with the professional and semi-professional personnel of public and para-public networks of the public service. (Houle, 2006)*

But chronic under funding of the community sector renders these groups overly vulnerable to measures derived from NPM and adopted by government agencies, other than the one responsible for the framework agreement secured between community groups and the Québec government. This is all the more true in that public services are increasingly amalgamated with community organizations on a sectorial basis. Regularly faced with community organizations' alternative practices (Houle, 2006) and with budgetary constraints, government agencies tend to consider the community groups as a solution for safeguarding public action in society. The social-democratic party (Parti Québecois) and the Liberal Party, each in turn, applied this vision in their own way. They did so by compelling under-funded community groups to adopt a project-defined approach; to participate (free of charge) in development planning with local and regional authorities; and by creating new local and regional intermediary organizations directly funded by government and mandated to deliver public services in youth employment, health care, and other fields. On the one hand, the territory of Québec is, indeed, currently dotted with community groups such as youth centres, women's centres, centres for street kids, housing committees, employability agencies, and groups engaged in food security (Houle, 2006). By better controlling their mandates and projects, the government's presence in these marginalized sectors has thus increased tenfold. On the other hand, rather than create new administrative structures that would facilitate its decentralization, the Québec government has created new non-profit organizations entrusted with a government mandate to decentralize its operations. It has thus been able to shape these structures by way of legislation (thanks to a reform of the legislation on non-profit organizations) and fund them directly: these new structures included the CRÉ, CLD, CLÉ,[13] and regional health authorities, established in every region of Québec.

Here are now some examples that illustrate how NPM, corporate culture, and new forms of neo-liberal governance have influenced community organizations. These *bad practices*, to be found to varying degrees in various sectors of community action and in various Québec regions, illustrate how community groups' original civic ethic can be shunted aside.

1. A COMMUNITY GROUP RESORTS TO CONSULTANTS FROM THE PRIVATE SECTOR FOR GUIDANCE ON ITS OPERATIONS

Certain community groups willingly incorporated the NPM's philosophy and practices into their internal management. The following describes the case of a board of directors, convinced that it had to reduce its human resource costs in order to enhance the community organization's performance by modelling itself on private corporations rather than on its own former democratic practices.

A tenants' rights advocacy committee from an underprivileged neighbourhood adopts the NPM model

At the end of the 1970s, citizens organized themselves in Neighbourhood X of City Y to develop housing cooperatives so as to escape the logic of rental housing and speculation. Federal and provincial funds had been made available to build cooperatives several years prior. Three community organizations, sharing the same board of directors, were created: a holding company for cooperatives, a housing committee (for information and tenants' rights advocacy) and a company to buy and renovate buildings.

When public funds for building housing cooperatives were cut in the early 1990s, the first organization was abolished and the second was merged with the company destined to buy and renovate buildings. Thus, in Neighbourhood X, only one organization remained, consisting of two sections, each with its respective coordinator: one linked to the housing committee and one to the development of cooperatives.

A decade later, the coordinator of the housing section leaves her job and the task of replacing her proves difficult. The Board of Directors thus decides to merge the two coordinating positions into one. It decides at the same time to restructure the whole organization and, to this end, hires a firm of management consultants. The firm's recommendations are modelled on the NPM: reduce employees' social benefits, reduce salaries for certain positions in order to match similar positions in the private sector, increase salaries for managers, and include on the Board of Directors (which had hitherto only been made up of citizens) "expert external" non-voting members.

These new measures were adopted by the Board of Directors without consulting the employees. The latter are thus subjected to a new job hierarchy, a deterioration of their

---

[13] Conférence régionale des élus (CRÉ), Centre local de développement (CLD), Centre local d'emploi (CLÉ).

> wages and working conditions, as well as the elimination of a seat on the Board of Directors reserved for their representative. This way of operating resembles private corporations much more than citizens associations and constitutes a practice contrary to a Board's role in advocacy, in democratic management, and in enhancing quality of life within the community organization.

2. ENCOUNTER BETWEEN A NATIONAL COALITION AND THE QUÉBEC GOVERNMENT

Other groups moved from a critical stance to supporting the ideological positions and tendencies of the Québec government. Here is an example of a national association, which was historically mandated to defend the rights of a highly vulnerable population, which endorsed a government proposal to reduce public funding in its own sector.

> **National Coalition Advocating for the Rights of an Underprivileged Segment of Society**
>
> The end of the 1980s and the start of the 1990s witnesses the emergence of a new coalition of associations advocating for a significant sector of the population. Gradually, it replaces an already established and more radical national organization. The government swiftly recognizes this new coalition as the agency that can speak for this sector. From the start, this new umbrella group renounces its predecessor's union-style struggle in the interest of lobbying, dialogue and cooperation with government. Its public stance reflects this choice and jars with the group's former position. In fact, rather than defend the rights of the population that it represents and suggest more beneficial alternatives, this new coalition endorses the implementation of NPM principles. It adjusts its stance and rhetoric to match these new tendencies in public management. The coalition endorses, for example, the imposition of performance indicators (comparable to the principle of competition between OECD countries) in its sector, even though the latter is of a social nature.
>
> Moreover, this group's organizational culture is modelled henceforth on the private sector rather than on the third sector. This involves centralized decision-making at the national executive, power concentrated in Montreal and little left to the other 16 regions, an absence of debate within its committees and assemblies (that exist only on paper), and a rubber-stamping role assigned to the Board of Directors. These tactics fuelled a revolt by certain members who created a new coalition whose platform opposed the Government's proposals and whose practices were more democratic.

3. NEW REGULATING MECHANISMS IN QUÉBEC'S REGIONS

In Québec, the gradual process of decentralization, initiated by the Québec government, was referred to as "regionalization". Over time, responsibilities and powers were devolved to 17 Québec administrative regions in accordance with successive reforms. They were entrusted to intermediary associations created by the Government for that purpose; they were ruled by the same chapters of the Québec Civil Code, and structured in the same way (Board of Directors, General Assembly, and so on) as are community groups. Their membership, however, remains vague and their operation does not resemble that of a citizens' association. Members of the Board of Directors are often appointed by authorities but remain without a mandate from the population. These members include provincial legislators, municipal councillors, as well as representatives of civil society co-opted by Government. Contrary to cities and to the muncipalities, the CRÉs (Conférence régionale des élus) have no taxation power and no electoral process. However, they are responsible for managing the social and economic development of the regions, whose territory at times exceeds that of England.

Here is an example of the way the idea to "rationalize" development in a region runs parallel to working "in partnership" with civil society. Operational procedures can easily irritate community "partners": professionals and managers, accountable only to their own Board of Directors and indirectly to the Québec State, take decisions internally and with no transparency or accountability.

Collaboration ("Concertation") in the Context of Political and Administrative Decentralization in Québec's regions

Regionalist social movements took shape in Québec *circa* 1965 in reaction to the centralization of the Québec State; in particular, it opposed a plan to modernize remote rural territories conceived in the capital without consulting targeted populations. In response, the Government created in each region a "Council A" responsible for a modest portion of this effort of decentralization. Economic development was the initial mandate of these councils. Their mandate widened somewhat in scope in 1993. In 2004 they were replaced by another council (the "Council B"), following the election of the Liberal Party. These new councils were swiftly entrusted with cultural and social mandates. However, neither the Councils A, nor the Councils B, created by way of legislation, were public institutions. Rather, they were non-profit organizations incorporated according to the "Loi des companies" (Corporations Act) Chapter 3 (of Québec's Civil Code), entities legally independent of the State, but designed to act as its representatives in their respective territories. Their mandate is broad: to develop their region and manage the budgets allocated by Government for such regional development. They also have to initiate forums designed to work with regional civil society in the context of regional development plans.

For several reasons, the establishment of Councils B produced much anxiety for democracy at a regional level. The main concern was their representativity, their legitimacy, and their accountability. Indeed, the structure of B Councils provides for limited civil society participation. While A Councils' Boards of Directors granted two thirds of their seats to representatives of civil society, elected by electoral colleges, the new legislation* granted no more than one third of the seats on the B Councils' Boards of Directors to civil society, and these were appointed by the Government upon the recommendation of the Directors of the B Councils. The presence of civil society on these Boards is thus tightly controlled. The other two thirds of the seats on the B Councils' Boards of Directors are occupied *ex officio* by local elected officials, often unfamiliar with regional issues. Indeed, they include mayors of rural municipalities or municipal councilors from larger cities, familiar with local rather than regional issues. The average citizen knows neither the B Council of his region, nor the people on its Board of Director, nor the decisions that are taken there. The media is scarcely interested in them and the B Councils are accountable only indirectly to the central government that finances them, not at all to the population that they serve. This being said, the B Councils have the power to confer legitimacy to community organizations on their territory, as a regional representative of a sector of civil society.

The internal structure of B Councils is variable but it typically consists of a certain number of commissions or committees occupied by delegates from sectorial community organizations or companies. As non-profit organizations, the B Councils thus have the power to co-opt the community group or company that they desire on to their commissions or committees, granting (or denying them) legitimacy by that very token. They can also terminate public funding of an organization or allocate such a funding to another community organization or company.

The process of planning and implementing five-year regional plans mobilizes significant resources within the community groups of each region and henceforth strongly influences each group's orientation. In several instances, the resources, the orientation, and the development of certain groups have been subjected to the decisions and the projects of the Councils B. Contrary to the Councils A, which favoured working in concert through inter-organizational structures, the Councils B wish, it would seem, to incorporate the organizations into structures controlled by elected municipal officials and development managers.

* Québec Government (2003), "Loi sur le Ministère des Affaires municipales et des Régions" (the Ministry of Municipal and Regional Affairs Act).

The Québec Government delegates regional governance to the B Councils, which are accountable to it, rather than to the population of their region. Important differences between the regions are noticeable here; for the modes of civil society's participation are subject to the discretion of each B Council. The state establishes the norms and the B Councils (which are legally, one must recall, non-profit organizations) are destined to perform the tasks; the state supervises the execution of tasks through mechanisms of accountability based on performance, results, and transparency (Lebel, 2009). Here is an example that illustrates how the Québec Government uses administrative mechanisms to manage regional collaboration with community groups.

Managing the Social through "Specific Agreement"

For the purposes of managing the development of its regions, the Québec government now favours "specific agreements". These are formal agreements between regional offices of government departments and agencies, para-governmental organizations, and third-sector or private partners, aimed at implementing regional development priorities. This contractual system brings together, around common goals, governmental and para-governmental resources in each region. The problem is that this system depends on civil society's contribution to government objectives by assuming that it will make these objectives its own. These "specific agreements" are, of course, achieved after a process of dialogue with civil society, but this process is firmly circumscribed by government objectives, policies, and administrative guidelines (Côté and Simard, 2010). This process takes place under the aegis and leadership of regional agencies and the actors they have themselves selected from civil society. It is a tightly controlled process, that does not rely on citizen participation, and that generates unequal relations. This being said, these "specific agreements" do acknowledge the importance of civil society, which was not the case a decade ago.

The Québec Ministry of *Culture, Communications* and of the Status of Women (MCCCF) issued an order in 2007 by which "specific agreements" on gender equality had to be achieved within each of the 17 Québec regions. While adapted to the regional realities, their objectives had to correspond to governmental priorities, that is to its 2006 Policy and 2007–2010 Action Plan (*Politique gouvernementale pour l'égalité entre les femmes et les hommes* and *Plan d'action en matière d'égalité entre les femmes et les hommes*). The women's groups' regional action committees ("tables régionales de concertation") were called upon to participate in the development and implementation of these "specific agreements". Their funding originates in part from the MCCCF's national envelopes, but mainly from regional departmental offices or from governmental or para-governmental agencies. The representatives of these agencies ensure therefore that the priorities established by the "specific agreement" of their region correspond to their own priorities and mandates since they are accountable to their head offices in Québec City. Thus, for example, the Ministry of Municipal and Regional Affairs (MAMROT) will finance projects to increase the number of female candidates in local elections and the regional health authority ("Agence de la santé") will finance projects aiming at reducing domestic violence.

The connections between Bill 34 (creating B Councils that oversee the "specific agreements", these "specific agreements", regional governmental agencies, and the community groups have scarcely been analyzed. However, they appear to follow a model set out by the "Loi sur la santé et les services sociaux" (Health and Social Services Act) which addresses the matter in more detail.* In practice, a region's resources are deployed in one direction only, and the community groups are mobilized around these government priorities. In this context, do the community groups succeed in fulfilling their own objectives? To what extent does their participation in these "specific agreements" mobilize their efforts beyond their own priorities? The power structure as well as the political culture of each region introduces here significant variations in this respect. Indeed, since the system of Québec regional governance is accountable to the Québec provincial government only rather than to the population of each region, and since the regional managers possess important discretionary powers, the community group's room for manoeuvre is often contingent on the political culture of a local or regional elite. A region whose culture is business oriented will tend to develop objectives that are scarcely sensitive to the needs of the community groups and will develop subcontracting relations; a region whose culture is more open to social movements will tend to develop more egalitarian partnerships with community groups.

In the best of cases, the community groups will, to a certain extent, influence decisions, but the sponsors and donors of "specific agreements" (which are always government agencies) will always wield the final decision-making power. Community groups are thus subject to acting as the mainspring of the "specific agreement": they can suggest projects that will be accepted, modified, or refused by the sponsors or donors; they can solicit funds within the context of "specific agreements", and become, if the project is accepted, subcontractors, accountable to the Council B and to the sponsors of the specific agreement. Their legitimacy before regional governmental agencies will have been obtained at the expense of their status and at times even at the cost of their mission. In certain cases, national objectives have been devolved through such subcontracting mechanisms to community groups possessing little financial resources. The cost of these projects is obviously less than the projects managed and borne by the civil or service or para-governmental agencies. However, the mechanisms of management and accountability to which community groups must submit seem more binding than within the civil service or within para-governmental agencies.

* Bill no. 7 or *Loi modifiant la loi sur les services de santé et les services sociaux*, 2003 and Bill no. 8 or *Loi sur les Centres de la petite enfance et autres services de garde à l'enfance*, took effect on December 18, 2003. See Masson, 2001.

4. COMMUNITY GROUPS' DISCOURSE AND DEMOCRATIC DEBATE

The NPM represents but one of many influences affecting community groups at this political juncture of ebbing social movements. The disappearance of global ideologies and meta-discourses on world affairs following the fall of the Berlin Wall also provoked among community groups a withdrawal into the delivery of services. Moreover, the government's legitimization of community groups as well as their professionalization contributed to the disappearance of the previously preferred conflictual approach to the promotion of the interests of the marginalized. This conflictual approach heralded an ethic of public debate and represented a barrier against what the French call *la pensée unique*.[14] With the disappearance of public debate and of counter-discourses, community groups are thus limited to "good management" of social issues that "cannot occur within a context of conflict", as well as to methods inspired by public relations rather than public debate or direct democracy.

A number of other factors incurred a certain institutionalization of Québec community groups: enduring community organizations (several community organizations are currently celebrating their 35th anniversary), the securing of more (albeit always inadequate) regular funding, pressures from staff seeking to improve their working conditions, and demands for the recognition of their expertise.

Capacity of critical thought on global conjuncture is now largely reduced; this is linked to the decline of militancy, in particular among intellectuals using their analytical and writing skills to the serve the cause of the underprivileged. The over-specialization of groups as well as the employees' surfeit of work can also explain why few critical analyses of macro situations are missing; community groups are rather focused on project management and the search for project funding:

Most of the material actually published by community groups is wanting in political analysis. How is our sectorial cause really faring? In what global context is it situated? Can one establish connections between our cause and that of others? Sanitized texts. For a movement made up of eighty-per cent of women, the word "patriarchy" seems forgotten and the word "capitalism" abolished from the dictionary ... Apart from hackneyed uses of the term "globalization", people rarely speak in clear terms, and in a spirit of demanding change in the population's living conditions and in the methods for improving them. People appear to have forgotten that if one does not criticize the system, one reproduces it ... This lack of opposition makes us

---

14 The expression "pensée unique" can be translated literally into English as "single thought". Coined in 1995 by Ignacio Ramonet, editor-in-chief of *Le Monde diplomatique*, it refers to the enforced reduction of political discussion by mainstream politics.

increasingly fearful of politicians. To assert our demands clearly and firmly is henceforth, it seems, categorized as radical demonstrations. (Brouillard, 2005)

Without a counter-discourse, without an analysis of the global situation, activist leadership within community organizations is now often relegated to the background, subordinated to the immediate needs of the projects, to the delivery of services, and to the ongoing search for funding. Admittedly, groups mobilize rapidly against certain legislative or administrative changes in their specific sectors: they still act as a political shield against the deterioration of social policies and programmes. However, they henceforth also play an internal regulatory role within social movements (Côté and Simard, 2010) and at times resort to anti-democratic methods to "control" activist initiatives from within their own organizations.

Global Mobilization and Hostile Takeover within a Community Coalition

Initiated by a coalition of community groups, a global mobilization effort is scheduled to take place within three years. Events are to be held in each of Québec's 17 regions. An activist from one region is co-founder the central organizing committee and subsequently returns to her region to organize a regional event there, directly related to this global mobilization. She establishes an organizing committee and works relentlessly with 20 other activists for more than a year.

Neither the paid staff nor the president of the coalition of community organizations of the sector to be mobilized awards any importance or funding to this initiative, because both give priority to collaboration with the regional authorities in their development plans. And yet, this mobilization effort fulfils the coalition's mission, a mission tied to advocating for the sector. Noting this, the activist-leader and a female ally seek election to the coalition's Board of Directors; both are elected. They believe that this will enable them to improve communications and to tie this mobilization effort more firmly to the coalition. The coordinator and the president of the group join forces against them and seek to take control of the event's organizing committee. The activist-leader and her ally refuse to surrender the leadership of the committee voluntarily. Ten months before the scheduled date of this world mobilization, the committee falls prey to a hostile takeover. Contrary to the private sector, no rule governs this type of situation in the community sector; the very idea that this could happen is denied. Everything takes place therefore in dark secret, since the global culture of community groups dictates omerta on this matter. The president and the paid staff's methods are brutal and diverse: the meagre funds allocated to the organizing committee are cut, false information is spread, false rumours are fabricated, the reputations of the activist-leader and her ally are sullied, parallel Board of Director meetings are held in the absence of the activist-leader and her ally. Seeing that these manoeuvres do not compel the activist-leader and her ally to yield, the paid staff, the president, as well as another member of the Board of Directors resign en masse, six months before the scheduled date of the world event; they believe, no doubt, that they will deal a blow to their "opponents". The activist-leader and her ally, without any preparation, take on the duties of the paid staff as well as the presidency on a volunteer basis. The resigning president then calls an illegal general meeting of the Board of Directors, accusing the activist-leader of embezzling funds and demanding that she be dismissed and that the Board of Directors be dissolved. A stormy meeting is held, each party

> being accompanied by his/her lawyer and putting forth legal rather than political arguments. The Board of Directors is not dissolved and the mobilization project takes place as planned. The activist-leader and her ally subsequently resign in order to give way to their opponents on the Board of Directors and are left with a bill of several thousands of dollars in legal fees. This mobilization effort in support of a "just" cause produced brutish power relations within the coalition that continues to claim to be working for a democratic alternative.

5. FORMS OF DEMOCRACY WITHIN COMMUNITY GROUPS

From their inception, community groups established various structures and avant-garde modes of operation, that they wanted more democratic than the institutional hierarchies they opposed, preferring participatory processes, mutual aid and sharing. These included very fruitful and diverse practices, which transcended representative democracy. In this respect, the process by which the Québec State recognized community groups, introduced when they first took shape and culminating when the Rochon Report was presented in 1998, seriously challenged the preservation of these activist, often radical, practices (Guberman et al., 2004). The introduction of methods intrinsic to the NPM and the ongoing relationship that community groups sustained with the bureaucratic systems led them to define their skills in function of a system of specialized expertise, incurring a depoliticization and an institutionalization of their movement (Couillard and Côté, 1995). Hierarchies and specializations were reintroduced; groups sometimes defined themselves around issues prioritized by the government's neoliberal policies. To such an extent that it becomes increasingly difficult to participate fully in decision-making processes within a community group short of a minimal level of expertise (Hamel, 1991). It is also increasingly difficult to operate as a collective or self-managed group.

Furthermore, the discussions on democracy within these groups are no longer a common occurrence. When they take place, they are often fuelled by the employees' perspective rather than by that of activists, members, users, or the population symbolically represented by the group (Guberman et al., 2004). This tendency to transfer power from grassroots members to the workers was already identified by Godbout (1991). As if the ideal of grassroots management had been reconfigured into an ideal of self-management (that is, management by the service producers) and then into an ideal of technocratic management (that is, management centred on the needs of the system).

Moreover, one notes the emergence of a certain form of unionism that preserves the illusion that community groups inherently defend the interests of all the underprivileged. Indeed, if the democratic practices of certain community groups are still alive and well, they have markedly eroded. But since internal democracy is in constant need of refurbishing (Côté, 1975), the ideal of social change within several Québec community organizations has masked a division of labour and an unequal distribution of power under the seal of omerta. Ever since class analysis waned in popularity, the creation of community group elites has, for all intents and purposes, disappeared as a theme from the literature and from debates. But the phenomenon has not, for all that, vanished, even if the elites of community groups have changed.

Sites of advocacy and counter-power have always welcomed individuals from the middle class and of radical, revolutionary, or reformist beliefs. Some among them are also willing to devote their career to the community group milieu as full-time community activists:

The spokespersons of the movement are not elected, except on rare occasions. These persons are, most often, employees of Boards of Directors, themselves composed of coalition employees ... In this way, many executive directors have occupied their positions for ten or fifteen years. This is a vast movement and a very small world. (Houle, 2006)

This structural characteristic carries within itself the seeds of a professionalization of the full-time salaried employees, and of the separation of the community group from its base. The opening of salaried positions can help reinforce a hierarchy between paid workers and volunteers. The possibility of representing a population external to the community group can favour the creation of a community group elite, endowed with a representative function rather than an executive one, just as in the case of political parties and trade unions.

The Death Throes of Activism within Community Groups

Within a number of community groups, activism has turned into voluntary work. Often "managed" by the employees, activism is no longer at the heart of group action and often even disappears from view: seldom mentioned in annual reports, it is easily seen as the equivalent of the work done by employees. Rarely recognized as expert (specialized) work or political work, activism is often converted into "help" granted to the group's salaried workers, who are chronically overburdened (but who do not do unpaid overtime). Activism remains central to the group's mission, less, however, as citizen participation than as compensation for its weak human and financial resources. Today, activist contributions within community groups are too often limited to membership in a Board of Directors, to services performed for the membership, or to carrying out the objectives of an organization's annual action plan, which, in turn, corresponds to a project financed by a government sponsor. As such, this activism increasingly resembles work performed within a voluntary association rather than an community group.

Conclusion

Within welfare systems, in Québec as elsewhere, social issues have become a phenomenon to be managed: the state has sought to do this by using its methods and techno-bureaucratic resources to its advantage. Far from reducing this tendency, neo-liberalism has reinforced it through different mechanisms such as governance and administrative decentralization. At the same time, it has incorporated a philosophy as well as methods inspired by the private sector, subsequently transmitting them to community groups to which it grants mandates and funding. Even if several community groups have been wary of these practices, they have in general had few means of resisting them and too often have fallen prey to them.

Of course, Québec community groups have helped extend democratic practices beyond the electoral process and party politics. They continue to have this impact today. Recognized in the rest of Canada, this democratic vitality of Québec civil society is indeed considered exemplary all over the world. Québec's community organizations have helped to establish a social safety net and to institute numerous reforms enabling a better redistribution of wealth as well as greater equality of opportunities. They have allowed individuals and marginalized groups to position themselves as equal political subjects. With few means and at the cost of bitter struggles to uphold the dignity of the socially and economically excluded, they helped establish social services, policies, and legislation. Finally, they channelled the creative ebullience of social solidarity, and did not wait for experts or persons mandated by the powers-that-be to look into their situation (Ravet, 2009).

Today, many groups are still fighting this tendency to privatize and to depoliticize social issues; they are helping to create "polemical communities" where opinions that diverge from the official point of view are being asserted (Lamoureux and Lamoureux, 2009). But too often this solidarity organized and encouraged by social movements is considered by the economic elites as being detrimental. They distrust the "political involvement of groups and 'popular' organizations" (Brunelle, 2005: 28). They resort to different means to stifle it, to "discipline it, neutralize or replace it with impersonal mechanisms [which cannot achieve anything other than emptying society of its] capacity to act and begin defining spaces of humanization" (Ravet, 2009: 11).

Techno-bureaucratic management is one of these methods of imposing within community groups a greater conformity to established authorities. The result is an erosion of community action as the groups' democratic structures and practices gradually disappear. This, in turn, has a major impact on democracy within Québec society. Indeed:

> *[...] community action [is an] essential component of democratic action – democracy being above all a particular way of acting on social reality. However, the latter is characterized by conflictual social relations and by the fact that relations of power are constantly interfering. What is at stake in democracy is the mobilization of individuals as subjects and as social actors, conscious of their common responsibilities and of their power in human affairs to engage in collective and coordinated action. (Ravet, 2009)*

The transformation of community groups' culture and practices also sets up a normative standard on their work that is all the more latent because it is not the object of discussion. For example, anti-poverty work is transformed to work on the poor or, in the best of cases, work accompanying the poor:

> *The obvious example of such a slippage is the work of the Collectif pour l'élimination de la pauvreté in recent years. The Collectif's proposal projected a solution that seemed all the more interesting in that it combined legal and expert technicity to reduce poverty, without however attacking the root of the problem. In doing so, it presented an image of a society able to expunge its ills through rational and consensual action, which underpins the illusion of a society reconciled through repairing its social fractures. Such a reconciled society is a pure fantasy ... (Houle, 2006)*

We are witnessing the normalization of neo-liberalism, of which one feature is precisely to proceed through local and regional actors that "manipulate the elements of local political culture". Neoliberalism "thus no longer appears as an exogenous force ... but as the new norm" (Boudreau and Keil, 2006: 98):

This reappropriation by the State and the economic elite of the democratic principles so dear to the socio-political movements opposing neoliberalism would thus suggest a normalization of neoliberalism. (Boudreau and Keil, 2006: 97)

If this normalization process is not irrevocable, it nonetheless appears to be in a phase of expansion and consolidation. Of course, there are always counter-examples to this dominant tendency, and new types of collective action, new structures and practices that are suggestive of tomorrow's democratic action.

References

Baines, D. (2004a). "Pro-Market, Non-Market: The Dual Nature of Organizational Change in Social Services Delivery," *Critical Social Policy*, Vol. 24, No. 1, pp. 5–29.

Baines, D. (2004b). "Caring for Nothing: Work Organization and Unwaged Labour in Social Services," *Work, Employment and Society*, Vol. 18, No. 2, pp. 267–295.

Baines, D. (2006). "'If You Could Change One Thing': Social Service Workers and Restructuring," *Australian Social Work*, Vol. 59, No. 1, March, pp. 20–34.

Basu, R. (2004). "The Rationalization of Neoliberalism in Ontario's Public Education System, 1995–2000," *Geoforum*, Vol. 35, pp. 621–634.

Belzile, G. (1999). "Le déficit zéro, enfin! Et après?" in *Québec 2000*, Montréal, Fides, pp. 363–368.

Boudreau, J.-A. and R. Keil (2006). "La réconciliation de la démocratie locale et de la compétitivité internationale dans le discours réformiste à Toronto: Essai d'interprétation sur le néolibéralisme normalisé," *Politique et Sociétés*, Vol. 25, No. 1, 2006, pp. 83–98.

Bourque, G.L. (1995). *Le néo-corporatisme comme angle d'analyse de la nouvelle politique industrielle au Québec*, Montréal, Cahiers du CRISES.

Brais, N. and W. Frohn (2002). "L'État local et le mouvement des femmes à Québec: une étude de cas," *Lien social et Politiques*, No. 47, pp. 55–66.

Brouillard, C. (2005). "Constitution d'un mouvement," *À babord!* No. 10, summer.

Brunelle, D., P.-A. Harvey and S. Bédard (2005). "La nouvelle gestion publique en contexte" in Brunelle, D. (ed.), *Main basse sur l'État: Les partenriats public-privé au Québec et en Amérique du Nord*. Montréal, Fides.

Caillouette, J. (2001). "Pratiques de partenariat, pratiques d'articulation identitaire et mouvement communautaire," *Nouvelles pratiques sociales*, Vol. 14, No. 1, pp. 81–96.

Chevalier, J. (2003). "La gouvernance, un nouveau paradigme étatique?" *Revue française d'administration publique*, 1–2, Nos. 105–106, pp. 203–217.

Clark, D. (2002). "Neoliberalism and Public Service Reform: Canada in Comparative Perspective," *Canadian Journal of Political Science*, Vol. 35, No. 4, pp. 771–793.

Côté, D. (1975). "L'animation sociale au sein de comités de citoyens de l'Assemblée générale de l'Île de Hull (AGIH)," Masters thesis, University of Ottawa, Department of Political Science.

Côté, D. and É. Simard (2010). *"De l'utopie radicale à la bonne gouvernance: le cas du Québec,"* *AmeriQuests*, Vol. 7, No. 1, pp. 42–53.

Côté, L., B. Lévesque and G. Morneau (2007). "L'évolution du modèle québécois de gouvernance: le point de vue des acteurs," *Politique et sociétés*, Vol. 26, No. 1, pp. 3–26.

Couillard, M.-A. (1994). "Le pouvoir dans les groupes de femmes de la région de Québec," *Recherches sociographiques*, Vol. 35, No. 1, pp. 39–65.

Couillard, M.-A. (1996). "Le savoir sur les femmes. De l'imaginaire, du politique et de l'administratif," *Anthropologie et société*, Vol. 20, No. 1, pp. 59–80.

Couillard, M.-A. and G. Côté (1995). "Les défis d'une interface: les groupes de femmes et le réseau de la santé et des services sociaux de la région de Québec," *Recherches féministes*, Vol. 42, No. 2, pp. 29–49.

Dawson, S. and C. Dargie (2002). "New Public Management: A discussion with Special Reference to UK Health," in McLaughlin, K., S.P. Osborne, and E.F. New (2002), *Public Management*, London: Routledge, pp. 34–56.

Debord, G. (1992). *La société du spectacle*, Paris: Gallimard.

Falquet, J. (2003). "L'ONU, alliée des femmes? Une analyse féministe critique du système des organisations internationales," *Multitudes* No. 11, Winter.

Gagné, J. (2008). "Les organismes communautaires au Québec: une sociologie de la mémoire," PhD diss., Montreal, Université du Québec à Montréal.

Giauque, D. (2003). "New Public Management and Organizational Regulation: The Liberal Bureaucracy," *International Review of Administrative Sciences*, Vol. 69, pp. 567–592.

Godbout, J.T. (1991). "Ce qui se passe aux frontières de l'État et de la société," *Politique*, No. 19, pp. 67–79.

Gouvernement du Québec (2003). Loi sur le Ministère des Affaires municipales et des Régions.

Guay, L. and D. White (2009). "Une politique novatrice sous observation," *Revue Relations*, No. 731, March, pp. 19–21.

Guberman, N., J. Lamoureux, J. Beeman, D. Fournier and L. Gervais (2004). *Le défi des pratiques démocratiques dans les groupes de femmes*, Montréal, Éditions St-Martin.

Hamel, P. (1991). "Les services urbains: le défi du partenariat pour le milieu communautaire," *Les cahiers de géographie du Québec*, Vol. 35, No. 95, pp. 257–283.

Hammer, M. and J. Champy (1993). *Reengineering the Corporation: A Manifesto for Business Revolution*, New York, NY: HarperBusiness.

Houle, M.-A. (2006). "Splendeurs et misères de l'autonomie. Les relations entre le communautaire et l'État," *À Babord!* No. 15, summer.

Ilcan, S. (2009). "Privatizing Responsability: Public Sector Reform under Neoliberal Government," *Canadian Review of Sociology*, Vol. 46, No. 3, August, pp. 207–234.

Klein, J.-L. (1995). "De l'*État*-providence à l'*État accompagnateur* dans la gestion du social: le cas du développement régional au Québec," *Lien social et politiques*, 33, Spring, pp. 133–141.

Lamoureux, D. (2002). "Le dilemme entre politiques et pouvoir," *Cahiers de recherche sociologique*, No. 37, pp. 283–201.

Lamoureux, D. (1990). "Les services féministes; de l'autonomie à l'extension de l'État-Providence," *Nouvelles pratiques sociales*, Vol. 3, No. 2, pp. 33–43.

Lamoureux, D. and J. Lamoureux (2009). "Histoire et tensions d'un mouvement," *Revue Relations*, No. 731, March, pp. 15–17.

Lamoureux, H. (1999). *Les dérives de la démocratie – questions à la société civile québécoise*, Montréal: VLB.

Latendresse, A. (2004). "Démocratiser radicalement la démocratie," *À Babord!* No. 3, January–February.

Lebel, G.A. (2009). "Du salariat au précariat en milieu communautaire: les partenariats public-communautaire," *À Babord !* No. 30, summer.

Loiselle, B. (2005). "Le mouvement communautaire dans les mailles des regroupements," *À Babord*, No. 9, April–May.

Masson, D. (2001). "Gouvernance partagée, associations et démocratie: les femmes dans le développement régional," *Politique et société*, Vol. 20, Nos. 2–3, pp. 89–115.

McAll, C. (1995). "Les murs de la cité: territoires d'exclusion et espaces de citoyenneté," *Lien social et Politiques*, No. 34, pp. 81–92.

Merrien, F.-X. (1999), "La Nouvelle Gestion publique: un concept mythique," *Lien social et Politiques*, No. 41, pp. 95–103.

Mouvement d'éducation populaire et d'action communautaire du Québec (MÉPACQ) (2004). *Bulletin spécial*, December 6.

O'Brien, D. (2006). *Post-Bureaucracy or Post-Public Good? New Public Management and the Policy Process Constraints in Ontario*, Working of Canadian Political Science Association, June 2: http://cpsa-acsp.ca/papers-2006/O per cent27Brien.pdf.

Paiement, G. (2009). "Des solidarités assiégées," *Revue Relations*, No. 731, March, pp. 12–14.

Paquet, G. (1989). "Santé et image sociale: un problème de distance culturelle," Québec, INRS.

Piotte, J.-M. (2010). *L'État social et l'action communautaire autonome*, edited by the committee Gouvernance de l'État du RQ-ACA. Montréal, RQACA.

Ramboarisata, L. and A. De Serres (2007). *Les partenariats entreprises/OBNL du* Québec dans le cadre de la mise en oeuvre de la stratégie de responsabilité sociale des entreprises, Montréal, ARUC-ÉS.

Ravet, J.-C. (2009). "Quel avenir pour l'action communautaire?" *Revue Relations*, No. 731, March, pp. 10–11.

Rochon, J. (1988). *Rapport de la Commission d'enquête sur la santé et les services sociaux*, Québec, Publications du Québec.

Rouillard, C. et al. (2008). *De la réingénierie à la modernisation de l'État québécois*, Québec, Presses de l'Université Laval.

Rubin, H.J. and I.S. Rubin (1992). *Community Organizing and Community Development*, New York: MacMillan.

Shragge, E. (2003). *Activism and Social Change: Lessons for Community and Local Organizing Action*. Toronto, Broadview Press.

Villeneuve, J.-P. (2005). *Citoyens, clients et usagers face à l'administration publique: Les balises d'une relation difficile*, Working paper de l'IDHEAP, UER: Management et marketing public.

CHAPTER 6

Knowledge Workers and Creativity Class: From Hopes and Ideals to Day-to-Day Reality

SILVIA PONCE

Introduction

Defined as a right, human dignity is inherent to human beings and it embodies both a capability and a privilege endowed to every man, woman and child. As De Koninck (2005) argues in his *Archeology of the Human Dignity Notion*, it is a requirement previous to any philosophical or ethical formulation, something human beings have because they are human beings. So, human dignity is not exclusively a contemporary issue or something we have nowadays due to the progress of our societies or the development of civilizations. What may have changed about is how it is conceived and how it is manifested, represented and expressed in our daily lives.

As a matter of concern, human dignity has been traced to the period of Enlightenment (Garbooshian, 2006). But as Khan observes "some of the ideas, principles, and values of human rights are common to all civilizations", and the basic principles and fundamentals of human rights and dignity "are rooted in universality, indivisibility, and inalienability" (Anonymous, 2006, p. 70). According to Ricard (2005), human dignity reaches people from all cultures and knows many representations although the concept itself is based on the notion of the *persona* from the Judeo-Christian and Roman jurisprudence; yet, its universal character is best expressed by Kant's *moral law of dignity* stating that nobody should ever treat himself, herself or others simply as a *mean* but always as an *end* in itself.

Etymologically, the Latin word *Dignus* refers to *Decet* – meaning "it is convenient" – and it is attached to two nouns: *Decor and Decus*. *Decor* refers to the body whereas *Decus* refers to soul or spirit and means "propriety or appropriateness, decency, dignity" (Isidore de Séville, cited by De Koninck, 2005). The fundamental dimensions of human dignity are then physical as well as moral, tangible and intangible, exteriorized and internalized. As intrinsic dimensions, they allow us to perceive human dignity manifestations in day-to-day life although much more attention seems to be paid to its physical and more tangible consequences; generally induced by high-tech computer culture in workplaces – stress, biorhythms and burnout (Rifkin, 1995) – new biomedical research and technologies (Melo-Martin, 2008), or in its relation to bioethics issues like autonomy and death (Belde, 2005; Larochelle, 2005).

As a right, human dignity also pervades every place, space and temporality, individually and collectively in all kind of human activity. In organized activities and at work – being the core of men and women contemporary activities – human dignity plays a key role by establishing the standards and references that maintain and guide collective interactions and individual aspirations, providing the principles and foundations in fulfilling our roles and responsibilities, shaping our ambitions and dreams. As such, human dignity is both individual and collective. Individually, it gives us the power and dominion over our own decisions, ambitions and dreams; collectively, it gives us respect and integrity in front of others and within our societies.

Acknowledging that "dignity at work is a complex phenomenon", Bolton (2006) has argued that it "can be more clearly explored if its multidimensional character is highlighted" (p. 46). It is under this perspective – that is, on human dignity tangible (physical) and intangible (moral) dimensions, individual and collective scope, interiorized and externalized expressions – that the present chapter is developed. We first present some antecedents on workers' stereotypes and knowledge workers to highlight human dignity at work and its implications concerning new demands management is requiring from workers – notably creativity and knowledge efficiency. Then, key aspects of human dignity manifestations at work are retrieved, along with some case-episodes that illustrate specific issues confronted by individuals in their respective activities; we also present a cross-case analysis. We conclude with some lines of inquiry in order to improve our understanding of human dignity in the current knowledge-based and creativity context.

Workers' Stereotypes

Industrial development, evolution, diversity, globalization, culture and individual fulfilment among others, are at the very heart of workers' stereotypes. Whereas craftsmen could be considered predecessors of industrial workers, knowledge workers in turn constitute the current model best describing the role information and technology is playing in productive activities of knowledge-based economies (Castells, 2004). Notably in Western societies, the development of informatics and telecommunication technologies, along with the expansion of the service sector, have given place to the rapid constitution of a knowledge worker class (Wuthnow and Shrum, 1983), a group considered the fastest growing workforce segment (Russette et al., 2007) shaping knowledge-based societies.

Actually, while different workers' stereotypes have been coexisting during the past century, an important shift took place in the ratio and distribution of workers types. From 1920 to 1980, the 2:1 ratio of manual workers to knowledge worker was reversed to 1:2, respectively (Ramirez and Nembhard, 2004). By now, knowledge workers total millions of peoples – near to 28 per cent in North America (McKellar, 2005), 32 per cent in the United Kingdom (Russette et al., 2005), and some even maintain that knowledge workers count for two-thirds of the workforce (Ramirez and Nembhard, 2004). Therefore, the different manifestations of human dignity in this newly developed context are worth to be explored. In so doing, let us start by reviewing the role knowledge has been playing under different managerial contexts.

MANAGERIAL ASSUMPTIONS AND KNOWLEDGE TYPES

In the management field, workers' stereotypes have best been characterized in line with production modes or manufacturing systems. As it is illustrated in Table 6.1, we have identified different knowledge types and repositories that are involved in *craft, industrial* and *post-industrial production*. These three generic types of production system are, in essence, different manifestations of management styles; accordingly, production objectives require specific skills, competencies, expertise and knowledge. In this sense, the term knowledge worker – coined by Peter Drucker in the fifties[1] – could be misleading because every kind of work requires specific knowledge generally embodied in product, processes, routines and tasks.

In fact, in their critical analysis of the American Corporation Florida and Kenney (1990) argued that "all workers must be elevated to the position of think-workers" (p. 194). And practice seems to demonstrate that considering "himself a knowledge worker and to think creatively" could have a significant impact on organizational performance, as it has been suggested by the Toyota's success case (*The Economist*, 2006, p. 9). Notwithstanding, Davenport (2005)has maintained that although "most jobs require some degree of knowledge to perform them successfully ... definitions of knowledge workers that incorporate anyone who uses knowledge on the job are also not very helpful" (p. 11).

From a cognitive standpoint, a turning point for knowledge at work was reached with Taylor's Scientific Management. Considered one of the first formal landmarks in the management field, this management style undertook the division of design and execution as two independent tasks (Taylor, 1911). Under this management approach characteristic of mass production of the industrial era (Table 6.1), workers on the shop floor were asked for the execution of tasks by *repeating* what others in their place had decided to.

Taylor's detractors have maintained that individuals were deprived of part of their human nature, because workers had to employ only their hands and body while executing physical labour, not necessarily using their brains. His supporters and followers instead have justified Taylorism in terms of efficiency and productivity. Others have rather explained and interpreted it in terms of the social, economic and historical conditions existing by the end of nineteenth century. Still, nobody can deny that the underlying steering principle of Taylor's "one best way" was resource maximization. Under these premises, Taylorism and all managerial approaches derived from do not conform to Kant's moral law of dignity. Expressions like "human resources" and "human capital" – adopted in management and economics fields – intrinsically and explicitly convey the concept of men and women at work as *means* of production, and knowledge workers are not the exception.

Current flexible production systems – the last column in Table 6.1 – are designed to offer the advantages of its two predecessors; that is, they are able to manufacture customized products (high-medium variety) in big quantities (high-medium volume). In this new manufacturing context, management has nevertheless kept traditional elements of Taylor's approach – for example, time and movement measurements, standardization logics, process analysis, reward systems, and other tools characterizing mass-production. Notwithstanding, at the opposite of Taylorist workers, knowledge workers are involved in both the design as well as the execution of their tasks. These new working conditions are not necessarily due to a certain progress at work; rather, the new business dynamics developed around and within flexible systems are responsible for them.

---

[1] Peter F. Drucker, (1959) *The Landmarks of Tomorrow*. New York: Harper.

Table 6.1 Workers' stereotypes and their production contexts

Production systems Characteristics	Craft production Pre-industrial era	Mass production Industrial era	Mass-customized Production Post-industrial era
Main driver	Development of commerce	Industrial revolution	Informatics and telecomm revolution
Management style	Entrepreneurship Individual in his/her collectivity	Coordination Hierarchical Production units	Cognitive style Teams and communities of practice, CoP Service orientation
Production logic (objectives)	Tailored products Selection (Raw materials) Low volumes High variety Uniqueness High quality	Standardized Products Maximization (Resources) Very high volumes Low variety Cost reduction Process efficiency Parts replacement	Modular products Optimization (Resources) High-medium volumes High-medium variety High flexibility Rapidity Innovation
Knowledge types and repositories	Tacit knowledge craftsmen	Codified knowledge Technical knowledge Machine, processes Engineers and machine operators	Tacit and codified knowledge Network Communities of practice (CoP) databases Software, hardware, firmware
Knowledge management approaches	Inventors copyrights Apprenticeships Mentorship Know-how transfer via person-to-person in the workshop	Property rights protection policies (patents, trademarks, licenses) Technology transfers Absorptive capacity development	Data and information driven Intellectual property Management Knowledge transfers via codification and virtuality Face-to-face technology facilitators
Underlying cognitive assumptions and roles	Crafts Manual dexterity Creativity Design and production (simultaneously)	Low-cost labour Taylorism (design activities separated from production) Learning curve	Knowledge-worker Analytical and abstract knowledge Design, production and service processes integration

Source: Adapted from Ponce and Dueñas, in press.

As Table 6.1 illustrates, whereas craft production is basically based on tacit knowledge and mass production on codified knowledge, flexible production systems require both tacit and codified knowledge plus team work and networks forms of organization. Challenging previous organizational structures and configurations, organizations who have adopted flexible systems have also institutionalized change and innovation. Changes in product and process technologies are increasingly faster and managers and workers are simultaneously asked for costs reduction, improved quality, flexibility and high performance levels.

Moreover, the many types of embedded networks – for example, networks of suppliers, production networks, networks of information and networks of innovators – also require constant organizational changes, specific skills, information exchange and relationship management. Consequently, tasks and activities need to be constantly designed, redesigned and rapidly executed. Under this dynamic, it became obvious that tasks design and execution separation, in manufacturing as well as in services, was no more convenient or adequate in fulfilling production objectives.

Florida and Kenney's (1993) descriptions of the new demands on workers in the new developed context are particularly eloquent. They wrote:

Capitalism is undergoing an epochal transformation from a mass-production system where the principal source of value was physical labor to a new era of innovation-mediated production where the principal component of value creation, productivity, and economic growth is knowledge and intellectual capabilities. Capitalism in this new age of innovation-mediated production will require deep and fundamental changes in the organization of enterprise, regions, nations, and international economic and political institutions. Survival in this new era will require the development of new organizational forms and systems, such as teams and new incentive systems, which decentralize decision-making, mobilize intellectual capabilities, and harness the knowledge and intelligence of all members of the organization. Perhaps the most fundamental element of capitalism in an age of innovation-mediated production is the transformation of the factory itself. The modern factory is becoming more like a laboratory – the place where new ideas and concepts are generated, tested, and implemented. (p. 635)

Another turning point for knowledge at work has then been reached with the transition from mass to flexible production – along with the development of the service sector and telecommunication technologies among others. During the last decades, the constitution of knowledge-based societies and knowledge-based economies has dramatically been changing and will continue to change workers' roles (Singleton, 1989; Florida and Kenney 1993; Drucker, 1994; Harvey, 1996; Chinying Lang, 2001; Castells, 2004; Davenport, 2005; Ehin, 2008). Nonetheless, management seems not to evolve accordingly in its conceptualizations and practices. But as Chinying Lang (2001) has claimed: "Hoary managerial assumptions and obsolete business practices will not survive in the knowledge economy" (p. 539). An effective and supportive managerial environment will not be built on anachronistic management practices that rather interfere and overload knowledge workers, making more difficult their tasks and goals achievements. In manufacturing as in service environments, while higher demands are made on knowledge workers, management is still acting on traditional premises in dealing with new emerging issues.

WORKERS IN THE SERVICE SECTOR

Services workers are more commonly considered knowledge workers than manufacture workers, mainly due to the customer-contact dimension that asks for workers' cognitive participation. Notwithstanding, similarly to production types (illustrated in Table 6.1), services can also be classified according to their processes; in fact, taking into account production and delivery processes characteristics, three categories of services are distinguished: *professional services, services shop* and *mass services* (Silvestro, 1999). In Table 6.2, we have characterized these three types of services, and accordingly to management styles, production logics also involve different knowledge types. Underlying cognitive assumptions (last row of Table 6.2), have, however, established that services involving professionals are considered the most representative category of knowledge workers.

Historically, the first two services types that we describe in Table 6.2 have coexisted for nearly the first two-thirds of the past century, whereas the third one was mainly developed in the seventies. Interestingly, at the same time manufacturing was evolving into flexible systems, the service sector instead took the opposite highway to industrialization (Levitt, 1972; 1976). Since then, in spite of the arguments in favour of de-industrialization (Teboul, 1988), mass services have been expanding and reinforcing their production logics by using, benefiting, integrating and promoting the development of soft (applications) and hard technologies.

Table 6.2 Services types and workers' stereotypes

Service types / Characteristics	Professional services	Shop services	Mass services
Main driver	Expertise	Economic development	Service industrialization informatics and telecomm revolution
Management style	Cognitive style	Decoupling (Front-office and back-office)	Taylorism-based
Production and delivery logic (objectives)	Customization Low volumes High contact time Uniqueness High quality	Customer participation Medium volumes Medium variety Customer satisfaction	Standardization Very high volumes Low variety Cost reduction Rapidity Process efficiency
Knowledge types and repositories	Tacit and codified knowledge Professional	Product and process oriented Contact employee (front-office) Service employee (back-office)	Data bases Equipment and contact employee
Underlying cognitive assumptions and roles	People focus Client interaction Autonomy Professional Knowledge worker	Coordination Service employee Customer participation	Equipment Focus Resources Maximization Productivity Minimizing customer participation Service employee

© S. Ponce 2009.

Furthermore, the service sector has increasingly been integrated into product manufacture; for instance, through customer service centres, financing, and other new service business models. Data and information – as intangible goods – have been placed at the very onset of new service types involving millions of people and workers in their exchanges and transactions. Once supporting tangible flows (transactions of goods), these intangible flows are now making possible the continuous emergence of new business models that create in turn new markets, new transactions modes and new knowledge-based jobs (Viardot, 2000; Florida, 2002; Castells, 2004).

Production and service frameworks, as described in Tables 6.1 and 6.1, respectively, bring to light that (1) all workers use and apply specific knowledge, and (2) management styles, approaches and production objectives play a key role in the knowledge type required to activities and tasks execution. Workers' stereotypes are then implicitly based on *knowledge use* and *application* but knowledge processes in organizations also involve creation, transformations, sharing, transfers, learning, integration, diffusion, appropriation, and so on. Consequently, although very insightful in the characterization of core productive activities, these frameworks also suggest that eliciting knowledge workers is complex, highly elusive and problematic indeed.

Traditional premises underlying production logics in service as in manufacturing have been developed by taking a restrictive perspective of workers and organizational knowledge. Actually, Nickerson and Zenger (2004) have described managers' key tasks in terms of accumulation and protection of "valuable knowledge or capability". But these authors have also argued that:

> *the key knowledge-based question the manager faces is not how to organize to exploit already developed knowledge or capability, but rather how to organize to efficiently generate knowledge and capability. (p. 617)*

On these matters, a knowledge-based view of the firm theory is underdeveloped. Previous analysis – such as the learning organization (Argyris and Schön, 1978), the intelligent enterprise (Quinn, 1992) or the knowledge-creating enterprise (Nonaka and Takeuchi, 1995), have certainly made insightful contributions but the new context is asking for a thorough re-conceptualization of the enterprise and its workers. On one hand, anachronistic management cannot contribute to "knowledge worker performance"; on the other hand, a partial or anachronistic conceptualization of the enterprise will not allow for a sound analysis of knowledge at work. A new knowledge-platform for organizations is required.

The state of the art concerning the knowledge-based view of the firm forces and gives the opportunity to re-conceptualize organizations – and enterprises in particular – under a new light. Under a different and *softer* perspective, we think that the integration of key human dimensions such at dignity at work is now possible and required.

DIGNITY AT WORK

Traditionally, dignity at work has commonly been associated to successful union fights translated into bills to protect employees from employers in their working environments. Among others, bills address offences, abuses, intimidation, unjustified punishments and detrimental changes attributed to employers' behaviours. Yet, as Meyer (1987) has maintained, human dignity includes much more than the capacity to claim rights; it also entails a human capacity for self-management. Effectively, Miller and Telles (1974) had previously observed that while human dignity at work is judged in terms of the assurance of a human treatment in working situations, it is also important in developing job motivation and equality of opportunities for individual's employment potential.

Different cultures construe human dignity in a different way but at work, it is often used to evaluate and critique the ethics of selected management practices (Koehn and Leung, 2008). Indeed, the need for developing dignity at work policies has emerged while discussing it in terms of the bullying problem (Peyton, 2003) although some authors have claimed for dignity while discussing downsizing and termination (Bayer, 2000; Greenspan, 2002).

Rayman (2001) has nevertheless approached human dignity under a balance perspective to multiple demands: work-family-community. In so doing, the author elicited three dignity pillars: (1) ability of gaining livelihood for oneself and the family; (2) self-respect, and (3) socially responsible individual contribution. On these premises, Rayman (2001) raised issues such as income inequalities, limited time available for children, elderly parents and community involvement, low-skilled-low-wages jobs, unemployment and job undervaluation, decreasing loyalty, work's social responsibility. However, the author also showed that improvements in workplace – in terms of increasing productivity and balance – are possible but efforts are isolated, fragmented and dependable on workers' ability to negotiate them.

Interestingly, Hodson (1996) had elicited the individual and collective dimensions of dignity while maintaining that "Dignity is contingent not only on protecting oneself from abuse, but also on having personal space for one's individual identity" (p. 722). At the same time, this author recognized two realms for workers at work: the task-related and co-worker-related domains. The first one describes workers' interface with both technology and management, and involves four aspects: job satisfaction, pride, *acquired knowledge* and effort (or commitment) levels. The second one takes into consideration the collectivity, especially the interaction with co-workers "to create and defend autonomous lives for themselves" (p. 723); therefore, it involves solidarity, peer training and social friendships.

Hodson (1996) had also correlated dignity to five production modes – craft, direct supervision, assembly line, bureaucratic, worker participation – asserting that (1) workers develop strategies for "protecting and maximizing their dignity in the workplace" (p. 722) – for example, resistance, search of meaning and group activities, among others; and (2) different production modes afford workers the opportunity to work with "greater or lesser dignity and self-realization" (p. 719). This ethnographic research, however, suggests that the collective domain appears less influenced by individual aspects – like skill and autonomy – than obviously do on the task-related domain. But Hodson (1996) also observed that personalized control and supervision fuelled solidarity; whereas direct supervision appeared to have a less mediated negative effect on peer training. The author then concludes that new concepts and new structures of work and co-workers' relations are needed to integrate dignity aspects in "the participative work-places of the future" (p. 735).

Knowledge Workers

The work-place of the future has always and will always be intimately grounded on technological advances and developments. It is in this context that the knowledge worker expression has been employed during the last decades, describing people who are developing and using sophisticated technological systems. Yet, McKellar (2005), the *KM World*'s editor in chief, wrote:

> today's technology is astoundingly sophisticated (and seductive). But often overlooked through all that allure and investment of time and dollars, are the people who will be using the systems – the knowledge workers. They aren't completely understood or given proper credit, nor do they themselves always contribute up to their potential because of organizational hurdles ... For me, knowledge management has always been an elusive term; so, too, is knowledge worker because it has been widely under- and over-used. (p. 14)

While defining knowledge workers has become a difficult task, their value is undeniable and critical in the context of knowledge-based economies (Martin and Moldoveanu, 2003; Bouchez, 2006; Edvinsson, 2006; Yigitcanlar, et al., 2007). Its importance has led countries and cities to rethink their future and to develop their strategies in terms of knowledge-based economies. Some of the key issues discussed are the design of knowledge cities to support "the value creation from and for the knowledge worker" (Edvinson, 2006: 6) as well as attracting and retaining this type of worker to develop knowledge-based industries (Yigitcanlar et al., 2007). Still, a key question for managers is if there is a particular trait that differentiates knowledge workers from traditional ones. Or else, isn't the knowledge worker concept rather reminding management of the integrity of human beings' capabilities and, consequently, human dignity at work?

KNOWLEDGE WORKERS DEFINITIONS

McCormick (2009) has recently asserted that knowledge workers are actually engaged in a great variety of activities although they spend an important part of their time searching for and evaluating information. Understandably, knowledge workers have been subjected to many definitions. As we show in Table 6.3, formal education, roles, experience, knowledge activities, capabilities, skills, and value are among the key elements employed to define them.

Davenport (2005), in particular, has argued that knowledge workers (1) have high degrees of expertise, education, or experience; (2) the primary purpose of their jobs involves the creation, distribution, or application of knowledge; (3) they *think for a living*; (4) they live by their wits – any heavy lifting on the job is intellectual, not physical; (5) they solve problems; (6) they understand and meet the needs of customers; (7) they make decisions, and (8) they collaborate and communicate with other people in the course of doing their own work (pp. 10–11). However, all these criteria also apply to traditional professionals – lawyers, professors, psychologists, engineers, architects, doctors, dentists, and so on – all of them actively contributing to economies well before the knowledge worker term was coined. What is therefore the differentiation?

In our knowledge, very few studies have examined differences between knowledge workers and traditional ones. For example, Benson and Brown's (2007) research found that routine-task workers and knowledge workers differ in their attitudinal commitment and intentions to quit; the first ones having lower commitment and higher intentions to quit. Withey's (2009) findings in turn suggest that knowledge workers place "more emphasis on factors that converge on autonomy, performance and shared values" (p. 213). Similar observations have previously been made by Davenport (2005): "Knowledge workers like autonomy; commitment matters." Notwithstanding, Glenday (1995) had previously observed that, in a same industry, comparisons involving new work environments from mass production were complex and not conclusive. Then, it seems that the universal character attributed to knowledge workers hides singular human's traits and challenges managers in their tasks.

Table 6.3 Knowledge worker definitions

Key aspect highlighted	Knowledge worker definition	Author(s)
Formal education	Those whose jobs require advanced and formal education	Russette et al. (2007)
Roles	Employees possessing specialist knowledge or know-how who is involved in consultancy based or research and development work for new products, services or processes	Lee-Kelley et al. (2007)
Education, experience and knowledge activities	Those who have high degrees of expertise, education or experience, and whose primary purpose is the creation, distribution, or application of knowledge	Davenport (2005)
Capabilities and context of their work	Those who are creators, manipulators, and purveyors of the stream of information that makes up the post-industrial, post service global economy	Rifkin (1995)
Skills	Employees who apply theoretical and analytical knowledge	Drucker (1994)
Value	Key employees who are a source of sustainable competitive advantage and create intangible value-added assets	Harrigan and Dalmia (1991)

Source: Bibliographic search compiled and analysed by S. Ponce, 2008–2009.

KNOWLEDGE WORKERS SEGMENTATION

Although very few authors have discussed knowledge worker diversity, the knowledge-based context cannot be approached under the "one best way" Taylorist logics. In fact, Bouchez (2006), in an effort for eliciting key knowledge worker characteristics, has segmented a group of them along with the nature of the main tasks they perform and the intensity of the client-contact. Thus, the author has characterized two big groups: (1) Knowledge workers, defined as those who *apply* knowledge and *treat information*; and (2) knowledge professionals, defined as those who *create knowledge* and *manipulate ideas and concepts*. On this basis, Bouchez (2006) identifies three dominant types of management control and coordination for professional knowledge workers: the organization, the capital and the profession.

Davenport et al. (2002) have also worked the segmentation of knowledge workers observing that managers resist to and do not always see the need for employees' differentiation. Taking into account the degree of segmentation of their work environment and the degree of individual choice, the authors developed a framework to characterize different working environments and the role workers could play in their design and configuration. The starting hypothesis of their analysis was that there is "an optimal level of segmentation and choice" (p. 29) to get knowledge work done.

Later, Davenport (2005) discussed the segmentation in terms of the complexity of the knowledge work and the level of interdependence, bringing indirectly to light the individual and collective dimension of the knowledge worker. Arguing that it is important to differentiate knowledge workers to prioritize, Davenport (2005) identified four knowledge-intensive processes involving different types of knowledge workers and organizational technologies: the transaction model, the integration model, the expert model, and the collaboration model. The first two focus on the process flow whereas the last two work with rather unstructured processes. In these four setting workers therefore deploy different capabilities and play different roles.

MANAGING AND "UN-MANAGING" KNOWLEDGE WORKERS

Literature review brings to light that the management of knowledge workers is essentially instrumental, intended to maximize their contribution, to enhance information sharing among them, to leverage knowledge networks, to improve knowledge worker performance (Harrigan and Dalmia, 1991; Drucker, 1994; Davenport, 2005). In knowledge-based economies, the logic of traditional competition is paradoxically shaping management demands and expectations on the basis of two premises: first, economic growth being necessary, it depends on increased productivity and innovation; and second, innovation (and therefore growth) depends more and more on knowledge workers. Consequently, management is looking for increasing knowledge work productivity and fostering creativity to innovate – mainly in products and processes – with the final goal of improving performance to maximize profits.

While authors are in general well aware that knowledge workers do not and should not be managed as industrial workers (Harrigan and Dalmia, 1991; Davenport, 2005; Ehin, 2008), the underlying logic is in practice still the same. Arguing for the need of new approaches and management techniques to deal with in a knowledge-based competition, Cooper (2006), for example, has recommended addressing autonomy, measurement and evaluation – of success, efficiency, quality, effectiveness and productivity – as well as thought capture for reusing knowledge and not to reinvent it. The author has stated the managerial challenge in the following words: "how best to approach knowledge work and knowledge worker in a way that helps them improve their performance or results" (p. 59).

Furthermore, when some authors relate dignity at work and organizational issues – such as mismanagement, over-long hours, bullying and poor working environments – the underlying cognitive assumptions are particularly referred to the mass production context. Therefore, the knowledge worker context is just being grasped in its dimensions and specificities, as we will see in this section with the discussion of managerial demands in terms of productivity, power and knowledge and creativity and innovation.

THE PRODUCTIVITY PARADOX

Predicting the impact of knowledge workers on competitiveness, knowledge worker performance and productivity are considered critical: "*the* great management task" of the past century, claimed Drucker (1999); "one of the most important economic issues of our time", asserted Davenport (2005). Still, it appears that the productivity paradox of the seventies (Skinner, 1986) takes a new form in knowledge-based enterprises. That is, it is not anymore a question of failed efforts conducted and elusive improvements. It is rather an elusive way for "knowing-how-to" proceed for improving, evaluating and measuring it without disturbing or interfering in it. Davenport et al. (2002) explained the problem in the following terms:

> Toward more productive knowledge work. *Although our research findings don't add up to a single, clear solution to the problem of improving the performance of knowledge workers, we do have some strong convictions that may help companies get started on finding the answers they need. (p. 27)*

So, in trying to solve the performance and productivity problem, authors have approached the issue under different perspectives. Weisbord (1987), for example, suggested that productivity is closely related and supported by intangible dimensions such as learning, participation, dignity and meaning, among others. Jennex (2005) instead has related productivity to *knowledge use* through knowledge management systems and knowledge management organization. The author concludes that, although the organization under scrutiny had not identified productivity improvement measurements, knowledge use had an impact on productivity in such a way that knowledge management systems improved the effectiveness/productivity of the organization.

At the opposite, Ramirez and Nembhard (2004) adopted a measurement approach. Recognizing that there is not a "universally accepted method to measure knowledge worker productivity" (p. 602), the authors developed a typology comprising a great number of measurement and tools previously published in the literature. The authors identified a set of 13 productivity dimensions, comprising among others, autonomy, innovation and creativity, responsibility level, timeliness, cost and/or profitability, effectiveness, efficiency, and customer satisfaction. But, they concluded "that more effort should be dedicated to find ways to measure productivity" (p. 625).

Jones and Chung (2006), in turn, approached the question from the standpoint of the individual contribution to productivity. These authors introduced the term "cognitive turnover, CT" – that is, mental absenteeism – to identify, describe and evaluate knowledge worker productivity; and suggested that team-based tasks could improve productivity by reducing knowledge workers' high levels of cognitive turnover when they perform isolated tasks. Under a similar perspective, Spira (2007) questioned information overload and interruptions during working hours whereas Appelbaum and Marchionni (2008) argued that multitasking behaviour does not affect productivity.

Thus, the collective dimension contributing to team effectiveness and efficiency constitutes a key issue in the efforts for improving productivity and performance of knowledge-workers. Janz et al. (1997) examined autonomy, interdependence, team process, and job motivation in their relation to knowledge workers team effectiveness. Interestingly, their findings suggest that interdependence – and especially tasks interdependence – could constrain autonomy, indicating that the trade-off between individual and collective contributions could only be solved by those teams that succeed in making the most of "each member's ideas and ability" (p. 901).

Courtney et al. (2007) developed a team model for high-performance knowledge workers teams to help its members in creating an understanding of organizational and environmental dynamics. Elliman et al. (2005) simulated knowledge workers daily behaviour to structure their activities while Davenport (2005) suggested that to improve knowledge work performance both organizational and individual capabilities have to be addressed although "sometimes improving the capabilities of individual workers can dramatically accelerate improvement at the organisational level" (p. 138).

POWER AND KNOWLEDGE

Access to information, technology skills and specialized competencies (managerial and technical), have empowered knowledge workers in organizations. In this high-end knowledge work, Davenport et al. (2002) have found that the most common management practice could be described as "hire smart people and leave them alone" (p. 27). Later, Davenport (2005), however, asserted that "A laissez-faire approach to knowledge work won't lead to improved performance and results" (p. 59). It has also been argued that the use of contingent knowledge workers to develop in-house knowledge capital could be considered as an effective and efficient means for achieving organizational knowledge goals (MacDougall and Hurst, 2005). However, the incongruence of advice, recommendations and observations led to maintaining that, as Maccoby (2006) has stated, "No one seems to have found the perfect way to manage knowledge workers, particularly those expected to create new knowledge" (p. 60).

Knowledge at work is certainly challenging managers in their core activities. Understandably, Foucault (1981) asserted that power and knowledge are correlated. Habermas (1973) indeed had differentiated three fundamental cognitive categories embracing social life: work knowledge, practical or interactive knowledge and emancipatory knowledge. At work, knowledge brings to light the inherent conflict between "knowing", as part of the individual working experience, and "knowledge" as a transactional economic commodity (Scarbrough, 1999). Thus, commitment, team players, critical thinking, problem-solving skills, motivation, training and retention of knowledge worker talent, all these elements lead to assert that knowledge workers need to be managed by knowledgeable managers; that is, by people that recognize the complexity and multidimensional character of knowledge processes and the integrality – mind and body – of knowledge workers.

CREATIVITY AND LEARNING

Based on the case of a film director, Arthur et al. (2008) have addressed the individual circumstances a knowledge worker confronts. A three-ways-of-knowing framework, centred in the individual's answer to three questions: why we work (reflecting values, interests, motivation, and work-family issues); with whom we work (reflecting personal relationships inside and outside the job); and how we work (reflecting the skills and expertise we have to offer) (p. 368). Yet, the central purpose of their study was to capture from a concrete experience how the individual could contribute to the organization, the industry and the community thus unfolding the knowledge economy.

Arguing that "knowledge workers cannot be managed in the traditional sense", Ehin (2008: 337) has elicited a series of principles – comprising among others self-organization, innate behavioural tendencies, explicit and tacit knowledge. Highlighting the multidimensionality of the issue but also the multidimensionality of knowledge workers, the author has maintained that fostering self-organization will give place to an organizational context "that is non-threatening and optimally supportive" (p. 348), making possible the expansion of tacit and explicit knowledge (internally and externally), and the increase of the innovative capacity.

Scott (2005), in turn, addressed the identity issue of knowledge workers in their flexible organizational environment. According to the author, knowledge workers construct meaning and identity through their interactions (social and working) and they perceive themselves as ontologically different from literature descriptions. Besides, Lee-Kelley et al. (2007) find that learning organization dimensions are related to knowledge workers retention and job satisfaction. Yet, a study of knowledge workers in a global context suggests that cultural differences could also have an impact in dealing with motivation, value perception and knowledge sharing (Forstenlechner and Lettice, 2007).

Summarizing, it is clear that important issues concerning knowledge worker are not yet thoroughly understood. Murray (2008) recently expressed his concerns in these terms:

We can, in part, describe knowledge workers in terms of what they are not. They are not factory workers, they are not labourers, they are not farm or field workers. But that doesn't tell us very much. (p. 26)

In spite of these unknowns, managers and economies have placed great expectations challenging and even threatening knowledge workers in terms of creativity and innovation. In so doing, managers themselves need to be creative and innovative in their approaches (Harrigan and Dalmia, 1991). We see the issue as a kind of double-loop, in the sense that every initiative for stimulating knowledge worker activities (and outputs), needs its counterpart on managers and management systems (Carrillo and Gaimon, 2004). Notwithstanding, to improve our understanding on creativity issues and innovation involving knowledge workers, we have started by exploring the individual worker and the dignity dimension at work. The next section describes our research.

Case Studies and Analysis

The central objective of the research was to explore knowledge and creative workers' issues in their relation to human dignity at work under an interpretive perspective. Because very little had been done and published about the subject, a case-based research was performed. Case studies are a powerful research methodology to approach complex issues previously unexplored (Eisenhardt, 1989; Yin, 2003; Eisenhardt, 2007). Although the methodology does not allow for generalization, all cases exhibit both specific and universal traits of phenomena under scrutiny. The methodology thus provides a solid basis for conceptualization and theory building (Eisenhardt, 1989; Meredith, 1998; Eisenhardt, 2007).

THE RESEARCH DESIGN

Methodologically, case studies were ethnographic-oriented. As we describe in Table 6.4, our research comprises a series of studies conducted on a convenience sample; that is, cases were purposefully selected not statistically, having as main criterion their theoretical relevance to be sure specific knowledge and creative contexts were approached. A total of 30 participants, all having acquired formal education,[2] and representing nine different knowledge contexts constituted our sample.

As we have summarized in Table 6.4, the unit of analysis was the individual in his or her working context. Data was collected through direct or participative observations (when possible), talks, semi-structured or in-depth interviews (one to four hours duration), and document analysis. Data was directly validated by reviewing case material with participants or by triangulation whenever three different data sources were available. We collected and validated data during two periods of time – from 1998 to 2003 (with scientists, researchers and computer workers), and from 2006 to 2008 (with artists, project manager, engineers and operators). Data was codified according to conventional procedures (Miles and Huberman, 1994; 2003) and cross-analysed to identify patterns, commonalities, differences and complementarities (Eisenhardt, 1989; 2007).

Table 6.4   The research design

Methodological elements	Descriptions	
Research nature	Ethnographic, interpretive	
Unity of analysis	Individuals in their working context	
Case selection	Convenience sample (all participants had formal education, technical, undergraduate, graduate, postgraduate)	
Data collection	Direct observations (first-hand observations of day-to-day activities and episodes, when possible)	Work processes Work environment
	Interviews and conversations (talks and in-depth interviews)	Work descriptions Requirements Challenges
	Participative observation (episodes, when authorized)	Team work
	Document analysis (public, private (when accessible), printed and electronic)	Organizational context
Data treatment	Journal (hand-written notes) and verbatim	Codification Case composition
Analysis	Cross-case	Common features Differences Patterns

© S. Ponce 2009.

---

[2]   Seven have technical degrees; 10 have under-graduate diploma from recognized universities (with two of them pursuing graduate studies when we met them); and 13 possessed graduated degrees (master or/and doctoral studies, PhD).

112   Human Dignity and Managerial Responsibility

In Table 6.5, we have initially classified cases representing the nine different knowledge contexts explored, in three groups according to key similarities: *thinkers*, *doers* and *dreamers*. Scientists, researchers and software developers who were involved in cases A to F constitute the first group. The second group is represented by cases G to K, involving people who worked in private enterprises (more precisely in service production, manufacturing and project management). These people classified as *doers*. The third group of participants, involved in case studies L, M, and N, were artists, initially described as *dreamers*. These three categories were initially adopted as case descriptors.

Table 6.5   Cases and their context

Categories	Cases	Context	Data collection
Thinkers	A: Seven scientists and researchers	Research team in a public Canadian institution	Participative observations (one year) and informal talks
	B: Two computer scientists C: Two technicians D: Four administrators E: Two vice-presidents	Research and development team in a semi-private Canadian R&D organization	Participative observations (10 months) and semi-structured interviews
	F: An engineer	Software development team (Canadian Enterprise)	Semi-structured Interviews (four hours)
Doers	G: An engineer H: A technician	Engineering consulting international enterprise (Canadian division)	Semi-structured Interviews (four hours) and visits to workplace (two hours)
	I: A production manager (engineer) J: Four operators	Manufacturing high-tech American enterprise (Latin American division)	Semi-structured interviews (two hours) and direct observations (one-day visit to the plant)
	K: A project manager	Creative Canadian Enterprise	Semi-structured interviews and direct observations (one to three hours, five visits to his office)
Dreamers	L: A cinematographer	In an international film festival (took place in Canada) (Latin American cinematographer)	Semi-structured interviews and talks (total of 12 hours)
	M: A musician	Previously and after studio recording (Canadian musician)	Semi-structured interviews (six hours) and video-tape observations (four hours)
	N: Two painters	In their atelier (Latin America artists)	Semi-structured interviews and talks (eight hours) and visits (two days)

© S. Ponce 2009.

Case-Episodes

To illustrate some key points identified in the research, in this section a series of representative episodes is presented. Episodes were selected according to specific characteristics observed, challenging common assumptions and underlying knowledge premises. In Popper's terms, the choice rested on challenging their falsification (Caldwell, 1991).

It should be noticed that headlines highlight key points illustrated. For example, case A illustrates love for knowledge, works conditions, recognition and appreciation, and mobility. All other episodes illustrate only one key point, written in the headline itself.

CASE A: SCIENTISTS AND RESEARCHERS IN A PUBLIC CANADIAN INSTITUTION

Love for knowledge

It is a team working on fundamental research. Their goal is theory-building to explain previous observations about the behaviour and characterization of a type of material. Nobody minded about the research process. It was impressively tacit. No deadlines were pre-established although a deep desire to get results as soon as possible was evident. Everybody worked long hours without counting them. Invested time in laboratory experiences was not a matter for discussions. Their work environment was more of a kind of "love for knowledge" and to discover. Questioned about if their work had some practical applications, the lead scientist answered: "Of course! There are many pending issues and problems that could be solved if we could demonstrate how the observed phenomenon works." But they did not take time in that kind of discussion. They rather enjoyed the wonder while reading printed results (graphics and numerical data) emerging from a digital device attached to a very expensive research equipment.

Work conditions

For an outsider, their working conditions could be questionable. All team members worked on a contract basis, only the lead scientist had access to work benefits. Yet, everybody said they were happy to have the opportunity to do research. "Money to perform research" they said "is not abundant." Actually, their fears turned around the renewal of their research budget. The lead scientist was particular aware of and very sensitive about the precarious situation. He even gave from his own money to pay a late payment to one of the team members. A new member said he was "atypical and strange".

Recognition and appreciation

The lead scientist used to share with his own family some comments about the way the most important equipment was performing. At one moment, I observed one of the members discussing a subject matter with him and he exclaimed: "If you do not publish, it is not useful!" and the researcher answered, "I know I have to, because is the rule in our milieu … but I really don't mind about publishing all the results."

Later, the same member explained, "I have read sociological studies on laboratory life but I could not find myself in their descriptions. According to my own experience in the

Lab, the sociological account rests on the surface of the real work and environment ... it is too external ... It is not easy to find the words to describe my expectations. I think, because my work is actually transcendental, existential. Knowledge in this case, is not a matter of social construction; I do not look after external recognition. I just need to understand the phenomena: to know about it. In fact, I chose to do research in this field because it is at the frontier of many disciplines. It is complex but it allows me to touch more than one knowledge domain ... Nevertheless, in the end, my research subject could be another one. What is important for me is the activity in itself, to explore the frontier of a knowledge domain. The research subject is therefore a pretext to push my thinking. What I really need is the intellectual challenge, the intellectual exercise. Food for thought! ... I think that's a better description of my work ... – What about productivity? ... Of course I am productive. My boss told me that he wanted to keep me in his team [most of the contracts were not going to be renewed] because my work is equivalent to five people's work. He knows I'm able to deal with many projects at the same time."

Mobility

Another member was going to leave soon. He was going to a foreign lab. He was in his thirties, recently married and was looking for a more stable position. His research field focused on a molecule. He got a new job because of this molecule. His wife was also having the opportunity to develop herself in a similar career. Yet, another member said she could not leave the lab. She felt she was not able to work in another field, no matter about the conditions. [Less than two years after she quit for a permanent position.]

CASE B AND C: COMPUTER SCIENTISTS AND TECHNICIANS – UNCONDITIONAL COMMITMENT

It was a team developing a software product. At the end of a working day (near 5 p.m.), a vice-president of the organization invited me to use the application saying next morning, the product was going to be presented to their client for final approval. Everybody was excited and very proud about the result and they just wanted to show it to me and eventually get another opinion (in fact, it was another trial or test). I started "playing with" the application and immediately I noticed that the user's interface was written in a mixture of two different languages. Nobody before me had noticed it! I made the comment to them and the vice-president said, "We cannot present a product like this to our client. It is unconceivable! It has to be corrected!" Nobody argued. Actually, I immediately saw them organizing the work to correct the problem and returning to their computer stations to work on.

I left the lab near 8.30 p.m., after testing as much as I could. The next day I heard that the client was going to launch the product in a few days. Everybody was happy, and nobody complained about the additional time spent in correcting the language issue. Actually, two of them spent the night at the lab ...

CASE F: A COMPUTER ENGINEER – ALIENATION

He was a computer engineer with a Masters degree in informatics and expressed his concern about his working conditions. He was working for a while in a private enterprise, developing software applications. He said, "I never expected this. I studied and worked hard because I didn't want to work in a line assembly. I just wanted to have a clean job ... but now, when I quit my workplace at 7 p.m. (I start every day at 7 a.m.), my own colleagues ask me: Are you leaving right now? They normally want me to work up to 9 p.m.! ... But I have a family ... beside ... doing programming since 7 a.m. is too much for me ... I am exhausted!"

CASE G: AN ENGINEER – LAY-OFFS

He was an engineer working in an international consulting enterprise. He explained, "The harder part of my job is not the project in itself but the conditions which we have to deal with, project after project. We establish our planning (goals, objectives, staffing, budgeting, and so on) but because *business are business* we cannot keep all our personnel under stable working conditions. This means that we constantly have to hire and fire very good people. They are always very knowledgeable, to work in the kind of projects we manage require high qualifications. So is not easy to tell an excellent worker that we do not need him or her anymore. Specially, when everybody in the Corporation is always repeating that *employees are the most valuable asset of our company!*"

CASE J: FOUR PLANT OPERATORS – LABOUR AND KNOWLEDGE EMBEDDEDNESS

I observed two of them working in the production line for about one hour and I am still not sure they were aware of my presence. One of them was doing the packing at the end of the line. At a first sight, I saw how hard and repetitive his task was; he never stopped the workflow while I was looking at him. But then, I thought about the kind of knowledge he was using to perform his task; and immediately, I noticed that he was also performing quality control on every package: he had to set and control the tagging device and checked every each product while packing.

The other operator was in the middle of the production line, moving continuously from one end to the other end of his work station, opening and closing bottles but also checking for the filling, verifying the right amount of product and the precision of the tags in conformance with tracing procedures. I was informed that soon his task was going to be automated because the production volume was increasing and it has been determined that an operator could not be able to work in this station for more than four hours without interruption.

Two other operators were at the beginning of another production line, working manually (and repetitively) because the production volume was low and the plant manager could not justify the investment for automating their tasks. Again, I thought about the kind of knowledge they needed to perform their work. Before asking about, the plant manager explained that to perform their tasks, these two operators were asked for specialized knowledge and skills such as precision and focus. He said they were hired because they had acquired very specific knowledge on industrial practices.

CASE K: A PROJECT MANAGER – AUTONOMY AND FINANCIAL TRADE-OFFS

He graduated from a recognized university but soon he realized that it was rather hard to find a stable job position in the creative environment he liked. For more than three years since he graduated, he had nevertheless succeeded in having a steady flow of projects and he just decided to pursue postgraduate studies for personal growth. He explained that what he most liked was his autonomy and the many opportunities he has to be creative; but in some way, he said, he was paying a big price for it because he had not work benefits (insurance, holidays, and so on) and had to deal with a permanent incertitude. Besides, every time he discussed a new project, negotiation on money issues had become a rule. He explained, "I don't really know if ever I will get paid as I think I should; that is, as other people who got a same degree. But it is not easy because they always said the company has no budget to paid more and they know my needs. I need projects to make my leaving … I know I am appreciated and recognized for the quality and professional work I am doing … But I do not perceive this appreciation translated into a fair financial retribution."

CASE L: A CINEMATOGRAPHER – AUTONOMY MYTH IN ARTS

Recognized worldwide, he agreed to meet me to talk about his life's work and creativity. I was deeply interested in trying to capture the creative process that characterized him. However, what most impressed me were his discipline and his consciousness of limitations. He made clear that his artistic expression was the result of a collective work. He said, "I cannot do it by myself; I need other people to produce a film. It is a collective work. Once everything is ready to work on – script, actors, setting, equipment, cameramen, and so on – I become a slave of my work during the realization!"

CASE M: A MUSICIAN – TO BE OR NOT TO BE, THE ONTOLOGY

I met her before and after one of her recording session; I also observed her by a video-camera during her recording session. She was definitely excited about the experience although she was also very conscious that it was only one step of his project. She felt prepared for the recording. She had previously been working many months on her compositions and rehearsals. And she explained that she particularly enjoyed and appreciated the time she invested in the preparation. It was in solitude, in a private place, but it was actually the fulfilment of a need. She said, "To feel I am alive … I need to play my music. It doesn't matter if people will like it or not. Of course, if people like my material, I will be extremely happy. But beside every other recognition, I need to play my instruments. It is as important to me as breathing."

CASE N: A PAINTER – EMOTIONS AND HARD WORK

He had to work hard to get the idea about his working activities accepted. Some members of his own family were worried about and resisted his decision. But for more than 20 years, he has been making his living through painting and teaching. He explained, "Since I was a 5-year-old child I knew I was going to paint … I grew thinking about it and when I finished high-school I started to work full-time on it. At first, I tried by myself but then I realized that I needed to go to the university. And I did it. Then, I was not satisfied with my style. Actually, I felt I hadn't a style of my own. I could paint and get excellent marks in my studies but I started searching and discovering my own way to express myself and see the world. After a couple of years, I started to paint differently … I started using simpler materials but I knew I had found my own way. What most surprised me was the emotional state I experienced when I was painting. I sweat a lot and painting became a hard working job, a labour, but extremely rewarding."

CROSS-CASE ANALYSIS

As previously explained, cases representing different knowledge and creativity contexts where compared to identify patterns, similarities, differences and complementarities. As expected – due to sampling criteria – it was observed that knowledge was a common acknowledged feature to all participants. Yet, people were involved with different types and knowledge processes at work. In general, *doers* said they used both tacit and explicit knowledge; *thinkers* said they primarily created and structured knowledge; whereas *dreamers* considered their knowledge was significantly tacit and embedded in their artistic works.

Comparatively, we observed that tasks design and creativity define a continuum going from high autonomy – that is, entirely dependent on individual choices – up to predetermined and dependent on collective working decisions. Besides, the intangible manifestations of human dignity were mainly associated with creativity and expression; specifically, with the need of having a cognitive space comprising emotional (feelings) and intellectual (knowledgeable) experiences. The tangible side of human dignity at work in turn was related to physical manifestations and interactions; for instance, non-abusive treatment, fair human conditions in the workplace, limited physical effort, air, temperature and environmental conditions, neatness, fair and respectful treatment.

As we have illustrated in Figure 6.1, if we relate task design and creativity to human dignity dimensions, we observed that a middle zone is defined – in between the darkest lines of Figure 6.1 – where autonomous artists are closer to the manifestations of intangible dimensions of human dignity and industrial workers are at the opposite side, that is, closer to the more tangible dimensions. In between these two types of workers, knowledge workers – as conventionally defined – appear "squeezed", feeling and experiencing both-side demands and working requirements.

All participants explained that work uncertainty and instability were the most important and difficult issues they faced; and everybody was concerned about it, directly or indirectly. *Thinkers* and some *doers*, in particular, expressed ambivalent feelings associated with dignity at work, oscillating between the heaviness of underemployment conditions and proud and delight with the kind of work and the opportunities they had. Interestingly, *artists* were those who were more aware of this kind of difficulty. All of them had been living a kind of a double working-life, formally involved in conventional activities to make their living – teaching, administration, publicity – saving money indeed to invest in their artistic projects. Besides, they explained they had consciously chosen this situation to keep their autonomy, not in terms of tasks design but in terms of their creativity. They said they could not accept the standardization of their artistic work and the normative character of production as imposed by big corporations.

Both *thinkers* and *doers* said that the knowledge-based economy has its rewards and recognitions but it is also asking more and more of them. Remembering the arrival of personal computers at workplaces, one scientist argued that they lost administrative support and had to absorb new tasks: "We were not scientists, thinkers or developers anymore: we became our own secretaries", and now, they feel they are also asked to be *artists*.

118 Human Dignity and Managerial Responsibility

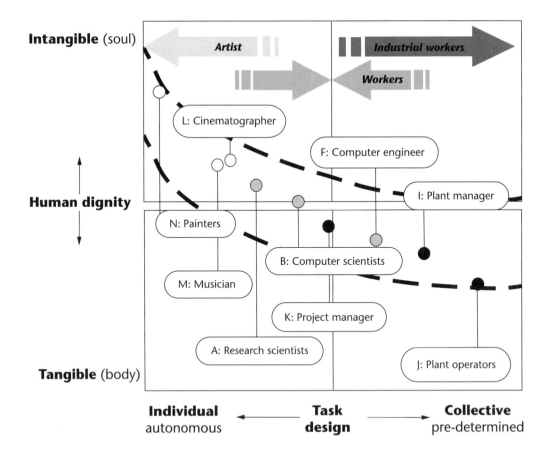

Figure 6.1 Task design characteristics
© S. Ponce 2009

Artists in turn said they are in some way living the automation era that plant workers experienced after the Second World War. Technological developments have made possible the replacement of painters, musicians and cinematographers by computers tools and applications. Nowadays, anybody could have access to informatics applications and electronic devices to paint, to compose, play and record music or produce media products with. Nevertheless, artists argued that a big difference exists between a hobby and authentic and original artistic expression. So, they do not fear such a replacement. Actually, they appreciate new technology and had harmoniously integrated it into their creative works. All the artists participating in the study had their own web pages, Internet sites and were very comfortable with related technologies and more complex user interfaces.

Productivity was also highlighted by everybody and there was a concern about its measurement. *Thinkers* and *doers* were particularly aware of because they are more and more confronted to performance evaluation. The way managers are measuring knowledge creation, knowledge processes and creativity was qualified as "ridiculous", "inconceivable" and "inappropriate". They argued that a serious effort should be done to define and select appropriate indicators, variables and methodologies to evaluate knowledge processes; otherwise, in their view, managers lose credibility.

Something similar happened with quality. *Thinkers* and some *doers* in particular maintained that managers were not qualified to establish quality measurement because they were unable to understand the knowledge they were creating. Consequently, only those directly involved with knowledge creation should assess quality and performance, and management should trust them about the quality of their work. In short, they argued that mass production management approaches and underlying conceptualizations were inadequate to assess knowledge production processes.

Invested time in work was also a particular characteristic for everybody. However, standardized tasks such as those performed by plant operators were easily quantified and consequently best rewarded. All others said that they were aware of but *thinkers* in particular argued that it was practically inevitable. They have more easily accepted that time is needed to create knowledge and that time and knowledge production are not always compatible; that is, it is not possible to accelerate or easily manipulate knowledge production and creativity processes.

All participants considered they were involved in innovative activities. *Artist* and *thinkers* said that they always were working on new ideas, initiatives and projects. *Doers* in turn considered that product, process and organizational innovation were inevitable and they all participated either as initiators or supporters.

Being aware of methodological limits intrinsic to the sampling procedure, cases still allowed for illustrating key elements identified in the literature also providing with a concrete starting-point to explore and analyse human dignity dimensions in knowledge and creativity contexts.

The Softer Side of Human Dignity at Work

During the last century, a departure was witnessed from a well-established premise maintaining that new employments were created when the economy exhibited a growth. Our research shows that in spite of the enormous importance attributed to knowledge and creative workers, they are not exempted from lay-offs, questionable working conditions, low salaries or precarious jobs. By definition, the knowledge working context requires formalized education – a diploma is normally needed to have a knowledge work – but it does not mean that if you have a diploma you will get that kind of job and fair working conditions.

Exploring knowledge workers activities and concerns bring out a softer dimension of human dignity at work. Previous research on knowledge worker – as discussed in precedent sections – have certainly identified important issues but very few studies (if any) had purposely addressed the individual knowledge worker in his or her working context. The privileged perspective has been the enterprise or management but not the knowledge worker himself or herself. Our cases have brought to light a series of elements, stimulating critical thinking about the way knowledge and creative workers have been approached up to date.

Knowledge workers are recognized and even defined by their talents, competencies and skills. They are certainly respected and appreciated by their creativity and knowledge they have acquired. Still, it is not clear how dignity at work is constructed and manifested in their specific contexts. But our research suggests that the intangible side of workers' dignity comprises a singular, individualized and inner dimension, as we have represented in Figure 6.2, along with the personal, cultural and universal ones. But as shown with the arrow in Figure 6.2, knowledge and creative workers' roles involve a shift from universal to singular aspects of human dignity. This conceptualization will necessarily raise new issues, mainly the ethics in seeking to exploit, for commercial purposes, the inner side of a human being and its creativity.

	Decus **Soul/Mind** ***Inner***	*Decor* **Body** ***Outer***
Individualized	**Singular** Interiorized Individually expressed Uniqueness, creativeness Originality	**Personal** Individually expressed but regulated (norms)
Collective	**Cultural** Shared values Underlying	**Universal** Equality Externalized

Figure 6.2   The inner and outer dimensions of dignity
© S. Ponce 2009.

A new context should go along with new conceptualizations and new approaches although redefining management in a knowledge-based economy is easier to think than to do. Traditional conceptualizations based on Fayol's management definition – planning, directing, organizing, coordinating, controlling – could not had considered the complexity of organizations, the systemic character of technologies, the instability installed due to constant innovations, the flexibility of production systems, the speed and volume of data and information flows, the embeddedness of individual and collective knowledge. Approaching management in knowledge-based contexts under the traditional perspective, with similar conceptualizations, tools and methodologies is therefore dysfunctional.

Our research nevertheless suggests that knowledge and creativity at work brings cognitive dimensions relevant to managerial re-conceptualizations. Human beings construct themselves individually and collective throughout their work activities and interactions. Thus, an original, creative and adequate starting point could be the consideration of human dignity at work. Although more research is needed to improve our understanding of human dignity in knowledge and creative contexts, by thinking creatively, cases-episodes seem to suggest the following four propositions:

P1: The intrinsic relationship between ontology-axiology and human cognition constitutes the soft, internal and singular side of human dignity; *unconditional commitment*, for example, is a knowledge worker's value (ontology-axiology) whereas *love for knowledge* and *emotions* are feelings pertaining to the domain of emotional cognition.

P2: External elements of human dignity – related to questionable work conditions, recognition and appreciation, alienation, lay-offs, mobility, financial trade-offs –, although undesirable are not necessarily detrimental to the ontology of a knowledge and creative worker, in the sense that they continue to perform their work in the best way possible.

P3: As a component of human dignity, autonomy has internal (mind) and external (body) dimensions but both do not impact in the same way knowledge worker's creative expression. Without compromising his or her internal autonomy while creating, a knowledge worker could accept less external autonomy, if necessary.

P4: Managers and all those who think that a knowledge and creative worker could be manipulated are unaware of the potential and value of the soft and inner side of human dignity that shapes knowledge worker's hopes, ideals, life-motifs and expectations.

These four propositions are intended to contribute to the understanding of human dignity in a creative and knowledge context. They could be insightful to managers that are looking for new ways of doing their jobs in an uncertain and new context but they also challenge researchers to study the human dignity subject in-depth.

Conclusion

We have explored human dignity in knowledge and creative contexts highlighting the importance of its inner and softer side. Knowledge workers are certainly a category of the workforce, yet every individual is knowledgeable in his or her working activities. Knowledge workers do not constitute a homogeneous group but knowledge and creative workers bring to light individual traits and singularity at work.

We are living in a transitional period where corporations, enterprises, institutions and organizations in general are slowly or radically being transformed. In so doing, some organizations are timidly searching for new ways of managing and doing business while others are audaciously experimenting with new organizational forms and technologies. The vast majority is rather at the mercy of evolutionary forces without taking the risk of playing a key role in the transformation, losing the opportunity to steer the changes. The moment nevertheless is particularly appropriate to change the course, by creating a dignified world where to live and dignify the future of new generations. We hope that the discussion presented here will foster a different way to think about people and enterprises. We think that a new turning point has been reached. May managers, workers and decision-makers be able to make a difference; a wise, creative, dignified and knowledge-based difference.

References

Anonymous (2006). The rights idea: Knowledge, human rights, and change. Interview with Irene Khan. *Harvard International Review*, Vol. 28, No. 2, p. 70.

Appelbaum, S.H., Marchionni, A. (2008). The multitasking paradox: Perceptions, problems and strategies. *Management Decision*, Vol. 46, No. 9, pp. 1313–1325.

Argyris, C., Schön, D. (1978). *Organizational Learning*. Reading, MA: Addison-Wesley. Vol. 1 and Vol. 2.

Arthur, M.B., DeFillippi, R.J., Lidsay, V. (2008). On being a knowledge worker. *Organizational Dynamics*, Vol. 37, No. 4, pp. 365–377.

Belde, D.M. (2005). Autonomy, human dignity, and death with dignity: Advancing a relational view of human dignity in end-of-life bioethics. Unpublished PhD thesis, Saint Louis University.

Benson, J., Brown, M. (2007). Knowledge workers: what keeps them committed; what turns them away. *Work, Employment and Society*, Vol. 21, No. 1, pp. 121–141.

Bolton, S. (2006). Dignity at work is about more than good people management practices. *People Management*, Vol. 12, No. 12, p. 46.

Bouchez, J.-P. (2006). Managers des travailleurs professionnels du savoir: Enjeux et perspectives. *Revue Française de Gestion*, Vol. 32, No. 168/169, pp. 35–53.

Brooks, Nita (2006). Understanding IT outsourcing and its effects on IT workers and their environment. *Journal of Computer Information Systems*, Vol. 47, No. 4, pp. 46–53.

Caldwell, B.J. (1991). Clarifying Popper. *Journal of Economic Literature*, Vol. 29, No. 1, 1991, pp. 1–33.

Carrillo, J.E., Gaimon, C. (2004). Managing knowledge-based resource capabilities under uncertainty. *Management Science*, Vol. 50, No. 11, pp. 1504–1518.

Castells, M. (2004). *The Network Society. A Cross-cultural Perspective*. Cheltenham: Edward Elgar.

Chinying Lang, J. (2001). Managing in knowledge-based competition. *Journal of Organizational Change Management*, Vol. 14, No. 6, pp. 539–552.

Cooper, D. (2006). Knowledge workers. *Canadian Business*, Vol. 79, No. 20, p. 59.

Courtney, H.S., Navarro, E., O'Hare, C.A. (2007). The Dynamic Organic Transformational (D.O.T.) team model for high-performance knowledge-worker teams. *Team Performance Management*, Vol. 13, No. 1/2 pp. 34–46.

Davenport, T.H. (2005). *Thinking For a Living. How to Get Better Performance and Results From Knowledge Workers*. Boston, MA: Harvard Business School Press.

Davenport, T.H., Thomas, E.J., Cantrell, S. (2002). The mysterious art and science of knowledge-worker performance. *MIT Sloan Management Review*, Vol. 44, No. 1, pp. 23–30.

De Koninck, T. (2005). Archéologie de la notion de dignité humaine, in De Koninck, T. and Larochelle, G. ~(2005). *La dignité humaine. Philosophie, droit, politique, économie, médicine*. Collection Débats philosophiques. Paris: Presses Universitaires de France, pp. 13–50.

Drucker, P.F. (1994). The age of social transformation, reprinted in *The Atlantic Monthly*, Vol. 297, No. 3, 2006, p. 47–48.

Drucker, P.F. (1999). Knowledge worker productivity: the biggest challenge, *California Management Review*, Vol. 41, No. 2, pp. 79–94.

Edvinsson, L. (2006). Aspects on the city as a knowledge tool. *Journal of Knowledge Management*, Vol. 10, No. 5, pp. 6–13.

Ehin, C. (2008). Un-managing knowledge workers. *Journal of Intellectual Capital*, Vol. 9, No. 3, pp. 337–350.

Eisenhardt, K. (1989). Building theories from case study research. *Academy of Management. The Academy of Management Review*, Vol. 14, No. 4, pp. 532–550.

Eisenhardt, K. (2007). Theory building from cases: Opportunities and challenges. *Academy of Management Journal*, Vol. 50, No. 1, pp. 25–32.

Elliman, T., Eatock, J., Spencer, N. (2005). Modelling knowledge worker behaviour in business process studies. *The Journal of Enterprise Information Management*, Vol. 18, No. 1, pp. 79–94.

Florida, R. (2002). *The Rise of the Creative Class*. New York: Basic Books.

Florida, R., Kenney, M. (1994). The new age of capitalism: Innovation-mediated production. *Futures*, Vol. 25, No. 6, pp. 637–651.

Forstenlechner, I., Lettice, F. (2007). Cultural differences in motivating global knowledge workers. *Equal Opportunities International*, Vol. 26, No. 8, pp. 823–833.

Foucault, M. (1981). *Power/Knowledge. Selected interviews and other writings*. 1972–1977. Colin Gordon (ed.). New York: Pantheon Books.

Garbooshian, A.M. (2006). The concept of human dignity in the French and American Enlightenments: Religion, virtue, liberty. Unpublished PhD thesis, Wayne State University.

Glenday, D. (1995). What has work done to the working class? A comparison of workers and production technologies. *The British Journal of Sociology*, Vol. 46, No. 3, pp. 475–948.

Greenspan, D. (2002). Downsizing with dignity. *Employment Relations Today*, Vol. 29, No. 3, pp. 39–48.

Habermas, J. (1973). *La technique et la science comme "idéologie"*. Paris: Gallimard.

Harvey, D. (1997). From Fordism to flexible accumulation. In Harvey, D. *The Condition of Postmodernity*, Oxford: Blackwell Publishers Ltd, pp. 141–172 (first published in 1990).

Hodson, R. (1996). Dignity in the workplace under participative management: Alienation and freedom revisited. *American Sociological Review*, Vol. 61, No. 5, pp. 719–738.

James, K., Brodersen, M., Eisenberg, J. (2004). Workplace affect and workplace creativity. *Human Performance*, Vol. 17, No. 2, pp. 169–194.

Janz, B.D., Colquitt, J.A., Noe, R.A. (1997). Knowledge worker team effectiveness: The role of autonomy, interdependence, team development, and contextual support variables. *Personnel Psychology*, Vol. 50, pp. 877–904.

Jennex, M.E. (2005). Productivity impacts from using knowledge. In Jennex, M.E. (ed.), *Case Studies in Knowledge Management*. Hershey, PA: Idea Group Publishing, Chapter XX, pp. 344–357.

Jones, E.C., Chung, C.A. (2006). A methodology for measuring engineering knowledge worker productivity. *Engineering Management Journal*, Vol. 18, No. 1, pp. 32–38.

Larochelle, G. (2005). La dignité du mourir: un défi pour le droit, in De Koninck, T. and Larochelle, G. (2005). *La dignité humaine. Philosophie, droit, politique, économie, médicine. Collection Débats philosophiques*. Paris: Presses Universitaires de France, pp. 51–86.

Lee-Kelly, L., Blackman, D.A., Hurst, J.P. (2007). An exploration of the relationship between learning organizations and the retention of knowledge workers. *The Learning Organization*, Vol. 14, No. 3, pp. 204–221.

Levitt, T. (1972). Production-line approach to services. *Harvard Business Review*, Vol. 50, No. 5, pp. 41–52.

Levitt, T. (1976). The industrialization of service. *Harvard Business Review*, Vol. 54, No. 5, pp. 63–74.

MacDougall, S.L., Hurst, D. (2005). Identifying tangible costs, benefits and risks of an investment in intellectual capital. Contracting contingent knowledge workers. *Journal of Intellectual Capital*, Vol. 6, No. 1, pp. 53–71.

Martin, R.L., Moldoveanu, M.C. (2003). Capital versus talent: The battle that's reshaping business. *Harvard Business Review*, Vol. 81, No. 7, pp. 36.

McCoby, M. (2006). Is there a best way to lead scientists and engineers? *Research Technology Management*, Vol. 49, No. 1, pp. 60–61.

McCormick, J. (2009). A day in the life of the knowledge worker. *InfoManagement Direct*, May 14.

McKellar, H. (2005). The knowledge (worker) economy. *KM World*, Vol. 14, No. 9, p. 14.

Melo-Martin, I. de (2008). Chimeras and human dignity. *Kennedy Institute of Ethics Journal*, Vol. 18, No. 4, pp. 331–347.

Meredith, J. (1998). Building Operations Management theory through case and field research. *Journal of Operations Management*, Vol. 16, pp. 441–454.

Meyer, M.J. (1987). Human dignity, rights and self-control. Unpublished PhD thesis, The University of North Carolina at Chapel Hill.

Miller, D.B. (1977). How to improve the performance and productivity of the knowledge worker. *Organizational Dynamics*, Vol. 5, No. 3, p. 62.

Miles, M.B., Huberman, M.A. (1994). *Qualitative Data Analysis: An Expanded Sourcebook*, 2nd edition, Thousand Oaks, CA: Sage.

Miles, M.B., Huberman, M.A. (2003). *Analyse des données qualitatives*, 2nd edition, Bruxelles: De Boeck Université.

Miller, J.F., Telles, R.L. (1974). The power of dignity: A matter of dignity. *The Personnel Administrator*, Vol. 19, No. 5, p. 47.

Murray, A. (2008). Goodbye, knowledge worker … Hello, knowledge entrepreneur. *KM World*, Vol. 17, No. 6, p. 20.

Murray, A.J., Greenes, K.A. (2007). From the knowledge worker to the knowledge economy. *The Journal of Information and Knowledge Management Systems*, Vol. 37, No. 1, pp. 7–13.

Nickerson, J.A., Zenger, T.R. (2004). A knowledge-based theory of the firm – The problem-solving perspective. *Organization Science*, Vol. 15, No. 6, pp. 617–632.

Nonaka, I., Takeuchi, H. (1995). *The Knowledge-Creating Company: How Japanese Companies Create the Dynamics of Innovation*. NY: Oxford University Press.

Peyton, P.R. (2003). *Dignity at Work: Eliminate Bullying and Create a Positive Working Environment*. Hove: Brunner-Routledge.

Ponce, S., Dueñas, H. (2010). Conocimiento y empresa (Chapter 7)), in S. Arcand et al. (eds) *Sociología de la empresa: del marco histórico a las dinámicas internas*. Bogotá, Siglo del Hombre Editores; Medellín, EAFIT; Cali, Universidad del Valle, 504 p., pp. 263–300.

Quinn, B.J. (1992). *Intelligent Enterprise. A Knowledge and Service Based Paradigm for Industry*. New York: The Free Press.

Ramirez, Y.W., Nembhard, D.A. (2004). Measuring knowledge worker productivity. A taxonomy. *Journal of Intellectual Capital*, Vol. 5, No. 4, pp. 602–628.

Rayman, P. (2001). *Beyond the Bottom Line: The Search for Dignity at Work*. New York: Palgrave.

Rifkin, J. (1995). *The End of Work. The Decline of the Global Labor Force and the Dawn of the Post-Market Era*. New York: A Tarcher/Putnam Book.

Russette, J.W., Preziosi, R., Scully, R.E., de Cossio, F. (2005). The twenty-first century incongruity: Perceptions regarding knowledge worker didactics. *Journal of Applied Management and Entrepreneurship*, Vol. 12, No. 2, pp. 15–43.

Scott, P. (2005). Knowledge workers: social, task and semantic network analysis. *Corporate Communications: An International Journal*, Vol. 10, No. 3, pp. 257–277.

Silvestro, (1999). Positioning services along the volume-variety diagonal. *International Journal of Operations and Production Management*, Vol. 19, No. 3/4, pp. 399–420.

Singleton, W.T. (1989). *Mind at Work*. Cambridge: Cambridge University Press.

Skinner, W. (1986). The productivity paradox. *Harvard Business Review*, Vol. 64, No. 4, pp. 55–59.

Spira, J. (2007). From knowledge to distraction. *KM World*, Vol. 16, No. 3, pp. 1 and 32.

Taylor, F.W. (1911). *Principles of Scientific Management*. New York: Harper and Brothers.

Teboul, J. (1988). De-industrialize for service quality, *International Journal of Operations and Production Management*, Vol. 8, No. 3, pp. 39–45.

The Economist (2006). Survey: Thinking for a living. (January, 21), Vol. 378, No. 8461, p. 9.

Viardot, E. (2000). Key features and importance of professional information technology-based services. *European Management Journal*, Vol. 18, No. 4, pp. 454–461.

Weisbord, M.R. (1987). *Productive Workplaces, Organizing and Managing for Dignity, Meaning and Community*. San Francisco: Jossey-Bass.

Withey, M. (2009). Some differences between knowledge-based and traditional workplaces. *The International Journal of Knowledge, Culture and Change Management*, Vol. 9, No. 1, pp. 213–226.

Wuthnow, R., Shrum,W. (1983). Knowledge workers as a "New Class". *Work and Occupations*. Vol. 10, No. 4, pp. 471–487.

Yigitcanlar, T., Baum, S., Horton, S. (2007). Attracting and retaining knowledge workers in knowledge cities. *Journal of Knowledge Management*, Vol. 11, No. 5, pp. 6–17.

Yin, R.K. (2003). *Case Study Research. Design and Methods*. 3rd edition, Applied Social Research Methods Series Volume 5. Thousand Oaks, CA: Sage Publications.

CHAPTER 7

Technological Change in Organizations: From Managing Resistance to Integrating Employee Creativity[1]

SYLVIE GROSJEAN AND LUC BONNEVILLE

Introduction

For over 20 years, information and communication technologies (ICT) have played a central role in organizations. The important rise of technological innovations within organizations has made necessary the development of strategies for change, whatever form this latter may take. In this context, technological innovation is considered by technological optimists to be necessary, indispensable and unavoidable, as shown by Bonneville in the computerization of health care organizations project (2003). Following this vision, this conception, technology is considered to be intrinsically "good" and to possess unto itself the power to improve the general performance of organizations that take advantage of its opportunities. Thus, it not surprising to observe that the actors that hold to this clearly functionalist vision consider the behaviour of any individual that does not use technology in the way in which it was intended, planed and calculated, to be problematic. These individuals were thereby labelled as "resistant", often accused of being against change and therefore in favour of inertia (Grosjean and Bonneville, 2006; Bonneville and Grosjean, 2007).

Now, we strongly suggest that this "resistance", interpreted as a refusal to use ICTs, masks an "insecurity" far more complex than the meaning generally lent to the concept of resistance alone. Could it be that, in fact, what we generally identify as "resistance" is rather the expression of what we have named, within the context of technological change, "digital insecurity" (Grosjean and Bonneville, 2007; Bonneville and Grosjean, 2007)? We propose to address precisely this question in the present chapter. Based

---

[1] The thoughts presented in this chapter were the subject of a presentation at the CREIS conference in June 2007, entitled *"From digital insecurity to social vulnerability"*. This chapter expands on the concepts and theories presented during this conference.

on examples drawn from our own research, this chapter offers a reinterpretation of a compilation of specific behaviours about computers and ICTs that, if one follows the history of managerial thought on the subject, have long been associated with behaviours symptomatic of resistance to change. We put forward the hypothesis that these behaviours are rather the expression of an insecurity that must be considered from the perspective of a combination of individual and collective strategies that equally enable actors to master their work environment (where ICTs are omnipresent) and to manage their diverse social and interpersonal relationships within the workplace.

We will thus consider the different ways in which "digital insecurity" is expressed during the process of computerization of organizations. We will notably present what strategies the members of an organization adopt in order to take back control of their work environment (where ICTs are omnipresent) and to reduce the *equivocality* (Weick, 1969, 2001)[2] that they are faced with. We will demonstrate how these strategies are more than simple expressions of resistance to change; they are a sign of the organization's member's ability to build upon structure, to restore meaning in their workplace, to show that they are creative beings.

The Computerization of Organizations: From "Resistance to Change" to "Digital Insecurity"

COMPUTERIZATION OF ORGANIZATIONS AND APPROACHES TO ICT INTEGRATION: A STARTING POINT

We must first call to mind the main approaches to ICT integration at work in organizations today. Let take us for example health care sector organizations, to illustrate our theories. In two previous articles, we analysed approaches to ICT integration in the health sector in Québec (Canada) (Grosjean and Bonneville, 2007; Bonneville and Grosjean, 2007). Based on the results of studies lead over the last few years, we have identified two approaches to ICT integration in health care organizations: a *techno-economic* approach and a *medico-integrative* approach.

The first approach, the *techno-economic* approach, rests upon a productive imperative that is based on the idea of a rationalization of medical practices. Generally held by the decision-makers, this approach imbues ICTs with the power to reduce the costs of health care work by increasing the productivity of health care professionals. A fundamental element of this approach consists of conceiving and integrating ICTs in such a way as they restructure health care work around planned administrative work standards. Health care professionals are thus expected to conform to what has been prepared, conceived, calculated, planned, standardized and broken down as tasks to be accomplished within a certain timeframe. This may be perceived as increasing control over their daily work (Bonneville, 2005a, 2005b). This approach is born, in great part, from a Taylorist vision of medical work made possible through the use of ICTs, which allow for an increase of

---

2 In Weick's model, the major goal of *organizing* is the reduction of *equivocality* in the information environment. *Equivocality* is the unpredictability that is inherent in the information environment of an organization. Weick defines the *process of organizing* as "the resolving of equivocality in an enacted environment by means interlocked behaviors embedded in conditionally related processes" (Weick, 1969, p. 91).

work resulting from long distance task planning that thus reduces health professionals to the role of simple executors.

This approach is based on a *technocentric* way of thought (Rabardel, 1995). In fact, in a study led in a 911 emergency dispatch centre[3] (Grosjean, 2008), this "top down" approach was found in the conception and integration of computer systems, designed largely to support the work of emergency dispatchers.[4] In fact, to meet production demands (particularly in terms of response and quick decision-making), the head of the organization values the computerization of dispatchers' workstations (particularly in developing numerous technological tools which aim to support cognitive activity and to facilitate the dispatcher's decision-making processes). Therefore, from these observations we can reason that the approach to the conception and integration of those technologies rest upon a *technocentric* vision, targeting primarily the internal coherence of the system and its harmony with organizational and structural demands, with no concern for the integration of the knowledge and practices of its various users (Brassac et al., 1998).

The second approach, the *medico-integrative* approach, is rather founded on a "creative imperative" (Cardon and Licoppe, 2000). While considering studies led by Bonneville (2003, 2005a, 2005b, 2005c, 2006), one may observe, in contrast to the operational objectives[5] prevalent in the *techno-economic* approach summarized previously, that health care professionals think that ICTs can and must be integrated in their daily practices to improve their clinical and therapeutic efficiency.[6] Here, ICTs are perceived as tools that can support, depending on the way in which they are used, daily health care work, on the condition that they be seen as offering the possibility of not only rationalizing medical work in itself, but rather of improving the quality of patient care. Thus, rather than being a key instrument supporting first of all and above all else, objectives to reduce medical work costs (in accordance with the *techno-economic* approach), health care professionals believe that ICTs can lead to a better management of work, founded on a better offer of health care services. To that effect, health care professionals assert that ICTs must be integrated with the intent to facilitate their work, so to avoid various perverse effects of the *techno-economic* approach (which prevail nevertheless in most tele-medical projects) that lead to numerous use problems (Bonneville and Grosjean, 2007) or even a failure to meet the goals of their daily work (Bonneville, 2003, 2006). This leads us to believe that ICTs should be put in place according to a complementary approach of negotiation

---

3   One of the objectives of the study was to describe the role of technological artefacts (computer systems that equip 911 dispatch centres) as resources that participate to the process of organizational remembering. The study was based upon an ethnographic approach (observations were recorded in the dispatch centre and interviews were held with the observed dispatchers).

4   The main duties assigned to the dispatchers were those of sending vehicles to emergency calls and of managing the deployment of available resources (emergency vehicles) in order to achieve optimal coverage of a territory (a geographic zone served by the organization). The computerization and the increasing complexity of the work environments, called dispatchers to use more and more often, sophisticated information and technological tools. There is therefore a high concentration of informational tools in their work environment. Thus, they must pass from one application to another, take down information in one place to then transfer it to another, all part of their daily work routine.

5   Operational objectives refer to the conception and integration of systems that regulate health professionals' daily practices to make them more productive and to increase their speed and intervention capability.

6   Clinical and therapeutic efficiency may be defined as the indicator of the quality of the clinical practice, in respect to health care professionals' capacity to obtain results (efficiency) that are measured in terms of improving both the economic and organizational health care services and technical conditions, that make this improvement possible. Health care professionals' ability to obtain "good results", adequate results, constitutes the fundamental criteria for clinical and therapeutic efficiency, which measures consequently the effects of the use of technology on the health professionals' current operations to study the best way in which to obtain results (operational efficiency) (Bonneville, 2003, 2005c, 2006).

rather than substitution or imposition (Gregori, 1999; Brassac and Gregori, 2000; Carré and Lacroix, 2001). Thus, ICTs are not considered to be an instrument of technical substitution of human medical work (in terms of increased productivity) but rather as an additional and complementary method of support for health care professionals, a method of improving the quality of health care services offered to patients, with a concern for their "well being" as Gadrey would say (2001).

This short detour toward the approaches to ICT integration in health care organizations allows us to look at organizational change management from a complex angle, where the interest for the organizations resides less in the object of change in itself (ICTs) than in the actors themselves that experience this change. The appropriation of ICTs remains organizations' fundamental concern, when faced with a tension arising from the coexistence of a "productive imperative" and a "creative imperative" within organizations such as those in the health care sector (Grosjean and Bonneville, 2007).

AN UNDERLYING DETERMINIST VISION IN THE CONCEPT OF "RESISTANCE"

The important rise of technological innovations within organizations has made necessary the development of strategies for change, whatever forms this change may take.[7] The "ideology of progress" soon made change management inevitable, as much on an organizational level (seen as a system, for the most part), as on an individual-worker level (that experiences or participates in the change). Organizations are in search of the highest level of performance possible, in a context marked by intense competition and a worship of excellence (De Gaulejac, 2005). When analysing the views of the Québecois government in regards to the integration of ICTs in their sector (Bonneville, 2003, Chapter 4), we discovered the resonance of a clearly determinist vision of ICTs which made these the driving force behind the enhancement of productivity and increased efficiency of health care organizations. These views became mainstream in most economic and social activity sectors, where a certain apologetic vision of new technologies reigns to justify and attempt to legitimize what was instantly thought to be necessary, that is to say to structurally reorganize organizations. Hence, the expectations that were expressed in regards to ICTs, by administrators and promoters of new technology, through prescribed applications. These applications, when not recreated on location by the workers, lead to reports of problems or even failures that demand immediate solutions. It is the concept of change itself, in its simplest form, that evokes automatically its opposite, "inertia", resistance (Teneau, 2006, p. 39), what is considered to be a pejorative concept in industrialized societies where "progress" is tied to "growth" (economic growth) which is itself strongly connoted with an idea of a movement. Furthermore, to not follow change is to automatically marginalize oneself from something – change – that we (administrators, heads of organizations, decision-makers, promoters of new technology, and so on) consider at first glance as desirable, "good", promising, and so on. As Collerette et al., stated so well, "the phenomenon of resistance to change is probably the bane of all those that express ideas of change. To the one that leads the project of change, resistances are

---

7   Change within an organizational context can truly take on various forms, as indicated by Bartoli and Hemel. They showed that change could in fact imply, for example, an evolution (a collection of transformations that work in the same direction), a modification (introduction of a new element in an already established, stable system), a mutation (a change that is often very quick and with what can be permanent effects), a transformation or restructuring (the passing from one particular form to a different form), and so on (1986, p. 23).

usually synonyms of hostility, intrigue, delays, polarization, conflicts, impatience, etc." ([translated by authors], 1997, p. 13).

Moreover, the etymology of the term "resistance", as indicated by Teneau (2006, p. 45) in reference to the Latin–French dictionary (Hachette, F. Gaffot, 1985), is as follows: *resistere, resisto* refers to the act of "stopping oneself, to go no further, to hold strong, to keep one's composure, to stand strong before". We believe that the fact that this term is now used, even misused, in most business management books, is a sign of the largely hegemonic conception of the term that prevails in management.[8] Teneau went so far as to retrace a few key definitions of "resistance", taken from big, well-known dictionaries. We have condensed these definitions in this concise table:

Table 7.1 A few lexicographical definitions of the term resistance

Robert pour tous, July 1994.	That which opposes free will, act by which one attempts to render powerless an act directed against them.
Le grand Robert de la langue française, November 2001.	Obstacle, hindrance.
Le Robert dictionnaire de la langue française, October 1989.	The variable ability to resist, to cancel or to diminish the effect of a force, an action undergone.
Markus (1983, p. 433).	"Behaviors intended to prevent the implementation or use of a system or to prevent system designers from achieving their objectives".

Source: Teneau, 2006, p. 45

According to these definitions of the term "resistance," a term that became a concept in management terminology and jargon, we view the individual that does not enter fully, blindly, into organizational change as being resistant, that is to say a deviant that we will label, implicitly or explicitly, as an outsider. Furthermore, we explain in most management or organizational behaviour books that resistance to change can be traced back to eight primary causes: "1) a fear of the unknown; 2) a lack of pertinent information; 3) a fear of losing knowledge; 4) a change that is perceived as or is really useless; 5) a fear of losing control/power; 6) a lack of resources; 7) poor timing; and 8) an attachment to habits" ([translated by authors], et al., 2002, p. 505).

Resistance is therefore seen as a problem, a problem to be resolved and to which many solutions are grafted; solutions that are in fact organizational change management strategies. Thus, as underlined again by Teneau, individuals' resistance to change is automatically regarded as an illness: "Resistance to change is frequently treated as an ailment that must be treated. As such, it may almost be considered to be an organizational deviance, a true 'hijacking' of efficiency" ([translated by authors], Teneau, 2006, p. 39).

---

8   Cazal makes the following remark in regards to books in management and organizational behaviour, when he speaks of the Americans standards and text-book cloning: "It is always a shocking experience to pick up an American text book in business administration. The structures are largely identical, only the examples, illustrations, cases and suggested aids differ. [...] The text books are cloned from other text books, the field of OB (Organizational behaviour) demonstrates this" (2005, p. 30–31).

Consequently, a majority of books in business management teach that one must be able to diagnose the problem (the alleged "illness"), so to determine thereafter a treatment: "The actor that faces resistance must refer to his diagnosis of the situation and to the explanation he can now make of the resistances to decide what attitude to adopt" ([translated by authors], Collerette et al., 1997, p. 102–103).

The organizational change strategies targeting resistance management are numerous and diverse and it would take far too long to discuss them now, and in any case they are not the object of this current chapter. However, tied to what was previously mentioned, we must note that all "good" strategies rely often on, or are at least inspired from, a vision developed by Lewin, who is one of the first psychologists to take on organizational change management. Lewin (1948) thought of change by analogy with what happens in chemistry when a compound is transformed: there is (1) an unfreeze; (2) a transition; (3) a refreeze (Collerette and Délisle, 1982, p. 27). As Teneau explains:

> *The steering of change consist of allowing for the passage from an organisational configuration A to an organisational configuration B (the target) passing eventually through intermediary phases, disregarding the subtleties associated to the organisational change model in itself. [...] The steering of change is therefore conceived in a very evolutionary manner. The steering of change consists essentially of calling to action the organisation's agents to work toward the target organisational configuration. ([translated by authors] Teneau, 2006, p. 41)*

This is also the method that is recommended by Bergeron, whose introduction to management books are widely distributed, at least in the francophone world:

> *Firstly, it is necessary to "thaw" pre-existing habits or attitudes. [...] Secondly, the necessary changes must be made in hopes of reducing dissatisfaction and establishing balance. [...] Thirdly, new predetermined attitudes and work methods are left to be "solidified. ([translated by authors] 1989, p. 233 and following)*

We therefore see very clearly, behind these conceptions, a functionalist vision of the organization and of change where obstacles are viewed as resistances. Furthermore, it comes as no surprise to have seen emerge among these management strategies, solutions where communication is key, ultimately as a persuasion strategy and as a tool that supports a will to fight against all forms of resistance. As Desmarais et al., indicated, to manage change well and to overcome resistances, one must:

> *1– first inform. [...] To inform does not mean say everything or anything. It is to give the necessary information, at the right time, so that people understand what is happening and what will happen. A lack of information creates fear and anxiety, and anxiety sets off resistances. [...] 2– let resistances be expressed. [...] 3– Listen to the expression of the resistances while refraining from all criticism. This reinforces the idea that the resistances are just part of the project and does not call immediately upon interpreters of these resistances. [...] 4– Remove all guilt. [...] Nothing indicates that it is anything but natural to feel apprehensive when a change is announced. This may not diminish the anxiety of the parties involved but it will show them that we do not think of them as embarrassments and will trivialise the phenomenon. 5– Study carefully each resistance that is expressed. [...] 6– Include the resistances in your project. [...] 7– Accept to take time. ([translated by authors] 1990, p. 51)*

Schermerhorn et al., calling upon the classic sources of resistances as we addressed them earlier, suggest different responses adapted to the very causes of resistance:

Table 7.2   Sources of resistance and suggested behaviours (responses)

Sources of resistance [translated by authors]	Suggested response [translated by authors]
Fear of the unknown	Offer information
Need for security	Clarify intentions and methods
No felt need to change	Demonstrate the problem or opportunity
Vested interests threatened	Enlist key people in planning change
Contrasting interpretations	Disseminate valid information and facilitate group sharing
Poor timing	Delay change and await a better time
Lack of resources	Provide supporting resources and/or reduce performance expectations

Source: Schermerhorn et al., 1992, p. 537.

Schermerhorn et al., (2002) explain that resistance to change management methods can even be based on "manipulation" and "explicit or implicit coercion", the first being attributed the advantage of "gaining more speedy and less costly results" while the second can be "quick" while "prevailing over all forms of resistance" ([translated by authors], p. 507). To that effect, manipulation and coercion are considered to be methods in their own right, and are ways for those who wish to steer the change to "react to all forms of resistance to change in a positive manner" ([translated by authors], Schermerhorn et al., 2002, p. 506).

Thus, we automatically lay the blame for problems related to organizational change on the backs of individuals, workers that "resist". Most of the time, managers assume that these individuals could not possibly understand all the issues surrounding change and it is for that reason that they resist, hence the importance of communication during the entire process:

What is most important is without a doubt to let those who show resistances to change, that are not objectively founded, realize that they express these exaggerated reactions without any real ties to the situation. Until they understand that no one wishes to cause them harm and that they are limiting their own opportunities to evolve. ([translated by authors] Desmarais et al., 1990, p. 51)

The resistant individual is seen as a generally worrisome individual, separate from the change:

All change is in some way a "leap into the unknown" that generates a certain number of psychological phenomena drawing up two worries: that of not accomplishing the change and that of ending up in a different situation that does not present any true benefit for the individual. ([translated by authors] Brénot and Truvée, 1996, p. 25)

In short, the point has been made that the concept of resistance to change is strongly ideologically connoted, in so far as we associate all forms of resistance with behaviours that we consider immediately to be roadblocks on the path to objectives that have been predetermined by the initiators of the change. Furthermore, it is believed that what one refers to as "resistance to change" is less a real "hindrance" than an insecurity revealing the meaning that the actors in the organization grant to each given situation. From that point of view, "resistance" only truly exists to the initiators, or agents, of change. We can therefore think that "resistance" to change hides other, more complex, social, psychological, organizational realities, as we hypothesized in our presentation of the concept of "digital insecurity" in this chapter.

MORE COMPLEX BEHAVIOURS: TALKING ABOUT DIGITAL INSECURITY?

The introduction of ICTs in organizations played a part in modifying employees' work environment (Bonneville and Grosjean, 2006) as well as freeing information from paper hard copy, this thanks in large part to the digitization of data. Thus, the launch of ICTs in organizations facilitated the transition from using sheets of paper to using computers, this could cause a feeling of insecurity associated with ICTs. Furthermore, the determinist view of organizational change recognizes the importance of the human dimension of the process, however emphasizing, above all, the "hindrances" and "blockages" that are perceived as "resistances" to change. Moreover, we hypothesize in this chapter that what is currently called "resistance" (when speaking of technological change) could actually be the expression of a form of "digital insecurity" far more complex than most theorists would have us believe. What is more, many researchers took interest in the communicational behaviours of managers hoping to thwart those resistances, forgetting that employees can be creative and that their perception of change evolves over time (Giroux, 1997). Thus, individuals can develop personal and collective strategies to take back control of their environment and reduce digital insecurity.

What do we mean by digital insecurity? Firstly, this term refers to an insecurity inherent to a new situation and created by the presence of ICTs in the workplace. In fact, as we will demonstrate later in an example, this insecurity is strongly tied to the physical transformation of the work environment and can have major repercussions in certain contexts (in our case, medical practices). It is therefore important for the subject to measure these transformations and progressively adapt his behaviour and ways of doing accordingly. Secondly, this term also refers to a form of insecurity that is caused by the fact that the introduction of ICTs in organizations stimulated the circulation of and access to information, information that has changed mediums (transition from hard copy to digital information). Individuals (having to manipulate and work with digital information) are therefore confronted with *equivocality* (Weick, 2001a/b). This notion of *equivocality* "refers to the presence of multiple interpretations of a same situation" ([translated by authors] Allard-Poesi, 2003, p. 99). In fact, the digital information available, via computers that are present in the workplace, is subject to multiple interpretations, even contradictions, that render the situation equivocal and thus problematic for the organizations' members. We will use an example to illustrate how individuals deal with this equivocality (generated by the multiplication of technical and digital tools within their work environment, that force them to work with digital data); we will also show how they take back control of their environment by being creative in their search for meaning. This second example (Grosjean, 2008) will illustrate particularly how, with time, individuals configured their work environment so to better integrate the digital infrastructure established in their organization in their daily practices, how they developed tools to support a "sense-making" process in order to reduce equivocality.

Through these two examples, we will put into perspective what may appear to be signs of resistance, roadblocks to the use of ICTs, which are in fact only the expression of the creativity of work groups seeking to control and master their work environment.

Expressions of Digital Insecurity within an Organizational Context

LOSS OF BEARING AND RELATIONAL UNCERTAINTY

During a study of the use of laptop computers in homecare work,[9] we discovered that caregivers expressed what we would qualify as a "rational" feeling of insecurity strongly associated to a fear of losing their bearings when coming into contact with patients (Bonneville and Sicotte, 2008). Here, it is not so much the technical knowledge that is problematic in most cases but rather the physical presence of the equipment that is needed to access digital data, be it the laptop computer in and of itself. As some of our informants stated in interview, their unease is caused by a fear of affecting negatively the quality of the interaction they have with their patients, as a social worker, an occupational therapist, a nurse and a physiotherapist explain:

I feel uncomfortable bringing my laptop to certain patients' homes. […] I worry about how it will affect patients' trust in me. […] I care about the human being. I speak with people, listen to people, and so on. I feel as though the laptop creates a barrier. […] I want to create a warm bond with people. I have to get to know the person before I bring in the laptop. […] The laptop can contribute to the severing of a relationship. The person will not feel comfortable. That is my impression.

To humanise the relationship I don't always use the laptop, not systematically. The human aspect of care is important.

If we do not want to break trust, we should not rush into things (by bringing the laptop to a patient's home).

I find that the approach of "direct" work with the patient and the computer, severs the relationship. […] I find that the computer cuts off my relationship with the patient.

---

9   Since 2006, we have had the pleasure of conducting over 20 interviews with health care professionals (mostly nurses, but also physiotherapists, occupational therapists and social workers). The central theme of these 45–75-minute long, semi-directive interviews was the effect of daily use of ICTs on the health care practice. Out of this group, twelve health care professionals (nurses, for the most part) known as using or having used laptop computers in home care work in the Québec city area (Province of Québec, Canada) were questioned. See Bonneville and Sicottte (2008).

These statements express an insecurity that is not related to the change (organizational change) that is caused by integrating laptops in home care, but rather directly tied to the effect of the use of this device on the everyday caregiver-patient rapport. This touches upon a fundamental aspect of the caregiver-patient relationship, the interaction, the social service relationship as Gadrey would say (1996, notably p. 171). Therefore, it is not the object of the change that is in question, the laptop computer, but rather adjusting to the use of the laptop at the patients' homes and the very purpose of the health care service that is expressed through a social *relationship* (Bonneville, 2003). In the context of health care work, a social relationship that depends upon the ability of the caregiver to gain the trust of the patient through their interaction: "the issue of trust is particularly important in medical communication that requires the sharing of deeply personal and private information" ([translated by authors] Richard and Lussier, 2005, p. 50). To gain this trust, one must be able to enter into "professional intimacy" (Bioy et al., 2003, p. 31) with the patient.

To offer health care is first and foremost to create a rapport with an individual by way of a particular interpersonal communication where listening is a fundamental aspect of the role of a caregiver. As Bioy et al., write "Listening entails a decision on behalf of the caregiver: a decision to make oneself available to the patient" ([translated by authors] 2003, p. 31). This is no more important than in homecare, where patients can be more reticent to expose themselves than patients that decide on their own to make their way to a medical centre: "The patient more often refuses or is hesitant about services in a case where he was not the one asking for help" ([translated by authors] Mégie, 2005, p. 779). Establishing "contact" with the patient is therefore vital, as this physiotherapist explains:

Already, to start with, we enter into peoples' homes. It is therefore already very different than the work of a physiotherapist that works in a clinic or in an institution. I go into their homes. I enter truly into peoples' privacy. It is not at all the same dynamic as a patient that makes his own way to a private clinic. The patient that goes to a private clinic usually goes with the intention consulting a doctor about ONE particular problem. Furthermore, we, in homecare, must open conversation up to other subjects. The approach is certainly different. [...] We often refer our patients to meet with other colleagues, for example, in the case of abuse, hygiene problems, aggressiveness, depression, etc. We really work as a team. [...] The human dimension of our work takes on it's true meaning in homecare. One can really not say the same in private clinics. [...] One must nurture the human dimension of health care and it is crucial in our healthcare centre.

At home, it is the patient who dictates what form the relationship will take. He is in his home, therefore master of his surroundings (Lofaso, 2000, cited in Mégie, 2005, p. 765). Thus, as mentioned in the previous statement, all health care professionals that enter into a patient's home step onto personal territory ("I enter truly into peoples' private space"). Without entire control of the interaction (as often is the case in classical medical environments (Mégie, 2005, p. 766)) the caregiver must make sure to really understand the patient not only on the basis of formal information that is divulged but also through information drawn from his living area (environment):

Physical places communicate precious information about the patient to the health care professional, information that must be handled with tact for it is ever more difficult to obtain during ordinary clinical consultations. ([translated by authors] Mégie, 2005, p. 767)

Thus and therefore at the heart of the health care professional-patient relationship lies the question of the quality of the interaction. To preserve, maintain, nay improve this quality, it must be founded upon a communication that is as adapted as possible to the frame of interaction. It is therefore not possible for health care professionals, in ambulatory care, to subsume systematically a technical device (laptop computer) into the frame of interaction which could cloud in many ways the bond of trust upon which this interaction founded. For in fact the interaction in the context of health care is a particular one, founded on a co-construction of meaning between the caregiver and the patient, that amounts to more than a simple transfer of information. Thus, dialogue, or conversation between the caregiver and the patient, constitutes the space within which the interaction takes place, whose purpose is to establish contact:

Conversation is not only used to exchange information: it is, in part, a creative process of construction of shared beliefs between two or more people, and in part a practical way of creating a relationship with someone. [...] There exists no situation where we can communicate information that is separate from social, interpersonal and relational dimensions. ([translated by authors] Richard and Lussier, 2005, p. 12)

Briefly, we now understand that the "relational" insecurity expressed by many caregivers in regards to the use of laptop computers in the homes of patients is not a matter of resistance to change (which would be a gross oversimplification), but rather a practical assertion of the very purpose of their work and the meaning they give it. It is not the laptop itself that is in question here, but again the balance between its use in all situations and the situation itself that does not always lend itself to technical interferences. Thus, we understand that when caregivers believe that the relationship that they have with their patient does not lend well to the use of the laptop, the laptop becomes an object that must be removed, whether it be by closing it completely (after it has been opened), or by moving it away for a moment (Bonneville and Sicotte, 2008). Even more so if the caregiver is dealing with a patient that is distraught, as a nurse and an occupational therapist highlighted:

When a patient is distraught and is crying in front of me, I close my computer.

When I am interacting with a patient and I have the computer in front of us and, while talking, the patient starts to cry, the first thing I do is close the computer. I do the same with all physical objects. I do not want to give off the impression that I want to continue doing that same thing at the same time.

In these statements, the interviewees clearly favour a strategy where the computer becomes an object that is considered to create discomfort. The computer therefore becomes a sort of intruder in the relationship, as though is passes from being an instrument, a tool, to an unfortunate object that caused uneasiness. There is therefore an insecurity that is inherent to the object itself, that is to say an insecurity based on the fear of seeing the social relationship (the caregiver-patient interaction) blurred. We therefore put the computer aside, out of "respect" for the patient as a central rule of acceptance and management of emotions (Richard et al., 2005, p. 231–265). As we evoked earlier, this strategy's purpose is to ensure that the communication that is established between the caregiver and the patient be the best it can be, hence the important role of listening in building trust as we spoke of earlier.

EQUIVOCALITY AND AMBIGUITY

During an ethnographic study in a 911 dispatch centre (Grosjean, 2008), we noticed on several occasions that emergency dispatchers are faced with a certain equivocality (Weick, 20021 a/b) that is expressed mainly as a loss of meaning (the situation doesn't make sense). We will see how they *"bricolent"*[10] (Weick, 2001) their environment so to reduce that equivocality.

Let us remember that a dispatch centre is effectively a coordination centre where 911 calls converge, where interventional decisions are made, and where the movement and intervention of ambulances scattered across the territory (in this case a territory in Québec, Canada) are coordinated. In order to fulfil their duty of ensuring that vehicles are well distributed over their covered territory, dispatchers must stay informed of all movements of emergency vehicles so to update their information in almost real time. To do so, a computer system allows them to (1) see on screen information concerning available ambulances and their location on the territory and (2) on another screen information on the address of the caller, their telephone number and other medical information if the caller is known to the service. The computerization and updating of data in real time is available to two dispatchers that access this shared data via their computer screens. However, observations and interviews held with the dispatchers allowed us to come to the conclusion that (1) on one hand, these dispatchers exchange a lot of information orally despite the fact that the information on their screens is updated regularly and allows them to access digital information simultaneously and (2) they also use sheets of paper for ambulance management which served the same purpose as the computer system.

During our observations, we noted that it is common to see dispatchers consult the information on the computer, and notice the movement of a vehicle only to then confirm this movement by speaking to a fellow team member. Now, this colleague not only confirms the information in the computer system but also places the movement of the vehicle into context by explaining how and why he/she chose to take that course of action.

The equivocality that dispatchers face and with which they must work seems to ban the exclusive use of digital information because it is void of context. In situations where members of medical staff and nurses must collaborate by correspondence, the lack of shared context can sometimes contribute to the deterioration of communication and misinterpretations can multiply and hinder the good coordination of actions. *Quid pro quo* situations are just one example of a lack of a common context and in these cases communication is interpreted with reference to a context that is not the one in which

---

[10] Weick used the French term *bricolage* in his work to refer to the use of all available resources to reduce equivocality and accomplish a task with which a team is confronted.

it was created, hence the misunderstandings that render our organizations vulnerable. Cahour and Karsenty (1996) gave examples of these communicational problems that result from *misframing*. Consequently, it is important to the dispatchers that the digital information displayed on their computer screens be explained in context. In the following conversation between two dispatchers (Excerpt 1), we will see how this gives meaning to the digital information that can be sometimes ambiguous.

Excerpt 1

[Three people are in the central dispatch office, two dispatchers (Claude and Paul) and one supervisor (Kevin)]

1. Kevin: *I am going to page Yves Blanc. Could you please ask him what his mileage is when he calls back?*

2. Claude: *The screen indicates that he's assigned to mobile 7, but he really has mobile 1.*

3. Kevin: *No, there it says that he should have mobile 7.*

4. Kevin: *Central to mobile 07.* [Kevin takes the radio to call the ambulance in question]

   [Paul enters the central dispatch office]

5. Claude: [Speaking to Paul] *He asked* [referring to Kevin] *whether Yves Blanc had mobile 1 or mobile 7.*

6. Paul: *Oh, yeah.*

7. Claude: *Well, that's that, he still has mobile 7. He also has mobile 1 at hand, but we call mobile 7.*

[A few minutes later, the paramedic confirms that he indeed has mobile 1, that is to say that he is assigned to ambulance 1, while explaining the events that led to the change.]

This excerpt shows that the second dispatcher (R2) quickly notices, while looking at his screen, that there is a discrepancy between the digital information and what is real ("The screen indicates that he's assigned to mobile 7, but he really has mobile 1"). Thus, the information on the computer is questioned. This phenomenon of erosion of meaning in a work group comes up repeatedly throughout our observations. The strategy, used by the dispatchers, to take back control of their work environment and reduce the equivocality of the situation, is to call upon members outside their two-person team (in this case, a paramedic). We can see how the dispatchers become "bricoleurs", Vidaillet, 2003), that is to say that they are able to make sense of and use the materials (oral and sometimes visual information) at their disposal. This example illustrates the dispatchers' ability to reduce the equivocality perceived in this situation by collecting new information. And, above all by creating meaning through discussion, by organizing the many messages and clues provided by their documents and their interlocutors (Huber and Daft, 1987).

However, what is more significant in this study is that the dispatchers created a sheet ("sheet management") that serves the same purpose as the computer system. This "sheet management" adds to the digital information and the dispatchers questioned will say that they consider it to be a "backup". They'll add that the information is better organized on the document, which allows them to react more quickly when an interventional decision must be made. We also observe that after a call the dispatchers ritually proceed to update this vehicle and team management sheet (Grosjean, 2008). This exchange of information amongst themselves is based upon that hardcopy and brings the teams at the end of a shift or on break up to date on the movement of vehicles on the covered territory, this in hopes of being able to make decisions efficiently when the moment comes, or to verify that all of the territory is well covered by ambulances.

One could interpret the use of this sheet as a way of avoiding use of the computer system, but this is not the case. In fact, a large part of the dispatchers' activities are tied to the computer system, specifically their ability to identify the information that is pertinent to their task. Here is what one dispatcher said when speaking of his relationship with technology (more specifically the computer system managing the dispatch centre) during the accomplishment his work assignment:

The computer provides information on the vehicles and the records of interventions. And with that we manage the vehicles. [...] It is the screen that talks to me. [...] For me it is 33 per cent screen, 33 per cent telephone and 33 per cent my mind.

This example shows us that digital information is sometimes a source of equivocality (generating a form of digital insecurity), which forces individuals to adapt to their work environment by developing collective methods (for example, the use of hardcopy tools and frequent conversations) that support the meaning reconstruction process and the reduction of equivocality.

Conclusion

The spread of ICTs in organizations quickly led to many changes, prior to and following the integration of ICTs. In some previous works, we have shown that these changes have meanwhile led to successes as well as failures (notably Grosjean and Bonneville, 2006). On one hand, the integration of ICTs within organizations favoured notably a redefinition of communicational processes, a more decentralized approach to the concept of decision-making, a recreation of practices based on new forms of temporality, a reconfiguration of daily tasks, and so on. More largely, ICTs were considered to favour a certain "sharing of information" where these were perceived at once as both a factor of flexibility and an instrument supporting collaboration and the sharing of knowledge (Benghozi, 2001). Moreover, we noted that ICTs tend to support the establishment of a Taylorian renewal reflected notably in an increase in work. Thus, we have seen in many organizations a considerable increase in tele-surveillance, tele-control, dismissals (thought possible by substituting ICTs to human work, that is to say the work of a living being) as well as the emergence of an excessively valued "ideology of emergency" (Valenduc, 2005; Bonneville and Grosjean, 2006; Aubert, 1998, 2003a, 2003b, 2004). Not to mention the many problems related to the use of ICTs that formed a specific field of research in information and communication sciences, sociology, and psychology or business management. Thus two realities appear (sources of tension) that are called to coexist within organizations and that can also challenge each other, especially during the integration of ICTs (Grosjean and Bonneville, 2007).

This complex dynamic led to (as we wished to demonstrate in this chapter) the emergence of a form of insecurity, called "digital insecurity", felt by the individual worker that is confronted daily not only by the use of ICTs but also by a "duty" to use the ICTs according to their design, a design that did not involve them. This insecurity is evidence of a discomfort with ICTs, with the technology itself, despite all its promises. Yet, this insecure behaviour has often been considered to be the expression of a dual resistance, technological and organizational. Now, in light of the examples we presented earlier in this chapter, we suggest that these forms of "resistance" to change are rather the expression of a digital security far more complex and nuanced than what many widely spread opinions would suggest. We believe that it is less a resistance to change as it is a collection of personal and/or collective strategies intended to control and reduce digital insecurity.

Organizational change has been the subject of studies and publications in business management and work psychology, and has even become "a star product" – as Giroux, 1993 says – for consultant committees. The failure of change attempts is often blamed on resistance to change or on communicational problems. And, as we have outlined, people are often thought to be the problem. However, as Giroux (1993) wrote:

To change an organisation, is to change the behaviours of its members and the relationships between them. It is to change at once their position in commitment networks and the context within which they create meaning. It is to affect their identity, their everyday life. In this perspective, resistance to change and communicational problems are no longer considered barriers to change but rather natural by-products of change. Unfortunately, resistance to change and communicational problems are too often perceived negatively, as enemies that must be eliminated.

Through our examples and by observing the tools *"bricolés"* ("sheet management" for example) by the members of an organization to give meaning to their environment, we wished to underline that administrators, leaders, cannot think of managing change on their own. They depend upon the cooperation of the other members of the organization. And, even if individual workers do not have the same resources as the managers have at their disposal, we have seen that they are dotted nevertheless with a large margin of error (Crozier and Friedberg, 1977), with a power to act that allows them to construct meaning and order and thus appropriate the change.

References

Allard-Poesi, F. (2003), "Sens collectif et construction collective du sens", in *Le sens de l'action* (B. Vidaillet), Paris, Vuibert, pp. 91–112.

Aubert, N. (1998), Le sens de l'urgence, *Sciences de la société*, Vol. 44, pp. 29–42.

Aubert, N. (2003a), *Le culte de l'urgence, la société malade du temps*, Paris, Flammarion.

Aubert, N. (2003b), "Urgence et instantanéité: les nouveaux pièges du temps", in *Modernité: la nouvelle carte du temps* (F. Asher and F. Godard), Éditions de l'Aube – Le Moulin du Château, pp. 169–185.

Aubert, N. (2004), Les entreprises face à l'urgence: Y-a-t-il encore place pour l'anticipation?, *Information sur les sciences sociales*, Vol. 43(3), pp. 309–402.

Bartoli, A., Hermel, P. (1986), *Piloter l'entreprise en mutation. Une approche stratégique du changement*, Paris, Éditions d'Organisation.

Benghozi, P.J. (2001), Technologies de l'information et organisation: de la tentation de la flexibilité à la centralisation, *Gestion 2000*, Vol. 2, Mars-Avril 2001.

Bergeron, P.-G. (1989), *La gestion dynamique – Concepts, méthodes et applications*, Montréal, Gaétan Morin Éditeur.

Bioy, A., Bourgeois, F., Nègre, I. (2003), *La communication soignant-soigné: repères et pratiques*, Rosny-sous-Bois (Seine-Saint-Denis), Boréal.

Bonneville, L. (2003), "La mise en place du virage ambulatoire informatisé comme solution à la crise de productivité du système sociosanitaire au Québec (1975 à 2000)", Thèse de doctorat en sociologie. Montréal: Université du Québec à Montréal.

Bonneville, L. (2005a), L'informatisation comme outil de contrôle et de surveillance de la productivité des organisations de soins et du travail médical au Québec, *Revue Terminal – Technologies de l'information, culture et société*, Vol. 92, pp. 173–185.

Bonneville, L. (2005b), La transformation des organisations de soins et du travail médical par le recours à l'informatisation au Québec: une analyse critique, *Communication et Organisation*, Vol. 26, pp. 205–225.

Bonneville, L. (2005c), A Paradigm Shift in the Evaluation of Information Technology in Health Care, *Journal of Telemedicine and e-health*, Vol. 10(4), pp. 477–480.

Bonneville, L. (2006), About the Evaluation of Computerised Health Care Services: Some Critical Points, *International Journal of Health Sociology*, Vol. 15(2), pp. 169–178.

Bonneville, L., Grosjean. S., (2007), Les défis que soulève l'informatisation de la pratique médicale sur le plan de l'innovation technologique, *Revue canadienne de communication/Canadian Journal of Communication*, Vol. 32, pp. 432–456.

Bonneville, L., Sicotte, C. (2008), Les défis posés à la relation soignant – soigné par l'usage de l'ordinateur portable en soins à domicile, Revue *Communication*, Université Laval, No. 26, Vol. 2, pp. 75–107.

Brassac, C., Grégori, N. (2000), Situated and Distributed Design of a Computer Teaching Device, *Journal of Design Sciences and Technology*, Vol. 8(2), pp. 11–31.

Brassac, C., Grégori, N., Remoussenard, P. (1998), "The User as an Actor in Educational Multimedia Software Design", in C. Branki and K. Zreik (eds), *Cyber Design*, Paris, Europia, pp. 385–395.

Brénot, J., Tuvée, L. (1996), *Le changement dans les organisations*, Paris, Presses universitaires de France.

Cahour, B., Karsenty, L. (1996). Contextes cognitifs et dysfonctionnements de la communication, *Interaction et cognitions*, 1(4), pp. 485–509.

Cardon, D., Licoppe, C. (2000), *Technologies de l'information et de la communication en entreprise: théories et pratiques*, Septième École d'été de l'ARCo, Bonas, France, 10–21 juillet 2000.

Carré, D., Lacroix, J.G. (2001), *La santé et les autoroutes de l'information. La greffe informatique*, Paris, L'Harmattan.

Cazal, D. (2005), "La communication: modèles et clichés, enjeux et contextes", in P. Gilbert, F. Guérin et F. Pigeyre, *Organisations et comportements. Nouvelles approches. Nouveaux enjeux*, Paris, Dunod, pp. 27–59.

Collerette, P., Délisle, G. (1982), *Le changement planifié: une approche pour intervenir dans les systèmes organisationnels*, Montréal, Agence d'Arc.

Collerette, P., Délisle, G., Perron, R. (1997), *Le changement organisationnel. Théorie et pratique*, Saint-Foy, Presses de l'Université du Québec.

De Gaulejac, V. (2005), *La société malade de la gestion. Idéologie gestionnaire, pouvoir managérial et harcèlement social*, Paris, Seuil.

Desmarais, J.-M., Hamel, B., Niewenglowski, P. (1990), *Anticiper et vivre le changement*, Paris, Éditions d'Organisation.

Gadrey, J. (1996), *Services: la productivité en question*, Paris, Desclée de Brouwer.

Gadrey, J. (2001), *Nouvelle économie. Nouveau mythe? Suivi de que reste-t-il de la nouvelle économie?* Paris, Flammarion.

Giroux, N. (1993), Communication et changement dans les organisations (introduction), *Communication and Organisation* [http://greco.u-bordeaux3.fr/article.htm?tpg_id=169].

Giroux, N. (1997), La construction discursive de l'organisation, *Colloque Constructivisme(s) et Sciences de Gestion*, IAE de Lille, 23 octobre, pp. 373–386.

Grégori, N. (1999), Étude clinique d'une situation de conception de produit. Vers une pragmatique de la conception, Thèse de doctorat en Psychologie, Université Nancy2 (France).

Grosjean, S. (2008), Communication dans un centre de répartition des urgences 911, *Canadian Journal of Communication*, Vol. 33, pp. 101–120.

Grosjean, S., Bonneville, L. (2006), TIC, organisation et communication: entre informativité et communicabilité, *Actes du colloque Pratiques et usages organisationnels des technologies de l'information et de la communication* (Rennes, France), 7–9 septembre, pp.

Grosjean, S., Bonneville, L. (2007), Logiques d'implantation des TIC dans le secteur de la santé, *Revue française de gestion*, Vol. 172, pp. 145–158.

Huber, G.P., Daft, R.L. (1987), "The Information Environments of Organizations", in F.M. Jablin, L.L. Putnam, K.H. Roberts and L.W. Porter (eds) *Handbook of Organizational Communication: An Interdisciplinary Perspective*, Newbury Park, CA, Sage Publications, pp. 130–164.

Lewin, K. (1948), *Resolving Social Conflicts: Selected Papers on Group Dynamics*, New York, Harper and Row.

Markus, M.L. (1983), Power politics and MIS implementation, *Communication of the ACM*, 26, pp. 430–444.

Mégie, M.-F. (2005), "La communication en soins à domicile", in *La communication professionnelle en santé* (C. Richard and M.-T. Lussier), Saint-Laurent, Éditions du Renouveau Pédagogique inc., pp. 763–787.

Rabardel, P. (1995), *Les hommes et les technologies: Une approche cognitive des instruments contemporains*, Paris, Armand Colin.

Richard, C., Lussier, M.-T. (2005), "Les manifestations et les composantes d'une relation", in *La communication professionnelle en santé* (C. Richard and M-T. Lussier), Saint-Laurent, Éditions du Renouveau Pédagogique inc., pp. 35–59.

Richard, C., Lussier, M.-T., Gerard, F. (2005), "La gestion des émotions", in *La communication professionnelle en santé* (C. Richard and M.-T. Lussier), Saint-Laurent, Éditions du Renouveau Pédagogique inc., pp. 231–265.

Schermerhorn, J.R., Hunt, J.G., Osborn, R.N. (2002), *Comportement humain et organisation*, Québec, Éditions du Renouveau Pédagogique inc.

Schermerhorn, J.R., Templer, A.J., Cattaneo, R.J., Hunt, J.G., Osborn, R.N. (1992), *Managing Organizational Behavior*, J. Wiley, Toronto.

Teneau, G. (2006), *La résistance au changement organisationnel. Perspectives sociocognitives*, Paris, L'Harmattan.

Valenduc, G. (2005), *La technologie, un jeu de société. Au-delà du déterminisme technologique et du constructivisme social*, Collection Sciences et Enjeux, Louvain, Academio Bruylant.

Vidaillet, B. (2003), "Exercice de sensemaking", in *Le sens de l'action* (B. Vidaillet), Paris, Vuibert, pp. 35–50.

Weick, K. (2001a), "Technology as Equivoque: Sensemaking in New Technologies", in K.E. Weick, *Making Sense of the Organization*, Blackwell Publishing, pp. 148–175.

Weick, K. (2001b). "Organizational Redesign as Improvisation", in K.E. Weick, *Making Sense of the Organization*, Oxford, Blackwell Publishing, pp. 57–91.

Weick, K.E. (1969), *Social Psychology of Organizing*, Reading, MA, Addison Westley.

Weick, K.E. (1995), *Sensemaking in Organizations*, Foundations for Organizational Science, Thousand Oaks, CA, Sage Publications.

PART III
Effecting Change

It is easy to think that individual customers have little power when faced with the power of large organization, from which goods and services must be purchased. Often there is a tendency to think that if we are not happy with those goods or services, or even with the organization itself, then our only alternative is to not purchase those goods and services. Thus we must either purchase alternatives from another organization or manage without. Of course this is a simplistic view of the relationship between customers and their suppliers as organizations are reluctant to lose customers. In general it costs around six times as much to attract a customer as it does to retain an existing customer, so organizations will inevitable try to retain customers as well as attract new ones. This view of the power relationship between individuals and organizations is also somewhat simplistic as customers have exerted significant influences upon organizations, particularly when acting in concert. In this chapter therefore we are going to consider the ways in which individuals can, and have, influenced organizations through their actions.

The Social Contract is a legitimating theory for CSR and describes the extent to which people and corporations surrender power for the benefit of a better functioning society. One of the perennial debates in CSR is the extent to which this should happen due to the ethical principles of those involved and the extent to which government regulation is required. In other words there is a debate about the relative merits of ethics and regulation, which has been heightened by the recent financial crisis. All the argument is situated in the debates about the free market system and its strengths and weaknesses so we must start by examining this and the philosophical underpinnings of it. The starting point needs to be Classical Liberal Theory and then Utilitarianism which was developed from it.

Classical Liberal Theory started to be developed in the seventeenth century by such writers as John Locke as a means of explaining how society operated, and should operate, in an era in which the Divine Right of Kings to rule and to run society for their own benefit had been challenged and was generally considered to be inappropriate for the society which then existed. Classical Liberalism is founded upon the two principles of reason and rationality: reason in that everything had a logic which could be understood and agreed with by all, and rationality in that every decision made was made by a person in the light of what their evaluation had shown them to be for their greatest benefit. Classical Liberalism therefore is centred upon the individual, who is assumed to be rational and would make rational decision, and is based upon the need to give freedom to every individual to pursue his/her own ends. It is therefore a philosophy of the pursuance of self-interest. Society, insofar as it existed and was considered to be needed, was therefore merely an aggregation of these individual self-interests. This aggregation was considered to be a sufficient explanation for the need for society. Indeed Locke argued that the whole purpose of society was to protect the rights of each individual and to safeguard these private rights.

There is, however, a problem with this allowing of every individual the complete freedom to follow his/her own ends and to maximize his/her own welfare. This problem is that in some circumstances this welfare can only be created at the expense of other individuals. It is through this conflict between the rights and freedoms of individuals that problems occur in society. It is for this reason therefore that de Tocqueville argued that there was a necessary function for government within society. He argued that the function of government therefore was the regulation of individual transactions so as to safeguard the rights of all individuals as far as possible.

Although this philosophy of individual freedom was developed as the philosophy of Liberalism it can be seen that this philosophy has been adopted by the Conservative governments throughout the world, as led by the UK government in the 1980s. This philosophy has led increasingly to the reduction of state involvement in society and the giving of freedom to individuals to pursue their own ends, with regulation providing a mediating mechanism where deemed necessary. It will be apparent, however, that there is a further problem with Liberalism and this is that the mediation of rights between different individuals only works satisfactorily when the power of individuals is roughly equal. Plainly this situation never arises between all individuals and this is the cause of one of the problems with society.

CHAPTER 8
The Management and Acceptance of Diversity

NATALIA DANKOVA

Introduction

The terms *multiculturalism* and *multilingualism* are most often used when speaking of a society. The term *multiculturalism* has become so common that it is rarely defined. I will use it as defined by Vinsonneau (1997):

> Multiculturalism is a social system in which diverse socio-ethnic groups coexist and maintain their respective characteristics. This occurs first because of the will of the actors involved who are motivated by a desire to protect their distinct identities, and second, because of the sheer impossibility of these groups achieving integration (or being assimilated), in the wider social scheme. (Vinsonneau, 1997: 180)

For modern society, multiculturalism has become both a problem and an ambition. By examining different laws, policies and other measures aimed at managing multiculturalism, it becomes clear that multiculturalism is seen as the sum of many cultures, languages and groups that share the same geographical space. One could ask: if the people who make up a society belong to a single culture or speak a single language, how can we build a multicultural and multilingual society? Tacking culture upon culture and language upon language only results in creating ghettos of varying sizes. We rarely speak of a multicultural individual. I would even go so far as to say that there is a certain fear of multicultural and multilingual people: at will, they can change their language, behaviour, references, country, passport ... *How many masks do these people wear? What is their true face?* For the people in question, there is no simple answer to simple questions such as *Where are you from?* or *What is your mother tongue?* Multiculturalism, as an integrated concept experienced by an individual, is not understood by those who see themselves as belonging to a single culture. Worse, it stirs up doubt: *Well, who do you feel you are?*

When speaking of countries, do people realize that, for example, 76 languages are spoken in France,[1] and in Canada,[2] over 100? Multilingualism, as a concept, is quite repressed.

The Linguistic Landscape

All of the languages spoken today have multiple roots; they are the result of a cyclical process of assimilation and diversification. Latin eliminated numerous languages along its path, while paving the way for new languages, the Romance languages, which have maintained traces of dead languages by integrating foreign linguistic material. Gallic peasants certainly had no idea they would be assimilated on the spot. What is more, they did not have any far-fetched ideas about going to live elsewhere. Today, many people move abroad, be it voluntarily or not. The practices of migration have led us to become conscious of the phenomenon of assimilation. Slow, imperceptible assimilation has become conscious and predictable assimilation. Unlike the Gallic peasants, immigrants know from the start, or learn later on, that a new language and culture will find their way into their lives, homes, and kitchens. They may come to miss the lost or threatened paradise of their culture. They will fight for their rights to protect the country they left behind. They will swear to return to their homeland. At the same time, they will learn a new language, new ways of doing things and of thinking. Learning is inevitable and will occur over a short period or a longer one. They will see their children speaking a new language without an accent. They can also cloister themselves in their ghetto for as long as they wish.

Canada remains one of the rare countries to promote immigration for demographic and economic reasons. Immigrants can take English and French language courses free of charge during their first five years in Canada, but the province of Quebec refuses to offer English classes to immigrants. In English Canada, language classes are given by community organizations, while in Quebec, the department of immigration and of cultural communities manages language training in a centralized manner.

In Canada, integration depends on the linguistic option chosen, as the desire to integrate in English or in French implies two different processes. First of all, Canada's Anglophone population is characterized by great cultural diversity: in Ontario, for example, one person out of five belongs to a visible minority[3] and one person out of four was born in a different country. In Quebec, visible minorities represent 7 per cent of the population,[4] while one person out of ten was born in a different country. Urban centres with high concentrations of immigrant populations, such as Toronto,

---

1   Source: "Les langues de la France", B. Cerquiglini (1999). http://www.culture.gouv.fr/culture/dglf/lang-reg/rapport_cerquiglini/langues-france.html#ancre84582/ consulted March 24, 2009.

2   Source: Statistics Canada, Census 2001. http://www12.statcan.ca/english/census01/Products/Analytic/companion/lang/canada.cfm/ consulted March 24. 2009.

3   Statistics Canada uses the following classification: Classification for visible minority: Chinese, South Asian (e.g., East Indian, Pakistani, Punjabi, Sri Lankan), Black (e.g., African, Haitian, Jamaican, Somali), Arab/West Asian (e.g., Armenian, Egyptian, Iranian, Lebanese, Moroccan), Filipino, South East Asian (e.g., Cambodian, Indonesian, Laotian, Vietnamese), Latin American, Japanese, Korean, Other. Non-visible minority: Aboriginal, White. Source: http://www.statcan.gc.ca/concepts/definitions/minority01-minorite01a-eng.htm/ consulted March, 24. 2009. Also, the term "audible minority" is used more and more, especially in journalistic texts.

4   Source: Statistics Canada, Census 2001. www40.statcan.ca/ consulted March 24, 2009.

Montreal or Vancouver, attract more immigrants than other areas. A foreign accent in an English speaker is more readily accepted than a foreign accent in a French speaker, notably in publicity, customer service and telemarketing.[5] There is no doubt that, in a North American context, English offers more possibilities than French. This is why many francophone immigrants choose to live in English. With regard to francophone immigration, the province of Quebec selects candidates for immigration. The desire to attract francophone immigrants stems from the political will to ensure the survival of the French language, the number of French speakers continuing to be on the decline. After two failed attempts at independence,[6] Quebec is shifting into survival mode with regard to French. In the past, Quebec's demands contributed to the awareness of duality and bilingualism in Canada. However, Canada's new official stance on multiculturalism aims not only at protecting the integrity of the country's territory, but at diluting separatist aspirations by putting all of the different ethnic groups on a level playing field. Canada must manage its diversity. The problem lies in how it will do this.

Canada's colonial past is reflected in the vocabulary Canadians use to describe themselves and others. Anglophones and Francophones refer to themselves respectively as English and French, even though typically, the French are understood to live in France and the English, in England. The term *Canadian*, in use since 1870, originally referred to the Francophones of Canada who were becoming aware of their identity after France's loss of Canada. Today, in principle, the term Canadian refers to a citizen of Canada, while in practice, *Canadians* are mostly Anglophones. But who are the others? When speaking of the Francophones of Quebec, it is politically correct to refer to them as "Quebecers". Quebecers become Canadians, briefly, when they go through customs. Different names are given to immigrants: we can say NewQuebecers, NewCanadians, newcomers. On the other end of the spectrum, there is an explicit, derogatory term used in Quebec, "les importés", which translates to "the imported". There are also concepts such as WASPs (White Anglo-Saxon Protestant). Despite mixed marriages and bilingualism on an individual basis, Canadians rarely introduce themselves as bilingual. At a time when multiculturalism and bilingualism are hot topics, there is no exchange programme between Francophone and Anglophone establishments that teach English or French as a second language (L2). The two solitudes are snubbing one another. Francophones learn English – they have no choice. Anglophones also learn French, but let's be honest; this is not always motivated by altruistic or philanthropic aspirations. Often, Anglophones learn French in order to be eligible for higher ranking positions, most of them requiring bilingualism. French immersion classes are very popular in English Canada and the number of classes offered has been on the rise in recent years. It is important to specify that there are language programmes offered in the two official languages, but the vast majority of people registered are those learning French as a second language. According to Statistics Canada, the number of people who identify as bilingual is growing. However, censuses do not validate these statements. It is difficult to evaluate second or foreign language skills, the frequency of exchange in these languages or the quality of these exchanges in that language. To this effect, McRoberts (1997) states:

---

5   No studies have been conducted on this issue. This statement stems from our own observations and personal experiences with both languages in Canada.

6   During the referendums of 1980 and 1995 in Quebec, the population was asked to make a decision about the sovereignty of Quebec. The motion in question was defeated both times.

> *The federal government's efforts have had a demonstrable and impressive impact in the case of personal bilingualism. No longer is bilingualism being restricted primarily to francophones; indeed, the proportion of bilinguals has increased in every province. Yet there are qualifications to this success. [...] One can question the meaningfulness of respondents' claims to census takers that they have a working knowledge of another language. In fact, a study of the graduates of high school immersion programs found that 90 per cent were unable to follow French-language university courses. (McRoberts, 1997: 108)*

The efforts of the federal government depend on an impressive budget geared toward language training. Nevertheless, it is still too early to rejoice in concrete results. The government has committed to offering services in both languages, but at times, access to these services, and their quality, leaves something to be desired. As an example, we can mention border services that are managed by a federal agency, the Canada Border Services Agency. Even in the large international airports of Toronto and Vancouver, bilingualism is not enforced: there are few bilingual agents working with travellers (while one could expect that they might all be bilingual), which results in longer waiting times for those wishing to communicate in French. Agents' comprehension and oral expression skills in French are often mediocre. There are few studies that focus on the quality of the services offered in French in places other than Quebec. In the document entitled *Services en français en Ontario pour les femmes francophones victimes de violence* (French services in Ontario for francophone women victims of violence), author Mélodie Guilbeault (2005) points out that:

> *It is not enough for the Ontario government to offer the possibility of obtaining services in French. In order to protect the Franco-Ontarian minority, to allow the progress of French and to promote its equality with English, French services must be reliable and of a comparable quality to those offered in English. Indeed, a lesser quality service in French encourages the use of faster, better quality English services and the assimilation of Franco-Ontarians, who get out of the habit of using their language and, eventually, le ability to function in French in an official context. (Guilbeault, 2005: 16)*

Guilbeault draws attention to the fact that "the lack of jurisprudence in establishing the application of the *Policy on Discrimination and Language*[7] (Ontario Human Rights Commission, 1996) stems from the services offered by the government" (2005: 11). Most human rights commissions in Canada do not recognize discrimination based on language as a pattern of discrimination on its own, in the same way as discrimination based on race, ethnic origin, ancestry, gender, and so on. Discrimination based on language is therefore associated with discrimination based on ancestry, place of origin or race, or to all of these motives.

Certain laws concerning linguistic issues are interpreted differently by different people. *The Charter of the French Language*, also called *Law 101*,[8] adopted in 1977 by the government of Quebec, proclaimed French as the language of labour relations and public signs; it also limited access to public education in English. For example, the children

---

[7] See the wording of the law at: http://www.ohrc.on.ca/en/resources/Policies/lang/view or https://ozone.scholarsportal.info/bitstream/1873/6901/1/10302365.pdf/ Consulted May 3, 2009.

[8] See the full text of Law 101 at: http://www.olf.gouv.qc.ca/charte/charte/index.html/ Consulted April 7, 2009.

of immigrants who move to Quebec must automatically be schooled in French. For immigrants coming to Quebec, it is not always clear why their children are not given access to English schooling or bilingual schooling in the name of the survival of the French language in Quebec, when at the start they knew they were immigrating to a bilingual country. They therefore don't have the opportunity to choose English schooling if they wish to.[9] Section 78.1 of *Law 101* stipulates that "No person may permit or tolerate a child's receiving instruction in English if he is ineligible therefor." Section 79 stipulates that "A school body not already giving instruction in English in its schools is not required to introduce it and shall not introduce it without express and prior authorization of the Minister of Education." *Law 101* was vehemently attacked by human rights defenders and caused a massive exodus of Anglophones living in the province after its adoption.

The fragmented nature of policies concerning languages and cultural diversity are mostly due to the organization of decision-making authorities: the federal government, provincial and territorial governments and municipalities each act at their level, which prevents the promotion and the realization of the dream of multiculturalism and bilingualism across the Canadian territory.

Immigrants quickly become aware of the tension between Anglophones and Francophones. They come to understand that issues surrounding Native populations are taboo, even though we are just beginning to talk about the violence inflicted upon these populations during attempts at forced assimilation. In all the talk about diversity and the improved integration of immigrants, we tend to forget the basics: the indigenous people who were here before the French and English colonizers, and whom we prefer not to speak about today. The gap between what is being said officially, and what is happening, is plain to see.

Official policies on multiculturalism and on the use of languages do not inhibit individual interpretation of diversity, which is often unconscious. The existence of these policies contributes to changing mentalities in this regard. We cannot help but be pleased that the desire of living in harmony in a multicultural society translates into a set of laws and policies. However, the fear of the other, of the stranger, continues to operate at an unconscious level (cf. Freud, 1919, Kaës et al., 1998, Dankova, 2007). This fear establishes psychic defence mechanisms that manifest themselves as xenophobia, racism and linguicism. The power of this archaic fear is often underestimated. Boris Cyrulnik (2008), who analyses individual and collective behaviour in the face of adversity or suffering, leading to the healing of the individual or the group wrote:

Persecutive violence lays the foundation of a group. The hatred of the persecutor cements the persecuted together and legitimizes their counter-violent defence. The other group responds the same way, which sets in motion a process of complicity of extremes in which each person reinforces the position of the survivors of the other group by seeking to destroy them. This classic phenomenon allows us to speak of "archaic socialization", "vendettas", "clan wars" and "submission to the past", since, a few generations later, everyone still think it necessary to destroy the other at the risk of their own destruction. This codestructiveness preserves the identity of the group, builds on its myth and helps it gain power. We can call this phenomenon "resistance", but certainly not "resilience", since in repeating itself, the past prevents new developments. (Cyrulnik, 2008: 77–78)

---

9   There are no English immersion schools in Quebec, contrary to the rest of Canada.

Consciously or not, *too much* diversity is perceived as a threat to the country: we have already heard Quebec's separatist ideas and the territorial claims of Native people. The "melting-pot" remains the dominant model, in the absence of other models. In order to accept diversity, one must first to know it. It is necessary to step outside one's frame of references and usual points of reference. The discovery of the other and the acceptance of that person is an individual and voluntary process.

Facing diversity inevitably leads people to doubt, to relativism and to comparison. A foreigner who arrives in Canada is troubling to Canadians. If Canada has separated Church and State, why are oaths still sworn on the Bible in courts of law and why are prayers still said at the beginning of meetings of certain public organizations? The discovery of diversity is a mutual process, a slow process that takes place through education, cohabitation, sharing, knowledge of the other and shared experiences in different contexts.

Once the multicultural ideal has been proclaimed, the next step is to make it happen. The *2006–2007 Annual Report on the Operation of the Canadian Multiculturalism Act* presents the achievements and challenges in this regard. For example, we can make reference to Health Canada's "$18.3 million investment to help internationally trained health professionals work in Canada"[10] or the creation, in collaboration with ethno cultural groups, of the *Canada Food Guide*[11] aimed at the parents of children aged 2 to 12 years old and to people in challenging socioeconomic situations (page 39). The *Guide* is available in 10 languages other than English and French. Among the achievements, there are training workshops given in the workplace that focus on the respect of diversity, on the perception of Aboriginal and Inuit peoples, on "Cultural Awareness Islam/Muslim" (page 23). We also learn that many federal organizations have hired "employees of ethno cultural backgrounds" (page 21). Beyond the awkward language used in the *Report* that can sometimes take on pejorative undertones, we can ask ourselves how we can learn about respect through a workshop such as the ones offered, how frequent is generalization and overgeneralization of cultural practices and traits, what are the clichés that represent others, what is meant by "Islam and Muslim cultures (!)" or "employees of ethno cultural backgrounds"?[12]

Talk about multiculturalism implies a stereotyped vision and the desire to classify people into categories, to separate them and to distinguish them based on language, religion, ethnic origin or culture, another word often used without any sort of definition. It also effectively masks certain people's incapability, on an individual level, of living with others. In the hope that established rules and a set of guidelines will allow the differences of society to be managed, these people feel released from the obligation of being interested in others and opening themselves up to them. It would be utopic to think that once the classifications are made and the rules put into place, the problems linked to intolerance and discrimination will disappear, since there will always be differences.

---

10   See http://www.cic.gc.ca/multi/rpt/105-eng.asp page 19 consulted May 13, 2009. In Canada, there is a dire need for doctors and nurses. Many people do not have a family doctor, and the waiting lists for certain surgical procedures are dangerously long.

11   See http://www.hc-sc.gc.ca/fn-an/food-guide-aliment/myguide-monguide/index-eng.php/ consulted May 13, 2009.

12   In French, the word "antécédent" is used for "background". This French word is often used in the sense of "record", as in "criminal record". We can therefore question the choice of this pejorative word in the French.

In trying to understand the problems linked to diversity as a whole, we looked into the issue of racial profiling in Canada. Racial profiling based on the connection between certain crimes and the frequency with which they are committed by people of certain ethnic groups is not a practice unique to Canada. In the document entitled *Le profilage racial: mise en contexte et définition* (2005) (Racial profiling: context and definition),[13] the Quebec Human Rights and Youth Rights Commission[14] reports:

> *These rules of practice were imported [...] to Canada during the 1990s, after members of the Royal Canadian Mounted Police received training in the United States. The people who were then generally victims of profiling were Black, Latino-American and Aboriginal. However, since September 11th, 2001, people of Arab descent and of the Islamic religion have been added to the list. (Le profilage racial: mise en contexte et définition, 2005: 5)*

While recognizing the existence of racial profiling in Quebec,[15] the Commission deplores the absence of recent data that would allow for the analysis of the depth of the phenomenon (*Le profilage racial: mise en contexte et définition*, 2005: 14). After analysing the definitions of racial profiling given by other organizations, the Quebec Human Rights and Youth Rights Commission has proposed the following definition:

> *Racial profiling refers to any action taken by a person or persons in authoritative positions with regard to a person or group, for reasons based on the safety, security or protection of the public, based on real or presumed factors of belonging such as race, colour, ethnic or national original or religion, without real motive or reasonable suspicion, that as a result, exposes the person to questioning or different treatment.*
>
> *Racial profiling also includes any action of a people in authoritative positions that disproportionately apply a measure on segments of society specifically because of their racial, ethnic, national or religious origin, real or presumed. (Le profilage racial: mise en contexte et définition, 2005: 15)*

How can we reconcile talk of multiculturalism and tolerance on the one hand, and the stigmatization of prejudices toward certain people on the other? Responding to complaints about discrimination is not simple. The accused can speak of security reasons or the confidentiality of the orders given by superiors. The absence of witnesses and of explicit proof, and the difficulty of accessing information make inquiries more complicated. Speaking of discrimination in public is not an easy task. Talk of multiculturalism reduces the vigilance of citizens: "What are you talking about? Canada is a welcoming country. What's more, it is the only country with a policy on multiculturalism. Discrimination must be something you are imagining. It's all in your head." And the dream of multiculturalism becomes a nightmare for those who experience discrimination regularly: "We look after Canadians first", we hear when looking for daycare for our children, or in the waiting room of a medical clinic of a doctor who is not taking any more patients. Of course, this

---

[13] See http://www.cdpdj.qc.ca/fr/publications/docs/profilage_racial_definition.pdf/ consulted May 14, 2009.
[14] The Commission des droits de la personne et des droits de la jeunesse du Québec.
[15] Every Canadian province has a human rights commission. The document quoted here was published by Quebec's commission, the *Commission des droits de la personne et des droits de la jeunesse du Québec*, and only concerns the province of Quebec.

does not happen every day. But how many times do we have to hear this before shut ourselves into our own ghettos? Official discourse will remain just talk until individuals have integrated the words into practice, each at their own level. To what extent are populations ready to adhere to an idea or a policy, and what do politicians and managers know about it?

Reasonable Accommodations

The importance given to the cultural diversity of immigrants in the receiving society was the focus of a public consultation organized in 2007 by the Bouchard-Taylor Commission on reasonable accommodations. While the purpose of this commission was initially to study possible accommodations of a religious nature – for example, whether or not Islamic headscarves or religious symbols should be allowed in public establishments – the survey launched a process of reflection on the spectrum of questions surrounding immigration and the diversity that goes hand in hand with it. The Commission's *Report* states "It is with regret that we had to remove from our mandate the aboriginal question" (Bouchard and Taylor, 2008b: 35); thus, the diversity in question is essentially linked to immigration and not to the diversity linked to the past (for example, the existence of Aboriginal people or Anglophone and Francophone Quebecers.)

It was decided that average citizens should be given the opportunity to voice their opinions, rather than launch an intellectual debate on the matter. This approach was criticized over and over again, but the choice to proceed this way can also be defended. The spectacle that resulted from the consultation and the reactions and comments of the rest of Canada deserve to be seen and heard. Based on the consultation, the *Report* presents itself frankly, stating that the identity of French Canadians is in crisis:

> *Quebecers of French-Canadian ancestry are still not at ease with their twofold status as a majority in Québec and a minority in Canada and North America. (Bouchard and Taylor, 2008b: 19)*

and

> *It must be noted that the French-Canadian past has been and always will be fraught with tension. A concern for survival has been a hallmark of this past, which has sustained a keen awareness of failures and a desire for affirmation. (Bouchard and Taylor, 2008b: 186)*

A subject that has been widely treated is that of the place of religion in the public domain: in schools, in places of work and within public organizations. Although Quebec society has become much less religious over the last few years and the Church has lost much of its influence and many of its followers, the loss of ground of religion is seen as a threat. In Quebec, there is confusion between religion, language and culture – the discourse on survival points to any of these elements to justify its *raison d'être*. The culture-language-religion blend finds its place in the Report of the Bouchard-Taylor Commission that attempts clumsily to convince readers of its merits:

> *Let us return to the identity-related anxiety that we mentioned. It is complicated, basically, because French-speaking Québec embodies traditions and values related to reception and solidarity, perhaps the legacy of over three centuries of Catholicism, perhaps also of the lengthy experience of settlement. […] We believe that these values do indeed exist but that they cannot fully express themselves.*[16] (Bouchard and Taylor, 2008b: 188)

We wonder whether the authors consider "values related to reception and solidarity" outside the realm of Catholicism and whether other communities and societies also "[embody] traditions and values". Certain questions arise upon reading the rest of the quote, in which we learn that these values, they believe exist, but "cannot fully express themselves".

The *Report* details the events and the measures taken in order to solve the problems linked to reasonable accommodations on a case by case basis. The recommendations published in the *Report*, all of them predictable in our opinion, are articulated around the following point: the redefinition of politics and programmes linked to interculturalism and to secularization, a better understanding of others and of diversity. Practices based on harmonization and the treatment of requests for accommodations, the integration of immigrants with a focus on francization and the improvement of their socioeconomic conditions, as well as the fight against different types of discrimination. That being said, many passages of the Bouchard-Taylor Commission Report, tone down the final recommendations. By avoiding the issue of Aboriginal people, the Commission also avoids that of Anglophones in Quebec. The discourse on survival remains a recurrent theme:

> *… the identity inherited from the French-Canadian past is perfectly legitimate and it must survive because it is a source of diversity*[17] *…* (Bouchard and Taylor, 2008b: 190)

The debates that took place during the inquiry into reasonable accommodations, that in our opinion were a waste of time if not a political blunder, highlighted the difficulty of combining the values of the Declaration of Human Rights with the personal values of different cultural and religious groups, specifically with regard to the distribution and the management of vital space. Wieviorka (2007) writes to this effect:

> *What is striking, beyond the anti-intellectual climate surrounding the commission, is really the mounting tensions surrounding "reasonable accommodations", that is, the principle of making an effort to refuse to choose between two wrongs … Universalists, frightened by the wave of communitarianists' demands, and sometimes propped up by a certain hostile form of nationalism towards immigration or Islam, want no more of what they see as a Trojan horse, a practice that, in the name of negotiation and tolerance, would end up calling into question the values they are attached to; and, on their side, communities seem to stiffen in the face of what they consider to be non-negotiable.*

---

16   Highlighted for the purposes of this text.

17   "A source of diversity" is the translation of the corresponding line in the French text "une source de richesse" – literally, "a source of richness". The English translation therefore does not communicate exactly the same message as the original French version.

The debates have shown that lack of knowledge about others inhibits reasonable accommodations in practice. Without better mutual understanding and intercultural exchanges between groups, diversity, rather than being a source of richness, remains a problem.

Conclusion

Canada is a young country still looking for its identity. But identity cannot be defined through negation: "We are not British, we are not French, we are not American". Things cannot be done in half measures. In everyday life, everyone takes on many roles without being confined to a single one. People who are truly multicultural understand that it is possible to speak several languages and to belong to many cultures, without having to divide themselves into different pieces. And when there are encounters, they are encounters between individuals, not groups. These encounters do not lead to assimilation, but to a crossing of cultures. Wieviorka (2005) points out that:

> *While cultural phenomena are destabilized as a result of the crossing of cultures, they also become movable, follow surprising paths and take root in unexpected places. Original cultural forms can therefore be invented without completely supplanting those from which they come from. (Wieviorka, 2005, p. 75)*

Communitarianism leads to segregation and slows down integration. Ghettos may very well operate autonomously, but they will always remain ghettos:

> *The temptation of "community" is the temptation of fleeing the fragility of the human condition to curl up in the illusion of the stability of calm and order ... Totalitarianism prospered in mass society. Communitarianism flourishes in a society of closed societies. (Macé-Scaron, 2001, pp. 125–126)*

Canada chooses its immigrants based on defined criteria. Diversity does not seem to pose a problem when comes time to select candidates for immigration. In fact, immigration has become a veritable industry. One could make the case that if the government is intent on "selling" immigration visas, it is also responsible for offering appropriate client services. To do this, it must reflect on the management and the integration of the diversity it wanted in the first place, to ensure a way of living together in which no one gets left behind, all in the respect of human dignity.

The kaleidoscope of Canadian policies, laws and practices allows us to reflect on the challenges linked to managing multiculturalism and official bilingualism. Even though each country has its own characteristics, the case of Canada is at the heart of the critical discussions stimulated by the cultural and linguistic aspects of modern society, as well as the increasing mobility of the population. A thorough study of local experiences will contribute to improvements at many levels, not only through the creation of new policies and programmes, but also through public consultations. Education and dialogue between representatives of different groups will also lead to the consolidation of the ideal of multiculturalism in a society that is more respectful of differences.

Translated by Julie Anne Ryan

References

Bouchard, G. and C. Taylor (2008a). *Fonder l'avenir. Le temps de conciliation*. Rapport final. Gouvernement du Québec. Disponible en ligne: www.accommodements.qc.ca/documentation/rapports/rapport-final-integral-fr.pdf/ consulted April 11, 2009.

Bouchard, G. and C. Taylor (2008b). *Building the Future. A Time for Reconciliation*. Final Report. Gouvernement du Québec: http://www.accommodements.qc.ca/documentation/rapports/rapport-final-integral-en.pdf/ consulted April 11, 2009.

Census 2001, Statistics Canada, http://www12.statcan.ca/francais/census01/Products/Analytic/companion/lang/canada_f.cfm#multilingual/ consulted March 24, 2009.

Cerquiglini, B. (1999). *Les langues de la France*. http://www.culture.gouv.fr/culture/dglf/lang-reg/rapport_cerquiglini/langues-france.html#ancre84582/ consulted March 24, 2009.

Commission des droits de la personne et des droits de la jeunesse du Québec. *Le profilage racial: mise en contexte et définition* (2005): http://www.cdpdj.qc.ca/fr/publications/docs/profilage_racial_definition.pdf/ consulted May 14, 2009.

Commission ontarienne des droits de la personne. *La Politique concernant la discrimination et langue* (1996): http://www.ohrc.on.ca/en/resources/Policies/lang/view or https://ozone.scholarsportal.info/bitstream/1873/6901/1/10302365.pdf/ consulted May 3, 2009.

Cyrulnik, B. (2008). *Autobiographie d'un épouvantail*. Paris, Odile Jacob.

Dankova, N. (2007). "De la peur de l'étranger – à l'intégration des immigrants diplômés ", in J. Archibald et J.-L. Chiss (éds). *La langue et l'intégration des immigrants*. Paris, L'Harmattan, p. 259–267.

Freud, S. (1919). "L'inquiétante étrangeté", in *L'Inquiétante étrangeté et autres essais*, Paris, Gallimard, 1985.

Gouvernement du Québec. *La Charte de la langue française* (Loi 101): http://www.olf.gouv.qc.ca/charte/charte/index.html/ consulted April 7, 2009.

Government of Canada. *Canadian Multiculturalism Act* (1988): http://www.parl.gc.ca/information/library/PRBpubs/936-e.htm/ consulted May 13, 2009.

Government of Canada. *Official Languages Act* (1988). http://laws.justice.gc.ca/en/showtdm/cr/SOR-92-48 or http://www.pch.gc.ca/pgm/lo-ol/legisltn/bill_s3_fact-eng.cfm/ consulted May 13, 2009.

Government of Canada. *The 2006–2007 Annual Report on the Operation of the Canadian Multiculturalism Act*: http://www.cic.gc.ca/multi/rpt/105-eng.asp/ consulted May 13, 2009.

Guilbeault, M. (2005). *Services en français en Ontario pour les femmes francophones victimes de violence*. Document rédigé pour l'AOcVF.

Kaës, R. et al. (1998). *Différence culturelle et souffrances de l'identité*. Paris, Dunod.

Macé-Scaron, J. (2001). *La tentation communautaire*. Paris, Plon.

McRoberts, K. (1997). *Misconceiving Canada: The Struggle for National Unity*. Toronto – New York – Oxford, Oxford University Press.

McRoberts, K. (1999). *Un pays à refaire*. Montréal, Éd. Boréal (French Translation).

Vinsonneau, G. (1997). *Culture et comportement*. Paris, A. Colin.

Wieviorka, M. (2005). *La différence. Identités culturelles: enjeux, débats et politiques*. Paris, Éditions de l'Aube.

Wieviorka, M. (2007). "La fin du multiculturalisme", *La Presse*, September 24, 2007.

CHAPTER 9
Enhancing Human Dignity through Philosophical Education

SERGIO CASTRILLÓN

The denial of basic human rights, the destruction of the environment, the deadly conditions under which people (barely) survive, the lack of a meaningful future for the thousands of children I noted in my story, ... [this] is a reality that millions of people experience in their bodies every day. Educational work that is not connected deeply to a powerful understanding of these realities ... is in danger of losing its soul. The lives of our children demand no less.
(Michael W. Apple, Remembering Capital)

How then is perfection to be sought? Wherein lies our hope?
In education, and in nothing else.
(Kant, 1963, p. 252)

Introduction

Just by looking at the newspapers, in any given day, it would be easy to notice that our contemporary world, characterized by economic upheavals, social inequality, cultural dislocations, political ruptures, famine, threats of terrorism, and so on, poses multiples threats to the human dignity of millions of people.

To a great extent the current dynamics in the world, with its positive and negative outcomes, could be explained in terms of the economic and social trends propelled by different kind of organizations; among which big corporations, multinationals, and other types of profit oriented businesses occupy a significant part of the scene.

These organizations are led by professional managers who are usually trained and hired to make decisions directed towards the maximization of profits, most often from a selfish and short-term perspectives.

No doubt that technological innovations as well as advancements in knowledge about economic phenomena have contributed to the rising of the standards of living. Nevertheless, since the very beginnings of the industrial revolution the pursuit of progress has been accompanied by the emergence of negative externalities, not always visible but always painful for some people, who unfortunately have seldom been given the voice to denounce the undesirable situations they must endure.

In the face of so many unfair circumstances displayed by our societies, and acknowledging the influence of business organization, as well as the power held by managers, in this chapter we explore the potentialities that managers might have to promote the human dignity of the people affected by their decisions.

Defining Dignity

Dignity can be basically defined as (1) the quality or state of being worthy, honoured, or esteemed; or (2) high rank, office, or position: a legal title of nobility or honour (Merriam-Webster, 2003). These definitions and potential meanings evoke particular challenges to managers. First: how can managers preserve the dignity and value of all the people affected by their actions and decisions? Second: how can managers themselves come to deserve the dignity of the offices they hold?

Both of these challenges require enhanced forms of education, different from the ones traditionally offered at business schools, which respond more to the mainstream concerns for maximizing profits or perfecting the operation of conventional business functions (Bennis and O'Toole, 2005; Des, 2003; Ghoshal, 2005; Kets de Vries, 1989, 1991; Marianne, 2004; White, 1995).

In this chapter I argue that a philosophical education, in orientation and contents, offers a unique possibility of contributing to the formation of a new breed of managers, capable of preserving and promoting the dignity and value of all the persons affected by the organizations they lead, while helping those same managers to become worthy and deserving of the dignity associated with the high positions, titles, honours and responsibilities that they hold.

The Challenge of Promoting the Dignity and Value of all Persons

The idea of human dignity necessarily evokes the ideals of greatness and noblesse to which all human beings are entitled, just because of the fact of being human. Let's remember that the first article of the Universal Declaration of Human Rights states that:

> *All human beings are born free and equal in dignity and rights. They are endowed with reason and conscience and should act towards one another in a spirit of brotherhood.*

From a philosophical perspective, Kant offers a simple but comprehensive justification about the dignity of humans, by stating that the rationality of human beings makes them autonomous and deserving of being treated as ends in themselves. To treat humans in a dignified way implies that each person is respected in her autonomy, and treated as an integral, purposeful being by herself, who shall not be treated in an instrumental way. In the words of Kant, the command for all of us is to:

> *Act so that you treat humanity, whether in your own person or in that of another, always as an end and never as a means only. (Wolff, 1969, p. 54)*

If managers were to accept and follow this form of the Kantian categorical imperative, new conceptions about their roles and responsibilities would have to be generated. In order to assure the dignity of all human beings directly involved or indirectly affected by the actions and omissions of the managers, organizations can no longer continue to ask of them the optimizations of economic transactions, or the supervision of business functions.

To foster dignity, while achieving other legitimate economic and social purposes, managers need to surmount certain limitations and develop a series of capabilities which are not nourished enough (or perhaps not at all in many cases) in the curriculum or the activities of many business schools.

To preserve and promote the inherent value and dignity of every person affected by a manager's job, it is first of all necessary that the manager becomes acquainted with the notion of dignity and its concrete manifestations in her own being, recognizing the pain of its absences and deficits, as well as the joy that its actualization represents.

After becoming genuinely familiar with the concept and reality of dignity in its own right, a manager can be truly capable of experiencing empathy towards others, and then become deeply concerned about the dignity of everyone affected by her/his decisions, and hopefully commits to actively promote their respect.

In order to do so, a manager willing to respect everyone's humanity, treating each one as an end, must exercise enhanced judiciousness and transcend the instrumental rationality which is precisely the kind of rationality conventionally used in the prevailing organizations of the contemporary world. Authors such as Max Weber denounced this situation about a century ago, and Theodor Adorno insisted by pointing out the unfortunate subordination of life to the technical and instrumental rationality.

If managers are to foster human dignity throughout organizational life, they must develop heightened emotional and cognitive capabilities. Besides, as Goleman has amply and sufficiently argued, emotional intelligence constitutes an avenue for success within organizations.

At the emotional level, the manager must learn to deal with the persons that represent and are represented by all the stakeholders, which involves the capacity to discern from different and often conflicting interests, and to get engaged in ethical dialogue, genuinely concerned in finding solutions through sincere listening and truthfulness.

This ideal attitude certainly involves the challenge of changing, and might not be considered convenient or feasible for most people that participate in business settings; nevertheless, in a world that faces so many aporias, perplexities and contradictions, that alternative becomes an inescapable quest. The inertial behaviour of doing more of the same will only exacerbate the negative problems engendered by current managerial practices.

The mastery of these new capabilities – emotional and cognitive – is required not only to better develop a conscious manager, but to make her capable of facing the resistances that will no doubt emerge as new ways of acting are proposed. Besides, a manager truly prepared to defend the idea of human dignity shall simultaneously be an embodiment and a spreader of the ideal concept, capable of ultimately helping others to develop such capabilities.

In other words, if managers are to promote the dignity and value of all the persons, they are to start nurturing the idea and reality of dignity within themselves, and afterwards emphatically nurturing and respecting it in others, while avoiding the traps and limitations of instrumental rationality.

The enhancing of all kinds of emotional and cognitive capabilities is highlighted as an indispensable quality in order to better communicate with different interest groups and experience authentic empathy towards them, therefore becoming more capable of overcoming the resistances that might rise when trying to manage organizations willing to adopt the idea of human dignity at their hearts. How can these ideals be achieved? As we will argue later, philosophical education provides a promising alternative.

THE CHALLENGE OF BEING *WORTHY* OF THE DIGNITY INHERENT TO THE POSITIONS, HONOURS AND RESPONSIBILITIES OF MANAGEMENT

Let us remember that the Merriam-Webster's dictionary provides a second sense of the definition of dignity, associating it with a high rank, office, or position or to a legal title of nobility or honour. From this perspective we can argue that another challenge for managers consists in turning the dignity inherent to a given position or title within the organization into one that is deserved on the merits of the performance of their work. In this order of ideas we ask: what are the responsibilities associated with the positions and titles of management? What does it mean for a manager to become dignified by her performance? How can she achieve this dignity?

In order to evaluate if a person is worthy of the dignity associated with the titles, ranks, offices and position of management, it becomes a *sine qua non* obligation to critically rethink the responsibilities associated with those same positions and offices.

Although a full reflection in this sense escapes the purposes and scope of this chapter, we can at least join the voices that denounce the short-sightedness of the *traditional* view that managers are mostly (some argue only) responsible towards shareholders; reclaiming that this view be replaced by a more holistic view that will favour the sustainability of all economic activities, and the respect for both human kind and the integrity of the whole ecosystem of life.

Because we share the conviction that management shall not be conceived as a simplistic, narrow, short-term oriented practice erected for the maximization of profits, but a complex art and social practice that is forged through the conjugation of multiple abilities of perception, action and reflection (among which we find the cognitive competences of several disciplines, usually taught in business schools, which are very relevant but to which management cannot and shall not be reduced), oriented towards the satisfaction of the legitimate risks of multiple stakeholders, we claim that managers, as key players within their organizations, play a unique role in society, which implies tremendous responsibility.

The worldwide ubiquity of organizations increases the expectations to comply with the challenge of truly deserving the honours and dignities associated with their power. In order to conquer that dignity, they must aspire and learn to operate in innocuous manners, while producing the goods and services that society requires.

How can this be done? What is the best way to prepare for and assume more comprehensive responsibilities? Absolute answers are not easy, probably impossible; but we argue that philosophical education can provide some useful clues.

Reflecting on the other questions proposed at the beginning of this section, and before elucidating the kind of philosophical education that we propose, we assert that if a manager is to be worthy of her position, she must earn the esteem of those potentially impacted by the direct and indirect consequences of any actions and omissions related to the attributes of the office and entitlements held.

A manager usually faces big threats towards the maintenance of the dignity of the post, as divergent interests, dilemmas and the pressures of the job might make it impossible to gain the approval of every stakeholder. Equally important is the fact that power asymmetries which usually favour the manager, even in relation to the shareholders, might lead to temptations that erode the dignity of a manager's job.

It is evident that managers hold privileged positions within the hierarchy of organizations which imply investitures of power and dignity that simultaneously oblige every manager (if they are to deserve the authority and respect needed to appeal to every stakeholder), to make every possible effort to develop and conquer a dignified position vis-à-vis themselves, their peers and other groups that deal with them. In this case the dignity granted by the position has to be confirmed by conquering it through a dignifying performance. But what does this mean?

We could equate a dignifying performance to an ethical performance, which necessarily implies the need for moral awareness and therefore for philosophical education. Or we could think about different frames to assess performance, for example, adopting a comprehensive model that might consider a manager's role from multiple perspectives, for example, interrogating the principles that inform managers' actions, or the actions themselves, along with their consequences (for a detailed proposal see Castrillón, 2007). Either way, articulating education through philosophy could really be part of a lofty solution to help managers assume their responsibilities and deserve the dignity embedded in their positions.

Explaining Philosophical Education

Let education be conceived on right lines, let natural gifts be developed as they should, let character be formed on moral principles, and in time the effects of this will reach even to the seat of government. (Kant, 1963, p. 253)

So far we have proposed philosophical education as a noble way to assure the dignity of both, managers and all the stakeholders they should care about, for philosophy serves the purpose of aiding the processes of learning, discovery, problem-solving, but especially of improvement of the self and of society through critical interrogation and the quest for the most sublime ideals.

Before we can demonstrate how philosophical education can contribute to nourish dignity in both of the senses discussed before, it's convenient to explain what we understand by the notion of philosophical education. Thus, and without pretending to be exhaustive in the approach, but aiming to provide a useful conceptualization, in the following segment we explain what we mean by philosophical education.

Let us recall that in essence philosophy means the love of wisdom, and education comes from the Latin word *educere*, meaning to lead forth. Combining both terms, philosophical education comes to mean: leading forth to the love of wisdom. Quite disruptive for a business school is not it?

Nevertheless, if we want to move towards a more comprehensive definition of management that transcends the immediate concern for resources and profits to gravitate instead around the idea of human dignity, while trying to harmonize the divergent interests of multiple stakeholders, we must recognize the benefit of aspiring towards more comprehensive ways of education, for example those involving the development of wisdom.

DEFINING WISDOM

Returning to our concern of conceiving an education capable of leading managers towards wisdom, it is important to recall that wisdom can be understood in several ways, all of them supportive of the ideal of human dignity.

Even though the concept of wisdom might represent different meanings, it is not necessarily ambivalent, for its possible senses are never contradictory. On the contrary they represent perspectives or attitudes that besides being compatible converge towards a common core which we will try to elucidate afterwards. As we will see, the singularity of each perspective reinforces the idea of wisdom as a complex and plural reality.

The word wisdom has been influenced by the Latin *sapiens*, (indicating rationality or intelligence, and linked to *sapience* or knowledge of God), but has its older origins in the Latin *sabius* and *sapius*, derived from *sapere*, which means having flavour or taste. This etymological rooting leads us to think that philosophy can never be insipid or dull, and that all its manifestations and avatars must always demonstrate good taste.

When we explore the possible definitions of the concept in French (*sagesse*), Spanish (*sabiduría*), and English (wisdom), we find the presence of varied shades of meaning, all of them gravitating around the same core of meaning and sense, which we relate to the Platonic idea of the good, for as Socrates said:

> *That which imparts* truth *to the known and the* power of knowing *to the knower is what I would have you term* the idea of good, *and this you will deem to be the cause of science, and of* truth *in so far as the latter becomes the subject of* knowledge; *beautiful too, as are both truth and knowledge, you will be right in esteeming this other nature as more beautiful than either ... (Plato, 1937, p. 770) (emphasis added)*

This brief quote synthesizes a significant dimension of the Platonic thinking that has so much influenced Western culture, and enables us to appreciate the links between the concepts of Goodness, Beauty and Truth, which emerge as constant aspirations in the quest for wisdom and a better ways of living, all throughout the human experience.

As we were saying, the definitions provided by the dictionaries of different languages are consistent with these ideals, that is, wisdom can be understood as (1) a prudent behaviour (*conducta prudente – comportement juste, raisonnable*), (2) Knowledge, insight (*conocimiento profundo – connaissance juste des choses, divines et humaines*), (3) Judicious judgment (*buen juicio – discernement*), or (4) a wise attitude, good sense (*cualidad de sabio, sensible – modération, calme supérieur joint aux connaissances, circonspection*).

These several meanings of the notion of "wisdom" demonstrate the presence of compatible senses, which could be manifested through specific behaviours, insightful forms of knowledge, decision procedures, the expression of values, or the embodiment of absolute principles.

The historic and multicultural permanence of compatible meanings indicates the unity, coherence and transcultural validity and force of the concept of wisdom, while inviting us to appreciate its rich diversity and stimulating plurality.

Thus, the concept of wisdom, although wide and polysemic, is never ambivalent or contradictory. The semantic flexibility is due to the varied spectrum of possibilities through which its related phenomena can be unfolded. All the nuances of meaning continue to gravitate around the conjunction of *sapiens* and *sapere*; that is, learning to behave, learning knowledge, learning to discern, and learning to be.

These different forms of learning, all immensely important for management, oblige us to rethink the education that is offered to those called to lead the organizations of the contemporary world, so they can be more responsible towards people and capable of respecting and promoting human dignity.

EDUCATING FOR HUMAN DIGNITY – ENACTING PHILOSOPHICAL EDUCATION

If we consider the several dimensions implied in the semantics of wisdom, then philosophical education must widen its scope in such a way that potential managers can be led towards (*educere*) each different form of wisdom; that is, those directed towards the praxis, the knowledge, the values and the being (Castrillón, 2008). In other words, it cannot be limited to just an intellectual activity, or a particular subject of study, as it is usually perceived through formal settings.

The philosophical education that we reclaim and propose addresses the integrity of the individual and the whole of society. It is simultaneously a concern about the contents and the methods, but mostly about the purposes.

Philosophical education as a set of contents

From the perspective of contents, we share the common expectation that "philosophy has as a distinctive subject-matter the most fundamental or general concepts and principles involved in thought, action and reality" (Mautner, 2000), and from that perspective suggest that managers have to become acquainted with those concepts and principles related to the lives of the people affected by their actions. It is our belief that that acquaintance must transcend a mere learning of descriptions, in order to involve actual experimentation and/or deep reflection about the realities and consequences triggered by the practices of management.

Which contents would help us to study the concepts and principles underlying organizational reality, and the thoughts and actions of the people involved? If we agree that managers are called to lead complex organizations, embedded in turbulent environments, and full of hectic internal dynamics, then we need to provide them with content material that will enable them to comprehend the basics of reality.

As Gareth Morgan explains, recalling Heraclitus and David Bohm, "the state of the universe at any point in time reflects a more basic reality. He (Bohm) calls this reality the implicate (or enfolded) order and distinguishes it from the explicate (or unfolded) order manifested in the world around us" (1997, pp. 251–252). This distinction between enfolded and unfolded orders leads us to argue that the education of managers would be better directed at helping them understand the essence of the implicate realities, while being able to deal with the subtleties of explicate circumstances.

In the face of multiple nuances and refinements of reality, being able to discern its core features becomes a great ability towards success. In this sense philosophical education contributes by helping those who receive it to elucidate the basic concerns of human beings, to whom organizations must be respectful. The selection of particular contents might be guided by criteria such as this, so that eventual selections and revisions of topics always prioritize those associated with the actions, thoughts and feelings of the people with whom managers relate, directly or indirectly.

Providing a definitive list of contents will be contradictory within an ever-changing reality, immersed in a philosophical quest; nevertheless arguments could be made in defence of texts that approach the quintessential elements of human experience, at both, the individual and the collective level. In this line of thinking, reflections about life, language, the experience of fear, the expectation of death, and so on, could be welcomingly included.

Generally speaking, in the philosophical formation of a manager, an anthology of the human sciences and their core concerns would have to be included, to the extent that they deal with the essential human problems. A prominent place in this educative agenda will be given to ethics, both normative and descriptive; its inquiry about human conduct and its assessment makes it indispensable when training philosophical managers.

To transcend a mere description of knowledge, the theoretical contents shall be presented in such a way as to help managers connect with concrete experiences of their own if possible, or else through vicarious learning. All this implies that managerial discourse will no longer be a collection of isolated abstractions, but a coherent set of apprehended notions and realities that inform the decision-making process of managers who try to be conscious and sensible about the consequences of their actions and omissions in other peoples' lives.

Some potentially useful contents could be found in the philosophy of religions, the history of mentalities – and why not, in the current events, which become an interesting prism to generate awareness about the vicissitudes of the human adventure in different latitudes? Beyond any specificity, we recommend that the contents be open, diverse, and stimulating to new sensibilities, for example inductive to beauty, truth, and goodness.

Philosophical education as a method

From a conventional Western perspective "the method of philosophy is rational inquiry" (Mautner, 2000). For our proposal of philosophical education it is nonetheless important to highlight that this rationality has be seen as substantial and not instrumental, and as a complement to experience and never reduced to cold speculation. We defend the rationality of philosophers such as Plato, Aristotle and Kant, who saw rationality as a human specific trait that vindicates the expression of human potential, enabling freedom and transcendence, a rationality that informs consciousness and action, contrary to uncontrolled determinisms.

Therefore, philosophy as a method for managers demands that they think and act reflectively and self-consciously, with an eagerness to learn and untamable inquisitiveness. The openness to inquiry shall be mindful about all of humanity, authentic and uncompromising to any kinds of power constraints. Probably the key necessary condition to foster this kind of method is a genuine love for wisdom, which is a true and ineludible philosophical orientation.

Philosophical education as a purpose

The kind of philosophical education that we propose for managers is not about conducting cold abstractions, isolated from people's needs and concerns. It shall never be about an arrogant display of erudition, for bookish learning is not truly philosophical and does not really help managers to run organizations in socially responsible ways.

When we propose philosophical education for managers, we never think about crafting pundits, but about developing pragmatic and ethical decision-makers, pragmatism as understood by William James and John Dewey, who pointed out that the true ideas are those that direct us to successful action; what ulteriorly works is what really matters, what could be taken as the truth.

When we propose the adoption of this pragmatic orientation, we recall the importance of overcoming the pitfalls of uninformed action and passive speculation. We believe that adopting a problem-solving approach, inspired by the love of wisdom and nurtured by its quest, constitutes a very adequate and legitimate aspiration which shall be complemented by the rigorous enactment of principles such as the protection of life and the respect of human dignity in all organizational dynamics.

Our twenty-first century world, its inhabitants, and the ecosystems that surround us urgently demand that the economic forces that seem to colonize other dimensions of life be tamed and subordinated to more dignified ideals, such as the respect of all forms of life, harmony in nature and, of course, the dignity of humans.

Within this philosophic-pragmatic perspective the purpose is to form managers capable of solving the defies of organizational life while contributing to the prevention and solution of problems that emerge within larger spheres of concern, among which we can signal the overall sustainability of economic systems, the harmonious development of society, and human well-being in general.

Philosophical education intends to endow those who follow it with phronesis: the practical wisdom necessary to conduct a good life and to distinguish, among all alternatives, proper ends of behaviour and the consequent adequate means to attain them. How can managers assure phronesis and project it to the organizations that they lead, while benefiting all stakeholders?

From the four dimensions of wisdom (derived of the possible meanings of the concept) proposed above, it follows that integral wisdom implies the conjugation of adequate knowledge, informed judgement and reflection about conflicting values, proper praxis, and authentic interiorizing of those principles deemed closer to goodness, beauty and truth.

From our perspective, managers must integrate wisdom at all these dimensions, and only by doing so, come to deserve the dignity ascribed to their office, and become capable of furthering the dignity of others; precisely the couple of challenges inherent to the definition of dignity. The following section indicates the specificities of how philosophical education contributes to the formation of managers capable of taking on those two challenges.

Philosophical Education and the Two Challenges of Human Dignity

How can philosophical education help managers to better face the defying situations of actualizing dignity on others and on themselves? The following lines suggest how philosophical education enables managers to successfully meet the demands and expectations associated with each one of the perspectives of dignity.

Initially we will approach the question of how can a manager comes to deserve the dignity of the inherent to the high organizational positions; and then we will demonstrate how philosophical education constitutes a *sine qua non* element to nurture the development of those capabilities needed to preserve and promote the dignity and value of every person.

DESERVING MANAGERIAL DIGNITY

How does philosophical education help managers deserve the dignity inherent to the high positions they represent within organizations and in relation to society? For a manager to come to deserve the entitlements of her office, she must first of all become aware of the privileges and influences associated with directive positions, for it is a fact that only a minority of the world's population enjoy well-paid jobs (let alone employment), and relative power and influence versus the rest of people.

Indeed, most persons in the world (including middle- and low-level managers) are subordinated to the will of others, while struggling to keep jobs that do not always satisfy their inner aspirations. Of course, it does not follow from this that top managers are necessarily following their inner motivations, but it is indisputable that they benefit from a larger share of power, control, and influence than most people in the world.

For a manager to be worthy of the advantages and honours to which she is entitled, she must recognize the corresponding responsibilities attached to the management positions. But what are these responsibilities? To whom is a manager responsible?

Although CSR and stakeholders' approaches to management are widely accepted in academic circles (Dima, 2008; MaryAnn and Kristi, 2008), and companies appear eager to embrace these theoretical developments (at least in highly publicized reports and self-produced advertisements), but most probably just for public relations motives, reality might be more inclined towards the conventional perspective that a manager is hired by the shareholders to act on their behalf, representing their interests above anyone else's.

Although this conventional view of managers as agents of shareholders has been sometimes criticized (Aubert and Gaulejac de, 1991; Bennis and O'Toole, 2005; Chanlat and Dufour, 1985; Freeman, 1983; Mintzberg, 2004; Sumantra, 2005), the mainstream still expect top managers to behave and make decisions as agents of the owners of the company, a situation which eventually leads to narrower perspectives and their subordination to the dictatorship of stock market indicators; ultimately to the evident reduction of their freedom of action.

From a philosophical point of view, a simplistic way of thinking is not acceptable; reality shall be assumed in all its complexity, acknowledging the causal links among actions and effects. With attentive regards, it is easy to corroborate that business organizations provoke multiple outcomes through their activities which are to a large extent the responsibility of the mangers in charge of running those organizations;

therefore we have the obligation to open our eyes to the web of causalities and effects triggered by organizational and managerial influence.

Although some excuses could be articulated by shifting this analysis to the macro level, blaming societal trends and impersonal economic forces, it is usually possible to track the genesis and evolution of most organizational phenomena at the managerial level. Without pretending to solve the subtleties of such a debate, we claim that even if managers are not ultimately responsible for everything that happens in the business world, they definitely play a decisive role, and can always act as vectors of change, for better or worse.

In this order of ideas, the responsibilities of management go beyond those due to shareholders, and they become accountable to any stakeholder impacted by their decisions. Of course, responsibility does not always imply guilt, blame or praise. It is basically about assuming the fact that the positions held by managers are characterized by decision-making and actions that generate consequences on others, therefore managers must become aware and develop that ability to respond to the claims that might come from different groups.

If managers are responsible to different stakeholders, how can those diverse responsibilities be discerned? How can a manager avoid being overwhelmed by multiple demands, many of which are not necessarily plausible or relevant? In this instance philosophy proves to be very effective, for it assists managers to distinguish between different kinds of demands, and equips them with a good dose of wisdom to face them.

For example, philosophical reflection will interrogate basics assumptions and differentiate the concepts of legal, social, and ethical responsibility, which unfortunately are randomly used and confused in the business world, the media, and even by the government. Philosophy props up managers to focus on the fundamentals, and decide what kinds of demands deserve to be answered. For example, let us recall that a social demand can exceed or even go against legal requirement, or that some legal requirements might be unethical (as in segregation regimes).

A manager informed by philosophy will be able to base the decisions not only on legal grounds (the ideal terrain for lawyers), or on social demands, pressures, and opportunities, (the territory of public relations and marketing people). The most adequate ground to decide on the claims of different stakeholders will be ethics, nurtured by philosophy. Here, reflection and true understanding of issues at play can be best decided with the support of philosophical theories, be it consequentialist, deontological, pragmatic, or some other. The wider the portfolio of perspectives, the wiser the eventual solutions can be.

Besides, if a manager is to deserve the entitlements of her office, she must acknowledge the leverage and limitations associated with the position being held. On one extreme, managers are not elected members of government nor chosen representatives of the public interest; on the other extreme, they do not have the authorization to penetrate the intimacy of families or to settle private concerns.

Nevertheless within their realm of action, they provoke many impacts, sometimes intended, sometimes unforeseen. Managers play the very influential societal role of guiding the organizations that drive economic forces while in charge of satisfying the legitimate economic needs of society; their decisions affect supply, demand, level of prices, employment quality and quantity, energy consumption, use and waste of raw materials, environmental pollution, and so on. In fact, a whole lot of impacts emerge as a consequence of the decisions and actions of managers.

Besides, for a manager to come to deserve the dignity of the inherent to the high positions held, we must as well recall the etymology of the verb deserve, which comes from French *deservir*, from Latin *deservire* to devote oneself to, from *de-* + *servire* to serve. That is, this old *transitive verb* (implies action), indicates that to be worthy or meritorious of something one has to be willing to serve. From this perspective emphasis must be placed on the importance of being capable to serve multiple stakeholders according to their ethical claims and not necessarily the legal or social ones.

ACTUALIZING THE CAPACITY TO PROMOTE HUMAN DIGNITY IN OTHERS

The discussion about the challenge of deserving the dignities associated with the entitlements of directive offices, leads us to the second one, concerning the need to develop capabilities to preserve and promote the dignity and value of all the persons affected by managerial practice. Among other reasons, when we think about who makes the calls about worthiness or who decides about the merits of someone, we believe that this can never be a narcissistic exercise; ultimately it is a collective decision, where others have a big say in deciding who is worthy of what.

As we had argued, all the privileges and power of the managers must be accompanied by the corresponding obligations of being able to respond to the legitimate demands of different stakeholders, which would be sorted out by philosophical analysis that will differentiate the regal regulations and social demands from genuine ethical concerns.

An indisputable managerial responsibility is to do everything possible to respect the dignity of every person eventually influenced by the outcomes of their action. Then we have to ask: how could philosophical education contribute to develop the capabilities to preserve and promote the dignity and inherent value of all the persons?

We believe that by stimulating the love of wisdom and its quest in actions, knowledge, values and the manifestations of being, philosophical education plants the seeds that, through proper care and cultivation, can eventually bear the desirable fruits of enhanced dignity for everyone affected by managerial practice: shareholders, labour, customers, the overall community, government, the natural environment and even future generations.

The following sections try to feature what managerial wisdom could be, according to the different meanings of the terms. Here it is important to highlight the analysis by segments is purely didactic, for true wisdom demands integration of the different parts, and a holism that transcends separated accounts. That is why at the end we will propose an integrative answer to how philosophical education can contribute to increase managerial respect of human dignity, through the several forms of wisdom.

PRAXEOLOGICAL WISDOM AND HUMAN DIGNITY

Let us recall that the first definition of wisdom has to do with fair, reasonable, prudent behaviour, which signals its praxeological dimension, that is, wisdom manifested through actions, doings and activity, which Aristotle contrasted with *poiësis* and *theoria* (Blackburn, 2005), *theoria* being speculation or contemplation (that will discussed in the epistemological), and *poiësis*, skilful production of something.

The importance of the concept of praxis resides in that it implies a goal-oriented action, by contrast to the mere execution of a given task exogenously imposed (like paid labour). Whereas *poiësis* demands dexterity, praxis involves the exercising of freedom and virtue to decide about the value of the activities to be pursued, as ends and their corresponding means.

From this perspective developing the praxeological wisdom of managers reclaims the need for comprehensive philosophical education, for true praxis has to be performed consciously, freely, and always under critical scrutiny of its motives, alternative means of achievement and possible consequences. As could be inferred when we discussed the ontological dimension of wisdom, the identity of any individual or of group can be defined by a large extent through their enacted praxis.

In this order of ideas, and keeping in mind the challenge of respecting the human dignity of everyone touched by their actions, herein we sketch a brief answer to the question of what could constitute managerial wisdom within the praxeological dimension.

If managers are to develop praxeological wisdom first of all they need to critically question their practices, become aware about their purposes, and possible contradiction with the proposed means. Wise praxis, capable of enhancing the human dignity of everyone affected by managerial action, implies balancing inspired creativity and ethical vigilance.

Ideally, a manager should be free to set her own goals, considering all legitimate stakeholders; subservience to short-term concerns of profit maximization must be replaced by reflective action. The ability to face emerging and unanticipated challenges should be preferred to the adroitness in executing business functions.

EPISTEMOLOGICAL WISDOM AND HUMAN DIGNITY

> *The solution which I am urging, is to eradicate the fatal disconnection of subjects which kills the vitality of our modern curriculum. There is only one subject-matter for education, and that is Life in all its manifestations. (Whitehead, 1929, pp. 18–19)*

Since wisdom can also be defined as knowledge, it evokes an inescapable epistemological challenge for managers. How can insights and understanding be generated? How can they foster human dignity?

A fair cognizance of human nature, potentials and limitations, aspirations and defining traits becomes a necessary condition for anyone willing to treat respect the dignity of others.

Another formulation of Kant's categorical imperative orders us to "Act only according to that maxim by which you can at the same time will that it should become a universal law". In order to develop such a maxim, it is indispensable to acquire the capability to interrogate and eventually discover such a deep knowledge about humans so that one could relate the particularities of anyone's concerns with the general realities of all. How can this be done?

Consistently with what was said a few pages above, concerning knowledge we deem that permanent interrogation about the contents, the methods, and the purposes constitutes the best means to provide provisional answers, which must be continually challenged.

Regarding the purpose of managerial knowledge, they should definitely be oriented to developing all the potentialities inherent in the human condition; the ones of the person acquiring the knowledge, and others' as well.

Regarding the method of managerial knowledge, it needs to foster curiosity, and eagerness to learn. Because of the influence and power that managers hold, they must interiorize reflexive and auto-critical skills; so critical thought will permeate not only the educational process, but the conception and organization of managerial dynamics. From our perspective, managerial knowledge is about being capable of transforming all the data and information into knowledge that makes sense, and is meaningful to people, in terms of achieving better living.

Regarding the contents, managerial knowledge should be nurtured by any kind of sources that will lead them to a more genuine comprehension of the human adventure and struggles in all its diversity. For example, we suggest management capacity will be potentiated by an engaging liberal education, which in the twenty-first century has to include among others a reflection about the impacts of technological innovation, new ethical dilemmas propelled by scientific discoveries and their plethora of potential applications, the contemporary challenges of socio-political organization, and so on.

Intuition and personal experience lead us to believe that unique understanding of human reality can best be grasped through the sublime message expressed by artistic expression. Literature, music, films ... contribute to enlightened the spectators about the diversity and plural authenticity of peoples' experiences.

A manager willing to seize a deeper comprehension of her fellow humans and their ideas and emotions can benefit a lot from the perspectives given by historical analysis, the study of mentalities, accounts about cultures, stories about myths, artistic expressions, and innumerable other sources that reflect the lives and creations of other humans but that unfortunately are shamelessly ignored by conventional management curricula.

Today's globalized world requires nothing less than a cosmopolitan manager, one capable of learning about the cosmos, capable of contemplating its integrality and sacred wholeness, a contemplative ideal located way beyond the shortsightedness and instrumentality of the knowledge sought in business schools. If managers are to respect others, their comprehension of the human condition has to be kept from being used in an instrumental way.

Situations where the most "enlightened" ones can manipulate the rest through some "illustrated despotism" have to be thoughtfully avoided by means of promoting the capacities for substantial rationality that will engender human dignity.

Through critically thinking about the purposes, methods and contents of managerial education, philosophy offers a unique possibility to overcome the dangers of instrumental rationality, while allowing its practitioners to enact a more substantial rationality that makes those who develop it capable of acknowledging and fostering the human dignity in others and in their own selves. As Brain Swimme said:

> Unless we live our lives with at least some cosmological awareness, we risk collapsing into tiny worlds. For we can be fooled into thinking that our lives are passed in political entities, such as the state or a nation; or that the bottom-line concerns in life have to do with economic realities of consumer lifestyles. In truth, we live in the midst of immensities. (Brian Swimme, The Hidden Heart of the Cosmos, quoted by O'Sullivan (2002), p. 1)

The knowledge we reclaim for our human-dignity aware and respectful manager needs to avoid the selfish pettiness and insignificant trivialities that chock the business world and suffocate deeper concerns. The knowledge we reclaim for our philosophically educated manager is one that nurtures her sensibility and makes her capable of appreciating the beauty, the truths, and untapped goodness of the immensities inherent to humans.

AXIOLOGICAL WISDOM AND HUMAN DIGNITY

> *Intelligence can only be led by desire. For there to be desire, there must be pleasure and joy in the work. The intelligence only grows and bears fruit in joy. ... It is the part played by joy in our studies that makes of them a preparation for the spiritual life. (Weil, 1951, p. 109)*

Legendary about his judgements and decisions, Solomon asked not for wealth or power but for discernment, and while he exercised it he became wealthy and powerful but, more importantly, widely respected. What can management learned from Solomon? Why should we place discernment above the thirst for power and profits?

Even if here we will not discuss the history of Solomon, we want to highlight the essence of his figure: judgement capability. Let us recall that the third semantic sense of wisdom addresses the concept of judgement, quite related to the concern for decision-making, a central issue for management. Here emerge the obvious questions of how judicious judgement can be enhanced, how good discernment can be acquired.

Keeping in mind the challenge of respecting the human dignity of everyone affected by management, the following paragraphs briefly outline an answer to the question about what could constitute axiological wisdom for managers.

Axiology as the branch of philosophy that studies value (*axia* in Greek) comes handy in this quest for improved judgement. What kind of values must be most eagerly sought by managers? How are they to choose the values to orient their action? How to judge among conflicting values of different stakeholders?

The notion of judgement evokes both the process of evaluating something and the result of such an evaluation. Recognizing the impossibility of axiologically neutral management scenarios is the first condition that managers with discernment need to be aware of; their actions are immersed in value-flooded settings, and decision-making outcomes reflect preferences among diverse alternatives.

This awareness about the value-laden organizational world should lead managers to become fully conscious about the normative nature of their work, and capable of exercising the power at their disposal. This implies displaying moral authority, which means the capacity to decide on issues, not relying on just opinions or mainstream inertia but on seasoned ethical reasoning and sensibility.

Wise wielding of judgement involves the responsibility to decide upon the value of alternatives in moral terms, that is, being able to discern good from bad, and acting in consequence. In this sense, managers with increased capacity must not be subjected to the dogmatic utterances of the most powerful players, or on the sentences given by tradition. Their actions and decisions should proceed from their own informed critical thinking, and not on the blind following of business and economic doctrine.

A wisdom-lover manager shall be able to develop her own ideas after conscious consideration of different alternatives and their underlying values, discarding unquestioned beliefs and positions of force. But how can this be done?

In a globalized world, where there are so many value claims, how to best judge among them? Since the dispute among absolutist and relativist is not yet solved – and might never be – and there is no need for managers to get lost in the maze of their argumentation, probably the most pragmatic avenue for action is to develop in managers the capacity to face emergent ethical dilemmas, and deal with unforeseen situations involving values, always oriented by the ideal to realize human dignity in themselves and others.

The aspiration of respecting the human dignity of everyone, and of enabling each person to actualize all her potential could be the ultimate guiding value. Let us recall the third formulation of the Kantian categorical imperative impelling us to "Act only according to that maxim by which you can at the same time will that it should become a universal law". Although it might seem paradoxical, the value of submitting each one's subjective preferences to the test of compatibility with the subjectivity of others might lead to an enhanced objectivity.

By adopting the ideal of the dignity of all human beings as the ultimate value, it becomes possible to have referential criteria upon which other values can be examined. In the light of the respect of the humanity in every person, diverging axiological premises can be scrutinized; for each conflicting alternative we can always explore which one propels most the consciousness and reason of which we are capable? Which values assure the treatment of humans and ends? Which maxims can be universally accepted as legitimate norms to guide our behaviour?

We believe that the quest for human dignity can be best achieved by the love of wisdom, and in axiological terms articulate the cornerstone of any normative foundation. The search for wisdom and those values compatible with its various forms constitute a disinterested basis for the diagnosis and remedy of those particular social pathologies engendered by unwise management.

While in this chapter we do not pretend to defend any particular value different from human dignity, we want to emphasize the importance of the philosophical method as a means of allowing its preservation and promotion. In this sense we believe that the ethics of discourse ethics proposed by Habermas really contributes to elucidate management principles and values compatible with the respect of the human nature and potential.

What if management replicated the process of discourse ethics that Habermas proposes for philosophical inquiry? If this were the case, all stakeholders should engaged in open dialogue about the purposes of organizations and the responsibility of management, regarding each other as equals, with the corresponding equal valuation of their interests. The recognition of everyone's interests demands of every actor active participation instead of passive expectations. Discussions should be based on rational argumentation, free from any kind of force or pressures. The conversation should always be open, which means that all assumption of management can be questioned any time, and that issues can never be settled on a definitive basis, for management is a social process, always in construction.

By seeking to emulate the process of discourse ethics, we might assuredly get closer to axiological wisdom, and what could be considered a discursive theory of ethical and dignified management, where organizations might be handled in deliberately ethical and dignified ways.

If managers were better discerners about values, they would be more prone and capable of respecting them, while increasing their capacity to make "better" decisions, among which we find the ability to face unanticipated dilemmas (for example, those derived of technological innovations, cultural encounters, new working rhythms, and so on).

A philosophically educated manager will be more capable of developing substantial rationality, and sincere introspection of her values while engaging in ethical dialogue and empathy about the concerns of others, thus deserving the trust of others, and embodying cosmopolitan values and the corresponding capability to respond to them. Like Solomon, a philosophical manager will avoid painful fragmentations, and be able to discern the legitimate interests, those necessary to preserve life.

ONTOLOGICAL WISDOM AND HUMAN DIGNITY

The good life is one inspired by love and guided by knowledge. (Russell, 1961, p. 372)

I am myself and my circumstances, and if I do not save them, I cannot save myself. (Ortega y Gasset, 1961, p. 322)

The fourth semantic nuance of wisdom has to do with the attitude and quality of being wise, with the sensibility and moderation of such state. From a managerial point of view, we ask what ontological wisdom might mean, and does it relate to the preservation of the human dignity?

Ontological wisdom in management represents the realization of the highest aspirations of human dignity in the persona of the managers by the preoccupation for its promotion in others. In a sense, a wise ontological manager is the one that is best aware about the nature of her position, but mostly about her own being, as well as about the relations she might hold with different actors of forces that exist interacting with management, such as all stakeholders, social trends (for example, consumptions patterns, unemployment), technology, power asymmetries, and so on.

The realization of human dignity, through the exercise of freedom and responsibility should be the ultimate end, the *telos* of management. This implies a qualitative breakthrough in the conception of managerial work, where moral development should replace economic growth as the urgency that propels action.

This moral development could take many forms, all of them compatible with the pursuit of wisdom and human dignity. For example, we could strive and materialize the ideals of liberty and justice proposed by Rawls, or nurture post-conventional behaviour such as defined by Kohlberg, or virtuous character symbolized by the noble Aristotelian aristocrats. Basically, many of these moral ideals epitomize the aspiration and longing for a truly moral embodiment of virtue, from which management can doubtlessly benefit.

Let's take for example the concept of ontological wisdom symbolized by the king philosopher proposed by Socrates. By experiencing life, learning from many sources – observation, contemplative reflection and conscious experience – it is eventually possible to leave the cave and question the prevailing assumptions of the illusory shadows of economic life, which quite often are mistakenly taken as the real concerns of management.

With a certain dose of stoic endurance, the emancipated manager, dragged upwards by philosophical inquiry, will be capable to face the dazzle created by the new excessive "enlightenment".

Ontological wisdom implies that the manager willing to defend human dignity is daring to live outside the cave, and assume the obligation to take part in leading roles. In this case, it would not be governing the Republic, but managing its omnipresent organizations, but seeking enhanced ways of seeing that escape the all blindness created by the excessive presence of business forces, and unquestioned goals and criteria.

The wise manager will need to foster all forms of intelligence, especially what we now know as emotional intelligence, but that Aristotle described and proposed as an ideal more than two thousand years ago. For emotional intelligence allows a person to better interact with other persons; its skilled cultivation enables managers to understand and deal with the authentic needs and aspirations related to the human dignity of others.

The ontologically wise manager could be seen as the personification of the search for, although not necessarily the achievement of, the dignity of everyone related to their actions and omissions of the organizations they lead. Goodness, truth and beauty do not have to be incarnated, but their pursuit must be actively manifested.

The eagerness to materialize and eventually exemplify humanity to its full potential might be the trait of managerial ontological wisdom, where all kinds of business circumstances shall be transcended and used to help every individual excel. Management could be the means to the good life proposed by philosophy, and as Bertrand Russell proclaimed, it shall be "inspired by love and guided by knowledge".

Philosophical Education and Respect of Human Dignity – Integrating Diverse Managerial Forms of Wisdom

> *Education must ultimately justify itself in terms of enhancing human understanding. (Gardner, 1999, p. 178)*

> *Radical pedagogy needs a vision – one that celebrates not what is but what could be, that looks beyond the immediate to the future and links struggle to a new set of human possibilities. (Giroux, 1983, p. 242)*

In the previous sections we tried to feature what managerial wisdom could be, according to the diverse meanings of the concept. As we said, the segmented analysis is just didactic, for true wisdom demands integration of all its dimensions. Now as a conclusion we propose an integrative answer to why and how philosophical education can contribute to increase managerial respect of human dignity, through the encompassing of the several forms of wisdom.

Any person should come to be fully aware of her rationality and inherent potentials, and in consequence, should actively seek to develop the dignity intrinsic to her human condition. In-depth consciousness about human dignity should trigger in the wisdom-lover the willingness to learn about how best to comply with the exigencies of materializing it in everyone.

For managers, who are so influential in the contemporary world, the challenge of wisdom is multidimensional, for their actions, ideas, values and concrete personifications, undeniably influence the unfolding of social reality. Wise managerial work, that is the one realized by persons capable of promoting the human dignity, demands nothing less than a sincere quest and coherent enactment of all forms of wisdom.

This obliges us to think about the best ways to lead forth every individual – particularly those privileged with directive positions – towards the recognition of their own dignity and their responsibility in assuring those of others.

In this sense, when addressing the education of managers we can say along with Howard Gardner that "education must ultimately justify itself in terms of enhancing human understanding", and in the business world, all cognitive training must be subordinated to this ultimate goal, of course with the ethical check of assuring that this human understanding will be used to multiply the actions in favour of humans, and not their manipulation.

In this sense, more than multiple forms of intelligence, what is really required is the ethical incorporation of the praxis, epistemic findings, axiological conquest, and ontological desires, into a coherent enactment of new personifications of management, eventually more capable of interrelating with different kinds of beings and varied manifestations of existing reality.

As we said before, philosophy serves as a purpose that justifies itself, wisdom, but that demands a concurrent method that must be respectful of truth, beauty and goodness. In other words, the dignified end of philosophy demands equally dignified means that call to be combined through education.

In a world with multiple wrongs to be righted, everyone's education needs to be radical, in the sense that it should address the inner roots in the formation of our beings. If we do not examine the roots of education, it is easy to be satisfied with only the mere replication of information; it would be very hard to notice deformations that might pullulate and pollute society. The potential for real formation of characters, and transformation of humanity, lies at philosophically oriented education, one that is critical and capable of establishing connections among the interrelated components of our complex realities.

Our suggestion to orient managerial work by the ideal of human dignity, nurtured by philosophical education, is supported by the radical practice of education envisioned by Henry Giroux, for whom true education "celebrates not what is but what could be, that looks beyond the immediate to the future and links struggle to a new set of human possibilities" (Giroux, 1983).

In the contemporary world, where economic and organizational dynamics generate significant outcomes, the positions and privileges of management imply outstanding responsibilities. The minimum acceptable to society cannot be less than the aspiration for the maximum of dignity. In this sense, managers shall be acquainted with the reality that they are part of a privileged class, invested with power, and accountable to all who are somehow at risk by their actions. Therefore, they should strive to be the best they can be, *aristos*, in the Aristotelian sense, and willing to assume their responsibility to others.

In this order of ideas, managers are to be seen as agents to the whole of humanity, and not just the shareholders. Contrary to the conventional thirst for profits and material accumulation, humanity requires wisdom in the practices, ideas, values and realities engendered by managerial work.

This redefinition of agency involves recalling the philosophical definition of agent, where the actions of a person are not necessarily of someone else's behalf, unlike the economic perspective where managers are seen as agents of shareholders. Philosophy empowers the agents, widening the conception of agency, and shifting the problem from executing the mandate of the capital holder to that of making managers conscious about the power of their action, and how ethical reflection cannot be absent from their job.

Under this redefinition, a manager must acknowledge the capacity of exerting power and the moral responsibility to assume the consequences of her actions, therefore becoming the principal of her own person. Necessarily, managers need to develop a wider perspective that shareholders aid these last ones to connect to the legitimate concerns of other stakeholders, unleashing an "ethical dialogue". Even from a selfish basis, the owners of business should become aware that their sustainability depends on the usage of substantial dialogue and rationality between all parties concerned.

In this light, the significant agency problem is not about conflicting goals and interests arising between management and stockholders, but about how human action could be simultaneously inspired and restricted by the ideal of human dignity, how to act in business promoting human dignity and avoiding the excesses or deficits that might undermine it.

We believe that through philosophical education it is possible for managers to come to embody all the entitlements of their job, and become capable of the moral reasoning necessary to ethically serve others in order to deserve the dignity of their societal status and condition.

References

Aubert, N., and de Gaulejac, V. (1991). *Le coût de l'excellence*. Paris: Éditions du Seuil.
Bennis, W.G., and O'Toole, J. (2005). How Business Schools Lost their Way. *Harvard Business Review* (May).
Blackburn, S. (ed.) (2005). *The Oxford Dictionary of Philosophy* (Second edn). Oxford: Oxford University Press.
Castrillón, S. (2007). Rethinking the Performance of Management Education, Some Elements for a More Socially Responsible Field. *Revista Universidad EAFIT*, 43(147), 26–46.
Castrillón, S. (2008). Administración y Sabidurías. Esbozando algunos nexos. *Revista Universidad EAFIT*, 44(149), 60–73.
Chanlat, A., and Dufour, M. (1985). *La Rupture entre l'entreprise et les hommes. Le point de vue des sciences de la vie*. Montreal: Éditions Québec/Amérique.
Des, D. (2003). The Dark Side of Leadership. *Business Strategy Review*, 14(3), 25.
Dima, J. (2008). A Stakeholder Approach to Corporate Social Responsibility: A Fresh Perspective into Theory and Practice. *Journal of Business Ethics*, 82(1), 213.
Freeman, R.E. (1983). Stockholders and Stakeholders: A New Perspective on Corporate Governance. *California Management Review (pre-1986)*, 25(000003), 88.
Gardner, H. (1999). *Intelligence Reframed*. New York: Basic Books.
Ghoshal, S. (2005). Bad Management Theories are Destroying Good Management Practices. *Academy of Management Learning and Education*, 4(1), 75–91.
Giroux, H. (1983). *Theory and Resistance in Education*. London: Heinemann.
Kant, I. (1963). *Lectures on Ethics* (L. Infield, Trans.). New York: Harper and Row.
Kets de Vries, M.F.R. (1989). Alexithymia in Organizational Life: The Organization Man Revisited. *Human Relations*, 42(12), 1079.
Kets De Vries, M.F.R. (1991). Whatever Happened to the Philosopher-King? The Leader's Addiction to Power. *The Journal of Management Studies*, 28(4), 339.
Marianne, T. (2004). Contemporary Issues in Organizations. *Development and Learning in Organizations*, 18(6), 4.
MaryAnn, R. and Kristi, Y. (2008). Moral Discourse and Corporate Social Responsibility Reporting. *Journal of Business Ethics*, 78(1–2), 47.

Mautner, T. (2000). *The Penguin Dictionary of Philoshophy*. London: Penguin Books.
Merriam-Webster (2003). *Merriam-Webster's Collegiate Dictionary*. Springfield, MA: Merriam-Webster.
Mintzberg, H. (2004). *Managers Not MBAs: A Hard Look at the Soft Practice for Managing and Management Development*. San Francisco: Barret-Koehler Publishers Inc.
Morgan, G. (1997). *Images of Organization* (Second edn). Thousand Oaks, California: Sage Publications.
O'Sullivan, E. (2002). The Project and Vision of Transformative Education. In E. O'Sullivan, A. Morrell and M.A. O'Connor (eds), *Expanding the Boundaries of Transformative Learning* (pp. 280). New York: Palgrave.
Ortega y Gasset, J. (1961). *Obras Completas* (Vol. I). Madrid: Alianza Editorial.
Plato (1937). *The Dialogues of Plato* (B. Jowett, Trans.). New York: Random House.
Russell, B. (1961). *The Basic Writings of Bertrand Russell*. London: Routledge.
Sumantra, G. (2005). Bad Management Theories Are Destroying Good Management Practices. *Academy of Management Learning and Education, 4*(1), 75.
Weil, S. (1951). *Waiting on God* (E. Crauford, Trans.). New York: Putnam's Sons.
White, B. (1995). Organizational Paradoxes: Clinical Approaches to Management. *Leadership and Organization Development Journal, 16*(4), 50.
Whitehead, A.N. (1929). *The Aims of Education*. New York: Mentor Books.
Wolff, R.P. (ed.) (1969). *Foundations of the Metaphysics of Morals: with Critical Essays*. Indianapolis: Bobbs-Merill Co.

CHAPTER 10
Managing Human Dignity and Corporate Performance

PIERRE-PAUL MORIN

Free Markets Laws

The business of business is business. The objective of durable private enterprise is clear: create value for their customers, at a cost lower than the value created, thereby generating profits for their owners. This will make long-term survival possible, providing jobs to employees and return on financial investments and risks. The greater the value generated, the higher the acceptable cost and/or the profits. Those are the basic rules.

In the context of a free market, generating greater value to the customer than one's competitor is another rule that adds to the one just described. This thereby creates pressure on the organization to generate the highest possible value to the customer at the lowest possible cost, increasing competitiveness and/or profits. This is where equilibrium between working conditions, price and profits is reached.

The conditions under which this equilibrium is established vary according to great many factors: the industry, corporate strategy, availability of resources, the specific product or service, and so on, Nevertheless, the basic rules staying the same, one can state that, for the same value to the customer being created, profits will be maximized by cutting costs. This will translate into a clear motivation to offer as skimp working conditions as possible.

On the other hand, authors state that the only long-term competitive advantage comes from hiring and keeping the best human resources available, using their knowledge and their ability to innovate. These will in turn generate greater value to the customer than the competitors and competitiveness. This will translate into a clear motivation to offer the best possible working conditions.

The balance between these two extremes should provide organizations with long-term success: offering attractive working conditions to employees while generating the profit margin necessary to provide for an acceptable return on investment being, at least theoretically, a winning combination.

But the free market is not always so free. For example, manpower mobility is far from being perfect. Therefore, for the same task being performed, organizations will pay less for a worker in developing countries than for one in industrialized countries. Or locally, a worker with more seniority will typically get a better wage than his newly hired counterpart, always for the same task performed. This possibility of lowering costs by using the cheapest suitable manpower is a clear motivation to hire and keep the most productive workers in the sense of their profitability.

Should this be encouraged or, on the contrary, be denounced? From a strictly commercial perspective, taking into account the costs of hiring and training new personnel, those of transportation and delocalization and fees related to general human resource management, using the person that can perform the task at the lowest cost is mandatory. Ignoring this rule would inevitably jeopardize long-term survival of the organization.

But is this acceptable from an ethical perspective? Are employers not complying to free market laws taking major long-term risks, compromising the survival of the organization? Is piece wages an acceptable compromise? What other working conditions can compensate for low salaries? At what point do legitimate productivity objectives become intolerable requirements? When does this become a threat to human dignity?

The technological revolution makes it possible today to control not only the organization of work but also the activities of the people that are responsible for its completion. Not only is the output monitored, but the effort required to generate this output can be closely measured as well. From the monitoring of emails to the information of the physical location of people, it is now possible to know at any time the exact nature of an accomplished task and the precise efforts that were required to carry it out. This control gives managers power over employees whose limits are ethical on one hand, and financial on the other, as one has to decide on the relevancy of exercising it. Other concepts, broader in their application, will be helpful in further understanding these issues, they are: human rights, respect and dignity.

Human Dignity, a Concept in Evolution

The concept of human dignity, as abundantly used in the Old and New Testament, is described as being "a gift from God". This interpretation gives dignity an extrinsic origin, thereby excluding any idea that it should be won or even deserved. Later described by Giovanni Pico della Mirandola (Kreis, 2004), in the middle of the fifteenth century, dignity clearly becomes an intrinsic characteristic of human beings. According to his interpretation, it is no longer God-given or even given by fellow humans. This idea was further developed in the middle of the eighteenth century by Kant, considered by many the philosopher who influenced the modern interpretation of dignity the most. The main idea underlying his theory is that human dignity stems from the fact that a human being is "free from all laws of nature, obedient only to those laws which himself prescribes" (Kant, 2002: 226).

His contemporary Nietzsche (Bonduelle, 1994) proposes a radically different conception of human beings, whom he describes as being closer to animals that angels. But he keeps nevertheless the idea of a dignity based on freedom, even though it may not be claimed by all. Darwin (Darwin, 2004) and Sartre (Caeymaex, 2007), as we will see later, agree with this idea of animals becoming humans, becoming capable of thinking.

The all-important Universal Declaration of Human Rights (1948) clearly states in its first article that "All human beings are born free and equal in dignity and rights" (General Assembly of the United Nations, 1948). Human dignity, in the last decade, has been reintroduced as one of the most important concepts governing the evolution of modern societies. It is an all-embracing concept, including not only all the rights but also the values of societies.

If laws define rights in a relatively structured way, the concept of dignity offers for its part relatively wide possibilities of interpretation. Several governments use their Charter of Rights and Liberties as the tool privileged to protect those who have no means to protect themselves. Administered by courts of justice, these laws referring to dignity are often competing with other laws that are meant to protect citizens. Judges are therefore more and more confronted with the choice of using the potentially more universal concept of human dignity rather than applicable laws in a specific context. This is to say that the changing nature of society's interpretation of the concept of dignity puts on tribunals a considerable burden, to the point where they may have to choose between the rights of the human being versus those of the citizen. For many people, this widely discretionary application of the concept can create a potentially abusive use of the term and what it represents. This would open the door not only to legislative laziness, but also to a progressive impoverishment of the concept itself. "The term has suffered a kind of inflation though undisciplined use to the point where its value is endangered" (Soulen, 2006: 2). Furthermore, "many authors consider it as a value, a non-legal concept: it inspires legal norms but is not one of them" (Martens, 2002: 69).

In order to illustrate the transitory and ephemeral character of the definition of the concept, Martens argues, for example, that "it is certainly referring to the respect of human dignity that sodomy has been included in the Penal Code. It is also in its name that it will be removed from it." (Martens, 2002). He adds:

> *we can see that the concept of human dignity, one that did not have any real legal standing in the past, is becoming a sort of all-encompassing concept for jurisdictional control. It allows judges to create interdictions, subjective rights, unconstitutionalities and even to impose positive obligations to states. (Martens, 2002: 71)*

This responsibility, delegated to courts of justice, is potentially hazardous in other ways. If, as Max Weber thought, "states have a monopoly on legitimate violence", (Weber, 1864–1920) Martens asks the question: "[…] when judges create a new norm that they call human dignity, don't they create for themselves a power that transforms democracy (government by people) into dicastocracy (government by judges)?" (Martens, 2002: 46). Societies are therefore confronted to a double bind: impose limitations to potentially abusive state powers while having enough of it to defend the weakest members of society against the strongest who abuse them. If going through the courts of justice looks like the most appropriate way to do it, how can governments make sure that judges will not eventually impose their own subjective perspective?

Individual and Collective Rights

Many think that there should be, to balance the effects of the Charter of Human Rights, a Charter of Human Responsibilities. The highest courts of justice in many countries have noticed the deep transformation in social climate created by legislation on rights and liberty. Among those consequences, the concept of collective rights, even though specifically recognized in the charters, is progressively weakened by the focus put on protecting individuals:

> *The traditional interpretation of human rights is imbedded in these texts and leads to a mostly individualistic presentation of them. This greatly influences the perception of economical, social and cultural rights. This perception limits deliberately the field of reflection; it is so restrictive that, after all, the only rights which are seen as fundamental are the individual rights, eminently subjective and devoid of links with the social and political environment ... collective freedom and rights, those of workers and citizens are thereby progressively ignored.*
> *(Koubi, 2008)*

From a strictly systemic point of view, if "infringing dignity of mankind is infringing dignity of every individual" (Edelman, 2002) it is also true to say that "… when individual dignity is impaired, it is that of mankind that is impaired" (Thomas, 2002: 44). Interestingly, this focus on individual rights has other consequences. As we will see further, those rights, if they are to be recognized and enforced, will have to be part of a consensus. This criterion is indeed one that is central to decisions in courts of justice.

Societal Values, also in Evolution

Along with this renewed focus on dignity, our society, in the last decade, is also confronted with a "value crisis". Typical frauds, dishonest and unethical behaviours used to have a limited impact, only a few years ago. This has changed dramatically lately, giving them quite another reach and impact. Globalization in conjunction with the increased dependency between corporations, as well as the ever increasing number of international transactions, have opened the possibility for unethical behaviours to have major impacts not only on large groups of people but on the world economy. This is how the large scale crisis and financial scandals that plagued the beginning of this century have demonstrated the urgency of having ethical issues at the forefront of corporate strategies and even at the societal level.

It is interesting to notice that these unethical behaviours, largely responsible for creating crises, are for the most part well known and done in the open. In fact, in most cases, they are not illegal. They are only in clear contradiction with an economical common sense that fosters long-term survival of financial institutions and structures. For example, several of the current usages, such as citizens going excessively into debts or executives getting paid outrageous salaries and bonuses obviously lead to long-term dead ends. These were nevertheless tolerated and even encouraged by a complaisant environment whose interests are well served, on one part. On the other, as we will see later, there is a rise of a new societal value, close to that of individual rights, that can be called global individual responsibility. It makes it possible for those who take advantage of unethical behaviours to be in peace with their conscience. Indeed, from this perspective, the burden of questionable financial behaviours will by more on consumers and board of directors than on those managers taking unethical decisions. How can anyone blame a manager or an organization that only makes available products that consumers cannot afford?

Furthermore, one must realize that the criteria differentiating acceptable ethical behaviours from those that are not are their financial consequences, in many instances. The questioning of the practices of the real-estate and stock-exchange markets indeed arose only when their medium-term failure was noticed. This questioning then gave place to a partial restructuring of financial institutions so that the behaviour at the origin of the problems is discouraged from now on. Like with many types of organization and social values, ethics in businesses behaves like a pendulum. It goes from a perspective where profits are maximized to one where the "moral issues" are prioritized and vice versa, as the adverse effects of one extreme or the other are felt.

But not everything is in the hands of institutions or businesses. Globalization, more specifically in its communications dimension, leads the way to new models in control and empowerment. The rise of the Internet fosters an unprecedented democratization of information around the world. Even if individuals seem to be more and more autonomous and even isolated, they can still rely on a virtual network of people sharing their interests and concerns. Some of the delinquent behaviours may thereby be denunciated immediately or in the short-term by an often structured mechanism. Public auctions on the Internet are a good example of this system. They give suppliers a satisfaction rating and give consumers access to comments from previous buyers. Consumers are thereby empowered as they are informed.

Divergent Schools of Thought

As we can see, those concerns about collective and individual responsibilities are not new. Already, in antique Greece, Socrates is at the origin of a school of thought that conferred individuals great autonomy and free will. He is the author of the famous "know yourself" philosophy. This thinking is further developed, in a modern version called "utilitarism" by Milton Friedman, among others. He further argues that employees are tools at the service of financial interests and at those of collective projects in which they are involved, for the greater good of the group. Their only concern should therefore be to maximize Return on Investment (ROI) for shareholders. According to this school of thought, managers' behaviours are governed by laws and their moral or ethical issues are strictly personal (Freidman, 1979).

In this perspective, the market is the ultimate regulator. Accordingly, the best interest of all stakeholders, including workers' working conditions, will be optimized by the freedom to change that they have. Nozik even describes this freedom as the only possible guarantee preserving them from potential abuses from overly profit-oriented employers (Nozik, 1974). The same author also questions egalitarianism as a social goal and justice as a mean to redistribute wealth. He indeed fears that, with the best intentions in mind, governments eventually become unduly powerful and have that monopoly on legitimate violence that we referred to earlier. They would then be capable of all kinds of abuses, in the name of a social justice interpreted end applied by a ruling minority. He further argues that this would go against the common good, in the long-term. This point of view is extended to both businesses and governments by Bonefeld and Psychopedis: "From within the logics of economic rationality and of political power, human values such as dignity and integrity are a scandal. They are rightly seen to resist the full utilization of technical efficacy of social labour power and its transformation into an effective and compliant resource that feeds well-oiled systems of economic production and political domination" (Bonefeld and Psychopedis, 2005: 3). This school of thought has many supporters today, well beyond those advocating what is referred to as wild capitalism.

Plato (428–347 BC) is a founder of a second school of thought called deontology. It was followed and reinterpreted by many, including Kant. It argues that social justice and universal rights should be prioritized. Employees, in this context, are considered as subjects and their well-being is a goal rather than a mean. The market is not the regulator any more, replaced by morality and logical thinking. Based on the reciprocity principle, treat others as you would like to be treated yourself, this perspective relies on the consciousness of acting for the good, respecting duty and law. It also advocates a consensual definition of ethical behaviours, describing the rules for respectful conduct in organizations. It is auto-regulated by agreements on social conduct, transgressions of which are potentially denounced by members of the group. A formal code of ethics is thereby created, facilitating proper behaviours. This school of thought has many supporters today, well beyond those advocating what is referred to as complaisant socialism.

Existentialism, Positivism and Constructivism

Jean-Paul Sartre is responsible for yet another school of thought, significantly different from the first two, but including them. It is based on the concepts of consciousness, responsibility, intentionality and finality. (Caeymaex, 2007). He first described his perception of ethics and morality in his "Notebooks for an ethics" (*Cahiers pour une morale*), between 1946 and 1948. Fifteen years later, he further developed his ideas in a conference in Rome, called "Ethics and Society" (free translation of Éthique et société). Those manuscripts, still unpublished in their complete form to this date, are the highlights of Sartre's ethical thinking, according to Simone de Beauvoir. He describes his interpretation of the concept of efficiency: "the mandatory influence of means over goals and that of goals over means". He thereby uses both utilitarist and deontologist principles, in a circular pattern, where they mutually influence each other.

Sartre asks himself: what is common between the various objective forms of ethics and between these and institutions? His answer refers to the concept of possibility. "It is a certain relationship with possibility: a specific behaviour appears, right from the start, as unconditionally possible" (free translation, Caeymaex, 2007: 80). Being unconditional, Sartre stresses the fact that the word "possible" in this context is interpreted radically differently from the positivist concept of being accidental but rigorously controlled. To illustrate this, Sartre further develops the concept of honour. The two concepts of honour and dignity are very close, especially considering Sartre's definition of honour, described as the hierarchical differences between social classes and closely related to the value of individuals.

Contrary to Kant's perception, Sartre does not see a universal ethical norm. He prefers to present it as an "individual possibility". It is "my possibility to create myself as subject" (Münster, 2007). In his interviews with Benny Lévy (free translation, Lévy, 1991), Sartre states:

> *In my early research, like the vast majority of moralists, I was looking for morality in a consciousness of others without reciprocity or without others (I prefer others to reciprocity) Today I think that everything that happens for this consciousness, at a given moment, is inevitably related or even often created by the presence or absence of the existence of others. In other words, any consciousness appears to me like self-created and, at the same time, like a consciousness of others and a consciousness for others. And it is this reality, this self considering itself as a self for others, relating to others, that I call moral consciousness.*

This is why Sartre is so often described not only as a freedom philosopher but also as a responsibility philosopher.

As Simone de Beauvoir (free translation, De Beauvoir, 1986) argues: "We are not born women, we become that", one can measure the distance between this perspective and the one stating that dignity is conferred from the simple fact of being human. Her constructivist approach reaffirms the primacy of acting over being and reinstates a dynamic in which human reality is recreated with every interaction. It cannot be interpreted in itself, without being contextualized both by finality and intentionality.

These ideas are resumed by several contemporary authors who advocate a determinedly constructivist perspective. One must then "find a way to justify personal choices in the context of a dialogue" (free translation, Legault, 1991: 20). This dialogue can even be at the entire human race level; "Thus, Human Rights are ethical ideal that should not be interpreted 'from a legalistic or procedural standpoint, but in terms of humanity'" (free translation, Durand, 1999: 368). "Personalism develops not only based on a representation of human dignity but also based on an anthropological representation of mankind" (free translation, Létourneau, 2006: 23).

How can one not refer to Charles Taylor's interpretation of work ethics, in the context of work organization and profitability? "Behavior system types, as referring to the concept of action, can be paired with the concepts of consciousness and intentionality. They describe individuals for whom things have a specific nature or description" (free translation, Gagnon, 1989: 74):

> *But Taylor does not believe collective consciousness comes before or is more important than individual consciousness or even as an independent free-standing entity, or as a super-ego. On the contrary, the idea of a community must stem, in theory, from a more authentic, even democratic, relationship between the individual self and others. Now, the theory of the committed Me relies on the relationship between this Me and the other Me in the presence of commitment, the relationship being impossible without it. For a relationship between the two to exist, it is mandatory that one dimension of their mutual commitment be concrete and shared. From this, comes the idea of a collective identity, a product of this shared commitment. (free translation, Gagnon, 1989: 237)*

For Taylor, "the reference to an external world, morally significant is necessary to create an equally morally significant experience. But this perception will elude us forever" (free translation, Gagnon, 1989: 278). Here is an interpretation of Taylor's work that should challenge the positivist idea that many have of his doctrine. Furthermore, his reference to sub-consciousness is in line with the theory that behaviours are not only influenced by intentionality but also by the role system.

This point of view is further developed by M.B. Edelman who says, in a document looking for ways to promote dignity: "[...] here, more than elsewhere, positivism is our worst enemy" (free translation, Edelman, 2002: 401).

The Systemic Perspective of Social Roles

In agreement with Sartre and Taylor, the principles of the modern Project management state that when a project or a company is born, they necessarily have an objective, a mission, an intentionality. It is around this purpose that tasks and relationships revolve. It is the conscious part of behaviours that Sartre and De Beauvoir were referring to. A complementarity then gets created between individuals, groups and subgroups, based on tasks, but also on competency and power. But another network is also created, more informal, subconscious, that of social roles:

> *Roles are the result of an instantaneous co-creation of a reality by consensus, not accessible to consciousness in the present. In all our relationships, we first subconsciously assign a social role to our vis-à-vis. We then behave in reference to this role, in the same way that we would have interpreted the role ourselves. The roles of the different actors are decided and implemented according to motivations and aptitudes of individuals on the one part, and needs and goals of the group on the other. (Free translation, Morin, 2008)*

So here is a perspective capable of interpreting behaviours that would otherwise be hard to explain. If, as demonstrated in the social role theory, the main objective for individual behaviours is to preserve systemic relationships, unethical conduct will only be perceived as such when the complementarity of roles will be in jeopardy.

Ethical behaviours, as we have seen, are influenced not only by the conscious perception of their fit within the set of values of the environment and the potential consequences on people's careers, but also by their unconscious effect on the system of roles. This leads us to consider yet another concept, closely related to that of dignity: the role of victim. It is indeed generally associated with the relative weakness of individuals and groups being oppressed. It is so important that a new discipline has been created: victimology.

How can someone keep his or her dignity in a victim's role? Our post-modern society, justly denouncing abuses against the weak has given victims a privileged status. To a point where we sometimes have a:

> *[...] "victims competition". When a group pretends that their sin is worse than anyone else's there will always be another group pretending to be the victim [...] of a worse one. This has been responsible, for the last twenty five years, for vile and endless discussions on the comparability of crimes and suffering. [...] (I)f, as some argue, the central conflict is not that of integration but that of insertion, the victim role may very well be the best claiming position. (Free translation, Chaumont, 2000: 167–168)*

The complementary role to victim is that of aggressor. These days, it is easy to associate the role of aggressor with jobs of power. Managers indeed can potentially put limitations on individual freedom to satisfy tasks requirements. From a contemporary interpretation of ethics, it is safe to say that a manager reprimanding a worker for sub-standard performance is more likely to be blamed by public opinion than the worker who does not provide his employer with an acceptable workload.

The pattern of victim/aggressor is one of the most difficult to change. It is embedded directly in the exercise of power. For it to change, the whole system around it has to change. Changing intentionality and finality of the project at hand typically will do that. Changing the relationships between many other members of the system will also do it.

Ethical Behaviours in a Work Environment

According to a recent survey performed with 15 Canadian managers, "we adopt ethical behaviors when protecting our reputation and professionalism" (free translation, Cherré, 2007: 283). This conclusion is in line with our previous findings: ethical behaviours aiming to protect dignity are often the result of what managers think represent an acceptable consensus in their workplace. It is also coherent with the fact that reputations can be ruined almost instantly on a large scale, using electronic means. Therefore it becomes increasingly important to behave "cautiously".

A New Dimension to Dignity: Reciprocity

In the 90s, France was the scene of a most unusual contest: the throwing of the dwarf. The objective, as the name says, was to throw a small human being as far as possible, above a thick carpet designed to protect him when he reached the ground. Spectators were asked to participate in the contest, hoping to win the competition and establish the record throw of the dwarf.

This contest, seen as funny to some but shocking to others, has had considerable consequences in Europe, as it was the object of a court ruling from one of the most important court of justice in France. The decision was to stop the competition, in the name of human dignity. But the person being thrown did not feel abused the least. As a matter of fact, he even felt valorized by the contest, feeling for the first time that he was equal in importance to tall people. The judge nevertheless decided that his perception of what he thought was a societal consensus on dignity in this case should overrule the "victim's" interpretation:

> *In opposition to fundamental civil and civic rights of citizens, dignity is therefore seen like a non-demandable right. Furthermore, dignity can be imposed on them like an obligation. (Thomas, 2002: 47)*

The concept of dignity, as described in the cause of the throwing of the dwarf, introduces the responsibility for the victim to behave in a way that preserves the integrity of the social norm of dignity. It is interesting to notice that this interpretation is very close to Confucius' code of ethics, written in China more than 2,000 years ago:

> *Human rights under the traditional Chinese political culture were conceived to be part of a larger body of morally prescribed norms of collective human conduct ... The Confucian code of*

ethics recognized each individual's right to personal dignity and worth, but this right was "not considered innate within each human soul as in the West, but had to be acquired" by living up to the code. (Tai, 1985:88; quoting Fairbank, 1972: 119)

But the purpose of political rights "was not to protect the individual against the state but to enable the individual to function more effectively to strengthen the state". (Nathan, 1986: 148) (Donnelly, 2002)

To enter the world of ethics is to accept to be taken hostage by what is most fragile and threatened. This way, the subject is elected, summoned to responsibility. (Doucet, 1997: 75)

The concept of dignity is therefore interpreted very differently in various cultures and eras. Not so long ago the word dignity referred to the aristocrats, the wealthy and the lords. In other words, those that had power. In India for example, for many years, human rights and responsibilities were a function of castes, as determined by birth, according to which group they belonged to. Those groups also determined a hierarchy, positioning people and groups as being superior or inferior to others. Since 1947, this system is officially replaced by the Charter of Rights making everyone equal. But the caste system is very much embedded in the culture and religion of this country. It will take many years before its influence completely disappears. The same holds true in organizations of any country. The interpretation of dignity is constantly changing, making it an elusive concept, constantly redefined by consensus. It is cultural, contextual and nevertheless a meaningful rallying point.

Conclusion

So, what is dignity? How can it be preserved in a work environment? Some define it in financial terms: "[...] (t)he public worth of a man, which is the value set on him by the commonwealth, is that which men commonly call DIGNITY" (Hobbes, 1996: 59). Others find an occasion to establish an empowering relationship with self, with colleagues and with the environment. "Dignity is the ability to establish a sense of self-worth and self-respect and to appreciate the respect of others" (Hodson, 2001: 3).

Dignity is not easily preserved. "Working with dignity requires purposive, considered, and creative efforts on the part of workers as they confront workplaces that deny their dignity and infringe on their well-being" (Hodson, 2001: 3). "Working with dignity thus entails both defending one's inherent human rights and taking actions that are worthy of respect by oneself and others" (Hodson, 2001: 4).

Are the concepts of business performance and human dignity compatible? There seems to be no simple answer to that question. One can say that they are probably competing but not contradictory. In a perfect free market, where competition for products and resources would be perfect, the answer would be no. As a matter of fact, the equilibrium between working conditions and productivity would foster the coexistence of both the best financial performance reached through hiring the best people by offering them the best working conditions. But despite the best efforts of individuals, governments and society in general, the free circulation of goods, services and people still remains a major challenge, one of the main obstacle being that of cultural differences.

So this is why many countries have rules and regulations making sure workers and citizens get "acceptable" living conditions. One of the most important examples of such is the Universal Declaration of Human Rights which uses, among others, the concept of dignity. Essentially based on consensus, values and beliefs, the interpretation of what is dignity is very variable. It is interpreted, in most instances, by courts of justice. The science of social systems helps us to understand how to interpret behaviours in a specific context. But the rise of the principle of the obligation for dignity has limited those behaviours to the ones that comply with social norms. Unfortunately, these norms do not seem to be able to guarantee the preservation of dignity in the long-term.

Workers and managers are therefore still confronted to their free will. It looks as though there is no simple substitute, to this day, for the dignity that comes from a job well done and from the respect of managers for such. Even though the interpretation of what a job well done means remains highly subjective, it is though this very subjectivity that our belonging to the human race gets articulated. All our individual actions will eventually become part of the whole and consequences will be shared by all. This should therefore be an opportunity to reflect on our long-term goals.

References

Bonduelle, P. (1994) *Fonder la dignité?: La notion de dignité*. Paris: Cerf.
Bonefeld, W. and Psychopedis, K. (2005) *Human Dignity, Social Autonomy and the Critique of Capitalism*. Burlington, VT: Ashgate.
Caeymaex, F. (2007) "L'éthique de l'existentialisme." *canal-u*. ENS Paris, November 12, 2007. http://www.canal-u.tv/canalu/producteurs/ens_paris/dossier_programmes/les_grandes_lecons/sartre_de_l_etre_et_le_neant_a_la_critique_de_la_raison_dialectique/l_ethique_de_l_existentialisme (accès le February 24, 2009).
Chaumont, J.-M. (2000) "Du culte des héros à la concurrence des victimes." *Criminologie*, Vol. 33 No. 1, pp. 167–183.
Cherré, B. (2007) *Études des représentations d'une décision éthique chez les gestionnaires*. Montreal: HEC Montreal, doctoral thesis.
Darwin, C. (2004) "The Origin of Species." The University of Adelaide Library. http://ebooks.adelaide.edu.au/d/darwin/charles/d22o/ (accessed on March 4, 2009).
De Beauvoir, S. (1986) *Le deuxième sexe*. Paris: Gallimard.
Donnelly, J. (2002) *Universal Human Rights in Theory and Practice*. Ithaca: Cornell University Press.
Doucet, H. (1997) "Éthique et discernement." *Les cahiers de la SFPL*.
Durand, G. (1999) *Introduction générale à la bioéthique. Histoire, concepts et outils*. Montreal: Fides.
Edelman, B. (2002) "La dignité." Dans *Les droits sociaux des étrangers*, de K. Michelet. Paris: L'Harmattan.
Freidman, M. and Freidman, R. (1979) *Free to Choose: A Personal Statement*. New York: Avon Books.
Gagnon, B. (1989) *La philosophie morale et politique de Charles Taylor*. Québec: Presse de l'Université Laval.
General Assembly of the United Nations (1948) *The Universal Declaration of Human Rights*. http://www.un.org/Overview/rights.html#a1 (accessed February 17, 2009).
Hobbes, T. (1996) *Leviathan*. Oxford: Oxford University Press.
Hodson, R. (2001) *Dignity at Work*. Cambridge: Cambridge University Press.

Kant, E., translation by Zweig, Arnulf (2002) *Groundwork for the Metaphisics of Morals*. Oxford: Oxford University Press.

Kendall Soulen, R. and Woodhead, L. (2006) *God and Human Dignity*. Cambridge: Eerdmans Publishing.

Koubi, G. (2008) *Distinguer entre droits individuels et droits collectifs*. http://koubi.fr/spip.php?article13 (accessed on February 17, 2009).

Kreis, S. (2004) "Pico della Mirandolla, Oration on the Dignity of Man." The History Guide. http://www.historyguide.org/intellect/pico.html (accessed on March 4, 2009).

Legault, G.A., Racine, L. and Bégin, L. (1991) *Éthique et ingénérie*. Montreal: McGraw Hill.

Létourneau, A. and Moreault, F. (2006) *Trois écoles d'éthique appliquée*. Paris: L'Harmattan.

Lévy, B. (1991) *L'Espoir maintenant*. Paris: Verdier.

Martens, P. (2002) *Théories du droit et pensée juridique contemporaine*. Collection de la Faculté de droit de l'Université de Liège. Larcier.

Morin, P.-P. (2008) "La gestion des changements profonds en gestion de projets: que faire quand rien ne va plus?" *La revue des sciences de la gestion,* No. 231–232, pp. 45–52.

Münster, A. (2007) *Sartre et la morale*. Paris: L'Harmattan.

Nozik, R. (1974) *Anarchy, State and Utopia*. New York: Basic Books.

Plato (428–347 BC) *La république*. Paris: GF Flammarion, 1996.

Thomas, H. (2002) "Du lancer du nain comme canon de l'indignité. Le fondement éthique de l'état social." *Raisons politiques*, Mai, pp. 37–52.

Weber, M. (1864–1920) *Politics as a Vocation*. http://www.ne.jp/asahi/moriyuki/abukuma/weber/lecture/politics_vocation.html (accessed on February 17, 2009).

PART IV
Conclusions

Practical experience demonstrates that if an organization is to be socially responsible then it needs the commitment of the senior managers of that organization. All organizations of course have leaders but this is not what we are concerned with – rather it is the leadership process which we are going to look at. Effect change management requires leadership to instigate and drive the process and an understanding of this leadership process will help you become a more effective change manager. Central to a consideration of leadership is the concept of power, and Rowlinson (1997) has argued that power is central to understanding organizations.

Equally one of the most used words relating to corporate activity at present is the word sustainability. Indeed some would argue that it has been so heavily overused, and with so many different meanings applied, to it that it is effectively meaningless. Thus the term sustainability currently has a high profile within the field of corporate activity. Indeed it is frequently mentioned as central to corporate activity without any attempt to define exactly what sustainable activity entails. This is understandable as the concept is problematic and subject to many varying definitions – ranging from platitudes concerning sustainable development to the deep green concept of returning to the "golden era" before industrialization – although often it is used by corporations merely to signify that they intend to continue their existence into the future.

The ubiquity of the concept and the vagueness of its use mean that it is necessary to re-examine the concept and to consider how it applies to corporate activity. In this chapter therefore we do just this – examining what is meant by sustainability – and looking at the various aspects of sustainability. For us there are two aspects to this – corporate actions and their consequences; and the distribution of the benefits accruing from such corporate activity. Furthermore both have to be set not just within the sphere of the corporation itself, or even the wider context of its stakeholders but also within the widest geospatial context – that of the global environment.

There is a considerable degree of confusion surrounding the concept of sustainability: for the purist sustainability implies nothing more than stasis – the ability to continue in an unchanged manner – but often it is taken to imply development in a sustainable manner (Marsden, 2000; Hart and Milstein, 2003) and the terms sustainability and sustainable development are for many viewed as synonymous. For us we take the definition as being concerned with stasis (Aras and Crowther, 2008); at the corporate level if development is possible without jeopardizing that stasis then this is a bonus rather than a constituent part of that sustainability. Moreover, sustainable development is often misinterpreted as focusing solely on environmental issues. In reality, it is a much broader concept. Sustainable development policies encompass three general policy areas: *economic, environmental and social*. In support of this, several United Nations texts, most recently the 2005 World Summit Outcome Document, refer to the *"interdependent and mutually reinforcing pillars" of sustainable development as economic development, social development, and environmental protection.*

References

Aras G. and Crowther D. (2008); Corporate sustainability reporting: a study in disingenuity?; *Journal of Business Ethics*, 87 (supp 1), 279–288.

Hart S. L. and Milstein M. B. (2003); Creating sustainable value; *Academy of Management Executive*, 17 (2), 56–67

Marsden C. (2000); The new corporate citizenship of big business: part of the solution to sustainability; *Business and Society Review*, 105 (1), 9–25.

Rowlinson M. (1997); *Organizations and Institutions: Perspectives in Economics and Sociology*; London; Macmillan.

CHAPTER 11
Governance, Dignity and Responsibility: Towards a Symbiosis

DAVID CROWTHER AND ANA-MARIA DAVILA-GOMEZ

Introduction

Recent corporate behaviour has exposed multiple misdeeds which have in turn demonstrated many failures in governance which need to be addressed. Although much attention has been paid to these governance failures, there still remain, however, a surprisingly large number of pertinent issues which have barely been mentioned – and have certainly not been explored in detail – despite the fact that they need to be addressed in order to create an environment in which a similar set of circumstances will not reoccur and cause the next crisis. One such issue – an extremely important issue – is the relationship between risk and rewards. Elementary economic theory teaches us that enterprise is concerned with taking risk and that rewards accrue to those taking risk if they are successful. Risk, of course, means that success is uncertain and that failure is also a possible outcome. So taking risks does not always lead to gaining rewards. It therefore follows that the higher the level of risk which is taken the higher the level of rewards for success that should accrue because the chance of failure equally rises. Finance theory was developed in order to quantify the relationship between success and failure and make the rewards commensurate with the risk. This quantification ensured that arbitrage would occur to equalize the risk/reward relationship across various enterprises in a freely operating market system. These are things that we all learn as part of an introductory economics course. This risk–reward relationship is a necessary part of economic activity and so a necessary part of business life. Its severing has led to irresponsible behaviour and arguably to a loss of dignity – certainly on the part of those who have suffered from the corporate excess. This chapter provides in effect a conclusion to this volume by seeking to reconnect these issues and to show that if all people are treated with dignity then not only is corporate behaviour inevitably responsible but also the crisis of governance will not recur.

It is clearly accepted that good corporate governance is fundamental to the successfully continuing operating of any company; hence much attention has been paid to the procedures of such governance. Often, however, what is actually meant by the corporate governance of a firm is merely assumed without being made explicit (Crowther and Seifi 2010); often it is assumed to be concerned with how the company conducts its annual meeting, deals with auditors and so on. Increasingly this has been extended into a more general concern with the management of investor relationships. In reality of course it affects all of the operations of a business and its relations with all of its stakeholders – a much more wide-ranging concern than is sometimes appreciated. It is being recognized everywhere that good governance is important for corporate performance. Indeed firms are being expected to make statements about their governance as part of their annual reporting and every corporate website makes a statement about the company's governance procedures. It is easy to claim that this is because of a reaction to all the corporate scandals which we have witnessed in the last decade, starting with the collapse of Enron.

The recent financial crisis, much as previous ones, has highlighted failures in governance and failures in regulation. There is of course one problem with managing the prevention of future financial crisis (Grabel 2003) and this is concerned with the recognition of and regulation of a truly global market for finance. The liberalization of financial markets instigated by the Washington consensus has made the free movement of funds a fact of financial life and has encouraged the parcelling together of doubtful debts into mystery parcels to be sold around the world. And of course the operators in all financial markets, always ready to accept a gamble in the hope of ever larger profits and bonuses have been quick to respond.

Regulators inevitably, according to their founding ethos, must focus upon a local market while finance escapes them through its ability to migrate around the world. Effectively this means that any realistic form of regulation does not and cannot exist (Becker and Westbrook 1998). One consequence of this regulatory failure of course is that contamination spreads and the dubious practices developed in one financial market become the norm in other markets. When the inevitable crisis appears this too spreads from one country to another as all economies are affected by both the consequences of dubious lending practices and by the ensuing crisis of confidence. This calls attention to the fact – recognized but mostly ignored in the financial models used to legitimate financial activity – that the financial market is a global market and a corollary of this is that any regulatory regime must also be global. In this chapter therefore we highlight the problems with the current regime and argue for a global regulatory authority capable of sanctioning even the most powerful actors in the market, including national and transnational governments.

Failures in Governance

One of the main issues which has been of concern to corporate managers, both before the crisis and much more so during it, is that of corporate governance (Aras 2008). Probably since the mid-1980s, corporate governance has attracted a great deal of attention. Early impetus was provided by Anglo-American codes of good corporate governance.[1] Stimulated by institutional investors, other countries in the developed as well as in the emerging markets established an adapted version of these codes for their own companies. Supra-national authorities like the OECD and the World Bank did not remain passive and developed their own set of standard principles and recommendations. This type of self-

---

1   An example is the Cadbury Report which went through several iterations to eventually become The Combined Code applied in 2003.

regulation was chosen above a set of legal standards (Van den Berghe 2001). After some big corporate scandals corporate governance has become central to most companies. It is understandable that investors' protection has become a much more important issue for all financial markets after the tremendous firm failures and scandals. Investors are demanding that companies implement rigorous corporate governance principles in order to achieve better returns on their investment and to reduce agency costs. Most of the times investors are ready to pay more for companies to have good governance standards. Similarly a company's corporate governance report is one of the main tools for investor' decisions. Because of these reason companies cannot ignore the pressure for good governance from shareholders, potential investors and other markets actors.

Good governance is essential for good corporate performance (Aras and Crowther 2008a) and one view of good corporate performance is that of stewardship and thus just as the management of an organization is concerned with the stewardship of the financial resources of the organization so too would management of the organization be concerned with the stewardship of environmental resources. The difference, however, is that environmental resources are mostly located externally to the organization.[2] Stewardship in this context therefore is concerned with the resources of society as well as the resources of the organization. As far as stewardship of external environmental resources is concerned then the central tenet of such stewardship is that of ensuring sustainability. Sustainability is focused on the future and is concerned with ensuring that the choices of resource utilization in the future are not constrained by decisions taken in the present (Aras and Crowther 2007a). This necessarily implies such concepts as generating and utilizing renewable resources, minimizing pollution and using new techniques of manufacture and distribution.[3] It also implies the acceptance of any costs involved in the present as an investment for the future.

The current crisis, and its effects, has meant that a great deal of concern is being expressed all over the world about shortcomings in the systems of corporate governance in operation and its organization has been exercising the minds of business managers, academics and government officials all over the world (Spence 2008). Often companies' main target is to become global – while at the same time remaining sustainable – as a means to get competitive power. But the most important question is concerned with what will be a firms' route to becoming global and what will be necessary in order to get global competitive power. There is more than one answer to this question and there are a variety of routes for a company to achieve this. Corporate governance can be considered as an environment of trust, ethics, moral values and confidence – as a synergic effort of all the constituents of society – that is the stakeholders, including government; the general public and so on; professional/service providers – and the corporate sector.

Of equal concern is the question of corporate social responsibility (Aras and Crowther 2007b); although there is an accepted link between good corporate governance and corporate social responsibility the relationship between the two is not clearly defined and understood. Thus many firms consider that their governance is adequate because they

---

2   Therefore, while addressing governance, managers should develop a sense of acknowledgment and awareness towards the importance of stewardship for external resources and the respect for the dignity of human beings with whom each organization interacts.

3   Thoughtfulness and forethought in managers' decision-making processes help them to consider the consequences towards the future of other stakeholders. To us, this thoughtfulness includes what Hume (1711–1776) discussed about the virtues of benevolence and generosity.

comply with The Combined Code on Corporate Governance, which came into effect in 2003[4] (Aras and Crowther 2008b). Of course all firms reporting on the London Stock Exchange are required to comply with this code, and so these firms are doing no more than meeting their regulatory obligations. Many companies regard corporate governance as simply a part of investor relationships and do nothing more regarding such governance except to identify that it is important for investors/potential investors and to flag up that they have such governance policies. The more enlightened recognize that there is a clear link between governance and corporate social responsibility and make efforts to link the two. Often this is no more than making a claim that good governance is a part of their CSR policy as well as a part of their relationship with shareholders.

The Free Market System

The Free Market system is of course based upon the philosophy of Utilitarianism, which was a development of Classical Liberal Theory. This theory started to be developed in the seventeenth century by such writers as John Locke as a means of explaining how society operated, and should operate, in an era in which the Divine Right of Kings to rule and to run society for their own benefit had been challenged and was generally considered to be inappropriate for the society which then existed. Classical Liberalism is founded upon the two principles of reason and rationality: reason in that everything had a logic which could be understood and agreed with by all, and rationality in that every decision made was made by a person in the light of what their evaluation had shown them to be for their greatest benefit. Classical Liberalism therefore is centred upon the individual, who is assumed to be rational and would make rational decisions, and is based upon the need to give freedom to every individual to pursue his/her own ends. It is therefore a philosophy of the pursuance of self-interest. Society, insofar as it existed and was considered to be needed, was therefore merely an aggregation of these individual self-interests. This aggregation was considered to be a sufficient explanation for the need for society. Indeed Locke argued that the whole purpose of society was to protect the rights of each individual and to safeguard these private rights.

There is, however, a problem with this allowing of every individual the complete freedom to follow his/her own ends and to maximize his/her own welfare. This problem is that in some circumstances this welfare can only be created at the expense of other individuals. It is through this conflict between the rights and freedoms of individuals that problems occur in society. It is for this reason therefore that de Tocqueville argued that there was a necessary function for government within society. He argued that the function of government therefore was the regulation of individual transactions so as to safeguard the rights of all individuals as far as possible.

Although this philosophy of individual freedom was developed as the philosophy of Liberalism it can be seen that this philosophy has been adopted by the Conservative governments throughout the world, as led by the UK government of Thatcher and the US government of Reagan in the 1980s. This philosophy has led increasingly to the reduction

---

[4] It was revised in 2006.

of state involvement in society[5] and the giving of freedom to individuals to pursue their own ends, with regulation providing a mediating mechanism where deemed necessary. It will be apparent, however, that there is a further problem with Liberalism and this is that the mediation of rights between different individuals only works satisfactorily when the power of individuals is roughly equal. Plainly this situation never arises between all individuals and this is the cause of one of the problems with society. This problem has been referred to periodically throughout this book in the context of the role of accounting in maintaining this disequilibrium in power relationships.

While this philosophy of Liberalism was developed to explain the position of individuals in society and the need for government and regulation of that society, the philosophy applies equally to organizations. Indeed Liberalism considers that organizations arise within society as a mechanism whereby individuals can pursue their individual self-interests more effectively that they can alone. Thus firms exist because it is a more efficient means of individuals maximizing their self-interests through collaboration than is possible through each individual acting alone. This argument provides the basis for the Theory of the Firm, which argues that through this combination between individuals the costs of individual transactions are thereby reduced.

The concept of Utilitarianism was developed as an extension of Liberalism in order to account for the need to regulate society in terms of each individual pursuing, independently, his or her own ends. It was developed by people such as Bentham and John Stuart Mill who defined the optimal position for society as being the greatest good of the greatest number and argued that it was government's role to mediate between individuals to ensure this societal end. In Utilitarianism it is not actions which are deemed to be good or bad but merely outcomes. Thus any means of securing a desired outcome was deemed to be acceptable and if the same outcomes ensued then there was no difference, in value terms, between different means of securing those outcomes. Thus actions are value neutral and only outcomes matter. This is of course problematical when the actions of firms are concerned because firms only consider outcomes from the point of view of the firm itself. Indeed accounting as we know only captures the actions of a firm insofar as they affect the firm itself and ignores other consequences of the actions of a firm. Under Utilitarianism, however, if the outcomes for the firm were considered to be desirable then any means of achieving these outcomes was considered acceptable. In the nineteenth and early twentieth centuries this was the way in which firms were managed and accounting information was used purely to evaluate actions and potential actions from the point of view of the firm itself. It is only in more recent times that it has become accepted that all the outcomes from the actions of the firm are important and need to be taken into account.

The development of Utilitarianism led to the development of Economic Theory as means of explaining the actions of firms. Indeed the concept of Perfect Competition is predicated in the assumptions of Classical Liberal Theory. This is a problem because it encourages selfish and exploitative behaviour (Crowther 2011). So we can either believe that the market will mediate in an optimal way – which is complete nonsense – or we can suggest that ethical understanding will compensate – also nonsense. Or we must look for an alternative.

---

5 It can be asserted that this was largely due to Thatcher's misunderstanding of Hayek's (1944) dogma in his *The Road to Serfdom*.

Gambling the Future

The proposed solutions to the crisis are themselves problematic. Firstly the Free Market system upon which much of the current economic system is based has been abandoned as governments have sought to support ailing banks, thereby signalling yet again that there is no cost to profligate irresponsibility as far as financial markets are concerned. For institutions therefore the cost of irresponsibility must be borne by society at large and particularly by future members of that society who must repay the enormous amount of government borrowings, or at best must service that debt. So the cost of irresponsibility now has been conveniently externalized into the future. While this public spending is in accord with the Keynesian economics which are the alternative to the deregulated economics of the Chicago school, Keynes himself actually advocated that the public spending should be utilized on the provision of public goods and infrastructure as an investment in the future. This time the spending has disappeared and the future has been mortgaged without any discernable benefit.

Although there has been much public discussion regarding how the responsibility should be apportioned this is not really significant, although it is apparent that those responsible are, in the main, avoiding sanction and penalty.[6] Similarly many people have discussed the failures in the system which have led to the crisis. Significantly, however, there does not seem to be any recognition that this is largely a cause of the incompatibility of a global environment with national regulation. And the voices of those calling for a regulatory environment to deal with this global environment are very quiet. So we argue that this needs to be solved in order to prevent future reoccurrences. Until this happens we are gambling with the future for no benefit.

It is unquestioned that all systems of governance are concerned primarily with managing the governing of associations and therefore with political authority, institutions, and, ultimately, control. Governance in this particular sense denotes formal political institutions that aim to coordinate and control interdependent social relations and that have the ability to enforce decisions. Increasingly however, in a globalized world, the concept of governance is being used to describe the regulation of interdependent relations in the absence of overarching political authority, such as in the international system (Rajan 2008). Thus global governance can be considered as the management of global processes in the absence of form of global government. There are some international bodies which seek to address these issues and prominent among these are the United Nations and the World Trade Organization. Each of these has met with mixed success in instituting some form of governance in international relations but they are part of a recognition of the problem and an attempt to address worldwide problems that go beyond the capacity of individual states to solve (Rosenau 1999).

To use the term global governance is not of course to imply that such a system actually exists, let alone to consider the effectiveness of its operations. It is merely to recognize that in this increasingly globalized world there is a need for some form of governance to deal with multinational and global issues. The term global governance therefore is a descriptive term, recognizing the issue and referring to concrete cooperative

---

6   The idea of faceless organizations evokes what, in reality, we witness nowadays numerous times when no individuals can be identified as responsible for actions of the organizations, as for instance, the organizations are many times considered as separate entities.

problem-solving arrangements. These may be formal, taking the shape of laws or formally constituted institutions to manage collective affairs by a variety of actors – including states, intergovernmental organizations, non-governmental organizations (NGOs), other civil society actors, private sector organizations, pressure groups and individuals. The system also includes of course informal (as in the case of practices or guidelines) or temporary units (as in the case of coalitions). Thus global governance can be considered to be the complex of formal and informal institutions, mechanisms, relationships, and processes between and among states, markets, citizens and organizations, both inter- and non-governmental, through which collective interests on the global plane are articulated, rights and obligations are established, and differences are mediated (Tobin 2000).

Global governance is not of course the same thing as world government: indeed it can be argued that such a system would not actually be necessary if there was such a thing as a world government. Currently, however, the various state governments have a legitimate monopoly on the use of force – on the power of enforcement. Global governance therefore refers to the political interaction that is required to solve problems that affect more than one state or region when there is no power of enforcing compliance. Improved global problem-solving need not of course require the establishing of more powerful formal global institutions, but it would involve the creation of a consensus on norms and practices to be applied. Steps are of course underway to establish these norms and one example that is currently being established is the creation and improvement of global accountability mechanisms. In this respect, for example, the United Nations Global Compact[7] – described as the world's largest voluntary corporate responsibility initiative – brings together companies, national and international agencies, trade unions and other labour organizations and various organs of civil society in order to support universal environmental protection, human rights and social principles. Participation is entirely voluntary, and there is no enforcement of the principles by an outside regulatory body. Companies adhere to these practices both because they make economic sense, and because their stakeholders, including their shareholders (most individuals and institutional investors) are concerned with these issues and this provides a mechanism whereby they can monitor the compliance of companies easily. Mechanisms such as the Global Compact can improve the ability of individuals and local communities to hold companies accountable.

Towards a Solution: The Role of CSR

Elementary economic theory teaches us that enterprise is concerned with taking risk and that rewards accrue to those taking risk if they are successful. Risk of course means that success is uncertain and that failure is also a possible outcome. So taking risk does not always lead to gaining rewards. It therefore follows that the higher the level of risk which is taken the higher the level of rewards for success that should accrue because the chance of failure equally rises (Aras and Crowther 2009a; b; 2010a). Finance theory was developed in order to quantify the relationship between success and failure and make the rewards commensurate with the risk. This quantification ensured that arbitrage would occur to equalize the risk/reward relationship across various enterprises in a freely

---

[7] See www.unglobalcompact.org/

operating market system. These are things that we all learn as part of an introductory economics course.

This risk–reward relationship is a necessary part of economic activity and so a necessary part of business life; it is what enables an assessment of the viability of any particular form of enterprise and what enables a potential investor to select between alternative uses for their investment – through an individual assessment of the risk – rewards trade off. If investors forget about this relationship between risk and reward then profligate investing ensues and unsustainable booms take place. We have seen many examples of this from the Dutch Tulip Bubble at the beginning of the seventeenth century through to the Dot Com Bubble at the end of the twentieth century as speculative fever takes hold and the risk–reward relationship is forgotten.

If this relationship is broken so that rewards accrue without the need to take risk then there is no basis upon which to assess investment possibilities and no way to adequately choose between the alternatives. It is likely therefore that investment decisions will be made which are plainly unsuitable and sometimes not even viable. This is the situation in the boardrooms of all major corporations where the chief executive is rewarded for success without fear of any penalty for failure. Indeed he[8] is often also rewarded for failure and is certainly more than adequately compensated for removal from office.

This situation is made worse because Attribution Theory operates in the boardroom but is not even recognized let alone challenged. Attribution Theory of course means that we, as individuals, take credit for successful outcomes – which we attribute to our particular abilities – while blaming failures upon circumstances outside our control. So we should be rewarded for success but never penalized for failure, effectively severing the risk–reward relationship.

In the boardroom therefore we see the cult of the hero (Crowther 2002; 2005) applied to the chief executive who becomes feted for success but never vilified for failure. And rewards have become skewed accordingly. Thus the rewards for a chief executive have increased fifteenfold in comparison with the average worker and the difference in pay is now vastly more than it was 50 years ago. At the same time incentive schemes have meant that between 5 and 10 per cent of the average corporation is now owned by its executives – simply as a reward for existing rather than for any abnormal performance.

This we would describe as legitimated theft as these people have not taken any risk. Risk remains firmly with the investors in the business who must pay the penalty for failure and with other stakeholders (such as employees of suppliers) who must equally take the risk without any rewards. Indeed JIT approaches are adept in transferring the risk away from the business – from the powerful to the less powerful.

So executives attract rewards without fear of penalty for failure. Indeed the balance is such that the risk takers cannot even remove those executives and cannot really determine what rewards they should receive. Moreover governance procedures which enforce this strange relationship have been accepted and are the norm for large companies. Indeed this is considered to be a part of good governance which leads towards successful and sustainable companies.

The strange thing is that this has not been questioned to any extent. When the economic climate is good then all stakeholders just sit back and accept their returns while praising the executives for their exceptional abilities. And it is simply expected

---

8   It will almost certainly be a man!

that this good economic climate will continue forever – even though history teaches us the opposite. When times are bad then scapegoats are sought – but these are outside the company: bankers, regulators, governments ... But never those executives who have received their rewards for merely existing.

There has been surprisingly little comment about this in the current crisis even though it seems clear that the re-establishment of the risk–rewards relationship is an essential component of creating an economic climate in which crises will not continually reoccur. It is our argument that this is a matter which needs to be raised and addressed in order for any form of sustainable economic activity to be able to take place. Without such a change then theft is simply legitimated – and legitimate theft cannot occur in a sustainable economy.

Governance and Social Responsibility

In the UK there has been a succession of codes on corporate governance dating back to the Cadbury Report in 1992. Currently all companies reporting on the London Stock Exchange are required to comply with the Combined Code on Corporate Governance, which came into effect in 2003. It might be thought therefore that a framework for corporate governance has already been developed but the code in the UK has been continually revised while problems associated with bad governance have not disappeared. So clearly a framework has not been established in the UK and an international framework looks even more remote. Indeed many of the codes in other parts of the world have been developed from the British code.

One of the problems with developing such a framework is the continual rules versus principles debate. The American approach tends to be rules-based while the European approach is more based on the development of principles – a slower process. In general, rules are considered to be simpler to follow than principles, demarcating a clear line between acceptable and unacceptable behaviour. Rules also reduce discretion on the part of individual managers or auditors. In practice, however, rules can be more complex than principles. They may be ill-equipped to deal with new types of transactions not covered by the code. Moreover, even if clear rules are followed, one can still find a way to circumvent their underlying purpose – this is harder to achieve if one is bound by broader principles. There is also the implication that what is not covered by the code is automatically acceptable.

There are of course many different models of corporate governance around the world (see Aras and Crowther 2009a). These differ according to the nature of the system of capitalism in which they are embedded. The liberal model that is common in Anglo-American countries tends to give priority to the interests of shareholders. The coordinated model, which is normally found in Continental Europe and in Japan, recognizes in addition the interests of workers, managers, suppliers, customers, and the community. Both models have distinct competitive advantages, but in different ways. The liberal model of corporate governance encourages radical innovation and cost competition, whereas the coordinated model of corporate governance facilitates incremental innovation and quality competition. However, there are important differences between the recent approach to governance issues taken in the USA and what has happened in the UK.

In the USA a corporation is governed by a board of directors, which has the power to choose an executive officer, usually known as the chief executive officer (CEO). The CEO has broad power to manage the corporation on a daily basis, but needs to get board approval for certain major actions, such as hiring his/her immediate subordinates, raising money, acquiring another company, major capital expansions, or other expensive projects. Other duties of the board may include policy-setting, decision-making, monitoring management's performance, or corporate control. The board of directors is nominally selected by and responsible to the shareholders, but the articles of many companies make it difficult for all but the largest shareholders to have any influence over the makeup of the board. Normally individual shareholders are not offered a choice of board nominees among which to choose, but are merely asked to rubberstamp the nominees of the existing board. Various incentives have pervaded many corporate boards in the developed world, with board members beholden to the chief executive whose actions they are intended to oversee. Frequently, members of the boards of directors are CEOs of other corporations – in interlocking relationships, which many people see as posing a potential conflict of interest.

The UK on the other hand has developed a flexible model of regulation of corporate governance, known as the "comply or explain" code of governance. This is a principles-based code that lists a number of recommended practices, such as:

- the separation of CEO and chairman of the board;
- the introduction of a time limit for CEOs' contracts;
- the introduction of a minimum number of non-executives directors, and of independent directors;
- the designation of a senior non-executive director;
- the formation and composition of remuneration, audit and nomination committees.

Publicly listed companies in the UK have to either apply those principles or, if they choose not to, explain in a designated part of their annual reports why they have decided not to do so. The monitoring of those explanations is left to shareholders themselves. The basic idea of the Code[9] is that one size does not fit all in matters of corporate governance and that instead of a statutory regime like the Sarbanes-Oxley Act in the US, it is best to leave some flexibility to companies so that they can make choices most adapted to their circumstances. If they have good reasons to deviate from the sound rule, they should be able to convincingly explain those to their shareholders. A form of the code has been in existence since 1992 and has had drastic effects on the way firms are governed in the UK. A recent study shows that in 1993, about 10 per cent of the FTSE 350 companies were fully compliant with all dimensions of the Code while by 2003 – when the Combined Code was introduced – more than 60 per cent were fully compliant. The same success was not achieved when looking at the explanation part for non-compliant companies. Many deviations are simply not explained and a large majority of explanations fail to identify specific circumstances justifying those deviations, although with the passage of time many more firms have become completely compliant. Thus the general view is that the UK's system works fairly well and in fact is often considered to be a benchmark, and therefore followed by a number of other countries.

---

9   The Combined Code on Corporate Governance.

Corporate governance principles and codes have been developed in different countries (see Aras and Crowther 2009b) and have been issued by stock exchanges, corporations, institutional investors, or associations (institutes) of directors and managers with the support of governments and international organizations. As a rule, compliance with these governance recommendations is not mandated by law, although the codes which are linked to stock exchange listing requirements[10] will tend to have a coercive effect. Thus, for example, companies quoted on the London and Toronto Stock Exchanges formally need not follow the recommendations of their respective national codes, but they must disclose whether they follow the recommendations in those documents and, where not, they should provide explanations concerning divergent practices. Such disclosure requirements exert a significant pressure on listed companies for compliance.

In its Global Investor Opinion Survey of over 200 institutional investors first undertaken in 2000 (and subsequently updated), McKinsey found that 80 per cent of the respondents would pay a premium for well-governed companies. They defined a well-governed company as one that had mostly outside directors, who had no management ties, undertook formal evaluation of its directors, and was responsive to investors' requests for information on governance issues. The size of the premium varied by market, from 11 per cent for Canadian companies to around 40 per cent for companies where the regulatory backdrop was least certain (for example those in Morocco, Egypt or Russia). Other studies have similarly linked broad perceptions of the quality of companies to superior share price performance. On the other hand, research into the relationship between specific corporate governance controls and the financial performance of companies has had very mixed results.

Human Rights Issues

Another thing which has become prominent is a concern with the supply chain of a business (Aras and Crowther 2010b); in other words with what is happening in other companies which that company does business with – their suppliers and the suppliers of their suppliers. In particular, people are concerned with the exploitation of people in developing countries, especially the question of child labour but also such things as sweat shops.

So no longer is it acceptable for a company to say that the conditions under which their suppliers operate is outside their control and so they are not responsible. Customers have said that this is not acceptable and have called companies to account.[11] And there have recently been a number of high-profile retail companies which have held their hands up to acknowledge problems and then taken very public steps to change this.

Interestingly the popularity of companies increases after they have admitted problems and taken steps to correct these problems. In doing this they are thereby showing both that honesty is the best practice and also that customers are reasonable. The evidence suggests that individual customers are understanding and that they do not expect perfection but do expect honesty and transparency. Moreover they also expect companies to make efforts to change their behaviour and to try to solve their CSR problems.

---

10 Such as, for example, the UK Combined Code referred to earlier.
11 See Marchand, De Coninck and Walker (2005) who also present a prospective of responsible consumer behaviour, which is a tendency that is increasingly gaining strength worldwide.

Companies themselves have also changed. No longer are they concerned with greenwashing – the pretence of socially responsible behaviour through artful reporting. Now companies are taking CSR much more seriously not just because they understand that it is a key to business success and can give them a strategic advantage, but also because people in those organizations care about social responsibility.

So it would be reasonable to claim that the growing importance of CSR and sustainability is being driven by individuals who care – but those individuals are not just customers, they are also employees, managers, owners and investors of a company. So companies are partly reacting to external pressures and partly leading the development of responsible behaviour and reporting.

Relating Corporate Governance and Corporate Social Responsibility

It is no longer questioned that the activities of a corporation impact upon the external environment and that therefore such an organization should be accountable to a wider audience than simply its shareholders. This is a central tenet of both the concept of corporate governance and the concept of corporate social responsibility. Implicit in this is a concern with the effects of the actions of an organization on its external environment and there is a recognition that it is not just the owners of the organization who have a concern with the activities of that organization. Additionally there are a wide variety of other stakeholders who justifiably have a concern with those activities, and are affected by those activities. Those other stakeholders have not just an interest in the activities of the firm but also a degree of influence over the shaping of those activities. This influence is so significant that it can be argued that the power and influence of these stakeholders is such that it amounts to quasi-ownership of the organization.

One view of good corporate performance is that of stewardship and thus just as the management of an organization is concerned with the stewardship of the financial resources of the organization so too would management of the organization be concerned with the stewardship of environmental resources (Aras and Crowther 2009c). The difference, however, is that environmental resources are mostly located externally to the organization. Stewardship in this context therefore is concerned with the resources of society as well as the resources of the organization. As far as stewardship of external environmental resources is concerned then the central tenet of such stewardship is that of ensuring sustainability. Sustainability is focused on the future and is concerned with ensuring that the choices of resource utilization in the future are not constrained by decisions taken in the present. This necessarily implies such concepts as generating and utilizing renewable resources, minimizing pollution and using new techniques of manufacture and distribution. It also implies the acceptance of any costs involved in the present as an investment for the future.

Not only does such sustainable activity, however, impact upon society in the future; it also impacts upon the organization itself in the future. Thus good environmental performance by an organization in the present is in reality an investment in the future of the organization itself. This is achieved through the ensuring of supplies and production techniques which will enable the organization to operate in the future in a similar way to its operations in the present and so to undertake value creation activity in the future much as it does in the present. Financial management also, however, is concerned with the management of the organization's resources in the present so that management will be possible in a value creation way in the future. Thus the internal management of the firm, from a financial perspective, and its external environmental management coincide in this common concern for management for the future. Good performance in the financial dimension leads to good future performance in the environmental dimension and vice versa. Thus there is no dichotomy between environmental performance and financial performance and the two concepts conflate into one concern. This concern is of course the management of the future as far as the firm is concerned.

Similarly the creation of value within the firm is followed by the distribution of value to the stakeholders of that firm, whether these stakeholders are shareholders or others. Value, however, must be taken in its widest definition to include more than economic value as it is possible that economic value can be created at the expense of other constituent components of welfare such as spiritual or emotional welfare. This creation of value by the firm adds to welfare for society at large, although this welfare is targeted at particular members of society rather than treating all as equals. This has led to arguments concerning the distribution of value created and to whether value is created for one set of stakeholders at the expense of others. Nevertheless if, when summed, value is created then this adds to welfare for society at large, however distributed.[12] Similarly good environmental performance leads to increased welfare for society at large, although this will tend to be expressed in emotional and community terms rather than being capable of being expressed in quantitative terms. This will be expressed in a feeling of well-being, which will of course lead to increased motivation. Such increased motivation will inevitably lead to increased productivity, some of which will benefit the organizations, and also a desire to maintain the pleasant environment which will in turn lead to a further enhanced environment, a further increase in welfare and the reduction of destructive aspects of societal engagement by individuals.

Relating Social Responsibility with Governance: The Evidence

There has been a variety of research over time investigating the relationship between the characteristics of a firm and its disclosure (for example Cowen et al. 1987; Gray et al. 2001) and equally there is research (for example Burke and Longsdon 1996) showing the benefits of CSR. It is clear that these benefits are also directly related to the sustainability of a firm and that firm's success. It would seem apparent therefore that there should be some attention paid to social responsibility within the corporate governance of a corporation. It is therefore apposite to conduct an investigation as to what exactly is mentioned about CSR within such corporate governance. It is to be expected that good corporate governance will foster social responsibility in general.

There has been much work undertaken which investigates the failures of corporate governance and the ensuing problems which arise and this could be adapted to a consideration of our concern with the relationship between corporate governance and

---

12   Essentially this is the Utilitarian argument, which we have expanded to take into account not just economic benefits but also welfare and spiritual benefits. We have argued elsewhere however (for example Aras and Crowther 2009c) that the manner of distribution – and its concomitant equity – is crucial to any consideration of sustainable society.

social responsibility. We argue, however, that this approach – akin to Popper's (1959) falsification theory – is not an appropriate methodology for this kind of research – companies which are not run perfectly are probably as common as black swans! Rather our starting assumption is that effective corporate governance will be largely unnoticed and that this will be manifest in examples of good practice rather than in the exceptional instances of poor practice.

The Social Contract

It has been widely recognized that the activities of an organization impact upon its external environment and therefore it has been suggested that such an organization should be accountable to a wider audience than simply its shareholders. Such a suggestion probably first arose in the 1970s and a concern with a wider view of company performance is taken by some writers who evince concern with the social performance of a business, as a member of society at large. This concern was stated by Ackerman (1975) who argued that big business was recognizing the need to adapt to a new social climate of community accountability, but that the orientation of business to financial results was inhibiting social responsiveness. McDonald and Puxty (1979) on the other hand maintain that companies are no longer the instruments of shareholders alone but exist within society and so therefore have responsibilities to that society, and that there is therefore a shift towards the greater accountability of companies to all participants.

Recognition of the rights of all stakeholders and the duty of a business to be accountable in this wider context therefore has been largely a relatively recent phenomenon.[13] The economic view of accountability only to owners has only recently, however, been subject to debate to any considerable extent. Some owners of businesses have, however, always recognized a responsibility to other stakeholders and this is evident from the early days of the Industrial Revolution. Implicit in this concern with the effects of the actions of an organization on its external environment is the recognition that it is not just the owners of the organization who have a concern with the activities of that organization. Additionally there is a wide variety of other stakeholders who justifiably have a concern with those activities, and are affected by those activities. Those other stakeholders have not the desirability of considering the social performance of a business has not always, however, been accepted and has been the subject of extensive debate.[14] Nevertheless the performance of businesses in a wider arena than the stock market and its value to shareholders has become of increasing concern. In many respects this can be considered to be a return to the notion of the Social Contract, which has been used to persuade business to accept their social responsibility.

Social Contract Theory is most often associated with the work of Hobbes (1651) and Rousseau (1762) where a contract, usually considered to be implied or hypothetical, is made between citizens for the organization of the society and as a basis for legal and political power within that society. An alternative to the attempts to explain, and regulate, relations between organizational stakeholders based upon the rationalities of economic theory is

---

13   Mathews (1997) traces its origins to the 1970s although arguments (see Crowther 2002c) show that such concerns can be traced back to the Industrial Revolution.
14   See Hetherington (1973) and Dahl (1972) for example.

the approach based upon the concept of the social contract. This social contract implies some form of altruistic behaviour – the converse of selfishness. Self-interest connotes selfishness, and since the Middle Ages has informed a number of important philosophical, political and economic propositions. Among these is Hobbes's world where unfettered self-interest is expected to lead to social devastation. A high degree of regulation is prescribed in order to avoid such a disastrous outcome, but in the process corporations sacrifice all the rights (human, labour, social) for others. Self-interest again raises its head in the utilitarian perspective as championed by Bentham, Locke and John Stuart Mill (Titus and Smith 1974). The latter for example advocated as morally right the pursuit of the greatest happiness for the greatest number. Similarly, Adam Smith's free-market economics is predicated on competing self-interest. These influential ideas put interest of the individual above interest of the collective. Indeed, from this perspective, collective interests are best served through self-interest. At the same time this corporate self-interest has come to draw disapproval in modern times, as reflected in the current vogue for the tenets of corporate social responsibility. The moral value of individualism has all but vanished.

The discourse of accounting can be seen to be concerned solely with the operational performance of the organization. Contrasting views of the role of accounting in the production process might therefore be epitomized as either providing a system of measurement to enable a reasonable market mediation in the resource allocation problem or as providing a mechanism for the expropriation of surplus value from the labour component of the transformational process. Both strands of the discourse, however, tend to view that labour as a homogeneous entity and consider the effect of organizational activity upon that entity. Labour is of course composed of individual people; moreover these individual people have a lifetime of availability for employment and different needs at different points during their life cycle. The depersonalization of people through the use of the term labour, however, provides a mechanism for the treatment of labour as an entity without any recognition of these personal needs. Thus it is possible to restrict the discourse to that of the organization and its components – labour capital and so on – and to theorize accordingly. The use of the term labour is a convenient euphemism which disguises the fact that labour consists of people, while the treatment of people as a variable cost effectively commodifies these people in the production process. In order to create value in the transformational process of an organization then commodities need to be used efficiently, and this efficient use of such commodities is measured through the accounting of the organization. When this commodity consists of people then this implies using them in such a way that the maximum surplus value can be extracted from them. The way in which this can be achieved is through the employment of young fit people who can work hard and then be replaced by more young fit people. In this way surplus value (in Marxian terms) can be transferred from the future of the person and extracted in the present. As people have been constituted as a commodified variable cost then they become merely a factor of production which can be exchanged for another factor of production, as the costs determined through the use of accounting legitimate. Thus it is reasonable, through an accounting analysis, to replace people with machinery if more value (profit) can be extracted in doing so, and this has provided the imperative for the industrial revolution which has continued up until the present.[15] Accounting is only

---

15 An endless search for productivity is nowadays the concern of many industrial engineers as well as the core of various well-accepted models of rationalization such as BPR (business process reengineering), ERP systems (enterprise resource planning techniques and integrated information systems), among others.

concerned with the effect of the actions of an organization upon itself and so the effect of mechanization upon people need not be taken into account. Thus if mechanization results in people becoming unemployed (or possibly unemployable) then this is of no concern – except to the people themselves.

This is at complete odds with any understanding of sustainability. As Aras and Crowther (2009c) show, sustainability must take into account the effects of corporate activity upon all of the people involved. This requires treating people as individuals and respecting dignity. It also requires a fuller accountability of organizations to their stakeholder community and a recognition of all of the effects of their activity (Aras and Crowther 2008b). This requires an adaptation and development of corporate governance to incorporate all of these things; at the moment the most enlightened companies do this (Aras and Crowther 2008) and the practice is gradually being extended. Indeed it is gradually becoming better understood that there is a clear connection between maintaining the dignity of the workforce and corporate performance.

Conclusions

It is clear that the definition of corporate governance has extended considerably beyond investor relations and encompasses relations with all stakeholders – including the environment. This is essential for the longer-term survival of a firm and is therefore a key component of sustainability. There is evidence that some firms understand this but they are still in a minority although increasing in number. So it is possible to say that good corporate governance will address this but that not all firms recognize this. It is equally possible to state that a firm which has a more complete understanding of the relationship between social responsibility, sustainability and corporate governance will address these issues more completely. By implication a more complete understanding of the inter-relationships will lead to better corporate governance, and therefore to better economic performance.

The current economic crisis has not just highlighted the importance of governance: it has also shown that CSR is a central part of governance and that both are essential for sustainability. Part of the problem is caused by failures in regulation and governance brought about by the nature of global markets but more local governance. So attention needs to be paid to the development of a truly global system of governance. This is the immediate need for action.

In the longer term further action is needed. We have also argued that a significant part of the problem is predicated in the underlying political philosophy upon which market economics is based – namely its basis in Utilitarianism. This too will result in future problems unless addressed and so in the longer term attention must be paid to addressing this and developing an alternative philosophical underpinning to economic activity – one which is not amoral as is Utilitarianism but one which has built into it a sense of morality. This is a more difficult but more important task. As we have shown in this book, the relationship between an organization and its people needs to change to enable not just better performance but also the sustainability of that organization.

References

Ackerman R. W. (1975); *The Social Challenge to Business*; Cambridge, MA; Harvard University Press.

Aras G. (2008); Corporate governance and the agency problem in financial markets; in D. Crowther and N. Capaldi (eds), *Ashgate Research Companion to Corporate Social Responsibility*; Aldershot; Ashgate.

Aras G. and Crowther D. (2007a); Is the global economy sustainable?; in S. Barber (ed.), *The Geopolitics of the City*; London; Forum Press, pp. 165–194.

Aras G. and Crowther D. (2007b); The development of Corporate Social Responsibility; *Effective Executive* X (9), September, 18–21.

Aras G. and Crowther D. (2008a); Exploring frameworks of corporate governance; in G. Aras and D. Crowther (eds), *Culture and Corporate Governance*; Leicester; SRRNet, pp. 3–16.

Aras G. and Crowther D. (2008b); Governance and sustainability: An investigation into the relationship between corporate governance and corporate sustainability; *Management Decision* 46 (3), 433–448.

Aras G. and Crowther D. (2009a); Corporate Governance and Corporate Social Responsibility in context; in G. Aras and D. Crowther (eds), *Global Perspectives on Corporate Governance and Corporate Social Responsibility*; Aldershot; Gower, pp. 1–41.

Aras G. and Crowther D. (2009b); Convergence: a prognosis; in G. Aras and D. Crowther (eds), *Global Perspectives on Corporate Governance and Corporate Social Responsibility*; Aldershot; Gower, pp. 313–336.

Aras G. and Crowther D. (2009c); *The Durable Corporation: Strategies for Sustainable Development*; Aldershot; Gower.

Aras G. and Crowther D. (2010a); Sustaining business excellence; *Total Quality Management and Business Excellence* 21 (5), 565–576.

Aras G. and Crowther D. (2010b); Sustainable practice: The real triple bottom line; in G. Aras, D. Crowther and K. Krkac (eds), *Proceedings of 9th Conference on CSR*; Zagreb, pp. 77–90.

Becker B. and Westbrook D. A. (1998); Confronting asymmetry: global financial markets and national regulation; *International Finance* 1 (2), 339–355.

Burke L. and Longsdon J. M. (1996); How corporate social responsibility pays off; *Long Range Planning* 29(4), 495–502.

Cowen S. S., Ferreri L. B. and Parker L. D. (1987); The impact of corporate characteristics on social responsibility disclosure: A typology and frequency-based analysis; *Accounting, Organizations and Society* 12 (2), 111–122.

Crowther D. (2002); *A Social Critique of Corporate Reporting*; Aldershot; Ashgate.

Crowther D. (2005); Modern epics and corporate well-being; in D. Crowther and R. Jatana (eds), *Representations of Social Responsibility Vol. 2*; Hyderabad; ICFAI University Press, pp. 125–166.

Crowther D. (2011); The Utilitarian fallacy; in G. Aras and D. Crowther (eds), *Governance in the Business Environment*; Bingley; Emerald, pp. 71–91.

Crowther D. and Seifi S. (2010) *Corporate Governance and Risk Management*; Copenhagen; Ventus.

Dahl R. A. (1972); A prelude to corporate reform; *Business and Society Review* Spring, 17–23.

Grabel I. (2003); Averting crisis? Assessing measures to manage financial integration in emerging economies; *Cambridge Journal of Economics* 27, 317–336.

Gray R., Javad M., Power D. M. and Sinclair C. D. (2001); Social and environmental disclosures and corporate characteristics: A research note and extension; *Journal of Business, Finance and Accounting* 28 (3/4), 327–356.

Hayek F. von (1944); *The Road to Serfdom*; London; Routledge.

Hetherington J. A. C (1973); *Corporate Social Responsibility Audit: A Management Tool for Survival*; London; The Foundation for Business Responsibilities.

Hobbes T. (1651); *Leviathan*; many editions.

Hume D. (1711–1776); *A Treatise of Human Nature*, Vol. 1 and Vol. 2; London; Dent and Sons, 1934.

Marchand A., De Coninck P. and Walker S. (2005); La consommation responsable – Perspectives nouvelles dans les domaines de la conception de produits, *Nouvelles pratiques sociales*, 18 (1), 39–56.

Mathews M. R. (1997); Twenty-five years of social and environmental accounting research: is there a silver jubilee to celebrate?; *Accounting, Auditing and Accountability Journal* 10 (4), 481–531.

McDonald D. and Puxty A. G. (1979); An inducement – contribution approach to corporate financial reporting; *Accounting, Organizations and Society*, 4 (1/2), 53–65.

Popper K. R. (1959); *The Logic of Scientific Discovery*; London; Hutchinson.

Rajan R. (2008); Reforming global economic and financial governance; in B. Eichengreen and R. Baldwin (eds), *What G20 leaders must do to stabilise our economy and fix the financial system*; London; CEPR; pp. 21–24.

Rosenau J. (1999); Toward an ontology for global governance; in M. Hewson and T. J .Sinclair (eds), *Approaches to Global Governance Theory*; Albany, NY; State University of New York Press.

Rousseau J. J. (1762); "*Du Contrat Social*" translated as "The Social Contract"; many editions.

Spence M. (2008); Agenda for the next few months; in B. Eichengreen and R. Baldwin (eds), *What G20 Leaders Must do to Stabilise our Economy and Fix the Financial System*; London; CEPR; pp. 11–14.

Titus H. and Smith M. (1974); *Living Issues in Philosophy*. New York: D. Van Nostrand Company.

Tobin J. (2000); Financial Globalization; *World Development* 28 (6), 1101–1104.

Van den Berghe L. (2001); "Beyond Corporate Governance", *European Business Forum* 5, Spring.

Index

acceptance 2–3, 8, 15, 17, 21, 52–3, 58, 78–9, 138, 147, 152, 197, 206
accountability 41–2, 51–2, 57, 62, 65, 73, 80, 85–6, 88, 201, 208, 210
acknowledgement 32, 52–3, 60–61
activism 7, 78, 91
Alcibiades 34
anthropocentrism 32–3, 60
assimilation 8, 148, 150–51, 156
awakening 7, 45, 62, 64, 66
awareness 2, 23, 34–5, 37, 62, 149, 154, 166, 173, 197
axiology 6, 13–14, 22–4, 120, 173

becoming being 13, 17, 25
benevolence 28, 34–5, 38, 42, 197

Cadbury report 196, 203
Canadian Multiculturalism Act 152
capitalism 24, 41, 88, 101, 186, 203
caring 7, 24, 42, 45, 57, 59–62, 64–6, 68–9
change management 17, 130–33, 193
Charter of Human Rights 8, 183
Charter of the French Language, the (Law 101), Canada 150
circular causation 53
Classical Liberal Theory 57, 145, 198–9
Classical Liberalism 145, 198
co-construction 17, 27, 137
coherence 129, 165
collaboration 3, 17, 22, 65, 78, 85–6, 89, 107, 140, 152, 199
collective, the 29, 33, 65, 67–8, 209
collective consciousness 187
collective rights 183
collective solidarity 57, 69
Combined Code on Corporate Governance 198, 203–4
communitarianism 156

community organizations 7, 75–83, 86, 88–91, 148
compassion 35, 60, 66
competition 81, 84, 107, 130, 188–90, 199, 203
competitiveness 15, 32, 108, 181
computerization 127–9, 138
computer workers 8, 111
concept of human dignity, the 31, 182–3
concertation 78, 85, 87
conciliation and mediation agents 21, 24
conformist selves 15
consciousness 7, 4, 33, 53, 62, 64, 116, 166, 174, 176, 186–8
constructivism 186
cooperation 35–6, 84, 141
corporate behaviour 9, 57, 195
corporate culture 7, 75, 83
corporate governance 28, 195–8, 203–4, 206–8, 210
corporate performance 1, 181, 196, 206, 210
corporate social responsibility (CSR) 1–2, 4, 11, 43, 62–3, 197–8, 206, 209
corporatism 80–81
corporate culture 7, 75, 83
corruption 31
cosmological awareness 172
creativity class 8, 97
crisis of governance 1, 9, 195
cultural awareness 152
cultural differences 110, 190
cultural diversity 8, 148, 151, 154
cybernetics 53

deontology 9, 29–31, 186
depersonalization 209
Dewey 64, 167
digital insecurity 127–8, 134–5, 140–41

dignity at work 98, 103–5, 107, 110, 117, 119–20
discrimination 150, 152–3, 155
distance learning 6, 18–22
domestic violence 78, 87
downsizing 68, 78–9, 104

economic accountability 41
economic crisis 210
economic performance 2, 4–5, 210
economic rationality 185
effectiveness 43, 107–8, 200
efficacy 63, 185
efficiency 19, 43, 80–81, 98–100, 102, 107–8, 129–31, 186
elucidating managerial responsibility 1
emotional intelligence 161, 176
emotional welfare 207
empathy 22, 24, 38, 45, 60, 161–2, 175
employee creativity 127
environmental conscience 34
environmental performance 4–5, 206–7
ethical behaviour 28, 184–6, 188–9
ethical conduct 47
ethical dialogue 161, 175, 178
ethical dilemmas 172, 174
ethical laxity 7, 41, 52
ethical management 41, 43
ethics of utilitarianism 9
European Commission (EC) 11
European Court 8
exemplarity 24
existentialism 6, 9, 36–8, 186

failures in governance 9, 195–6
fairness 30–31, 34, 41
financial crisis 145, 196
forethought 37, 60, 66, 196
fortitude 30, 36–7
Frankfurt School 61
free market 41, 51, 53–4, 79, 145, 181–2, 190, 198, 200, 209
Freud 15–16, 151

General Assembly of the United Nations 8, 182
generosity 28, 30, 32, 34–5, 52–3, 197

global competitiveness 15
global environment 7, 193, 200
global warming 54
globalization 30, 36, 41, 48, 58, 67, 74, 80, 88, 98, 184–5
goodness 6, 3, 28, 34–6, 59, 60, 164, 166–7, 173, 176–7
governance failures 9, 195
government decentralization 7
guilt 16, 132, 169

healing 151
hero, the 202
holistic approach 6, 34, 37
honesty 6, 30, 205
hope 33, 35–8, 159, 196
humility 34
human qualities 17
human resource 63, 65, 83, 182
human rights 1, 5, 8, 11, 41, 43, 73, 97, 150–51, 153, 155, 159–60, 182–4, 187, 189, 190–91, 201, 205
Hume 28, 33–5, 197

idealism 6, 30, 33, 37–8
individual responsibility 60, 184
individual freedom 9, 146, 188, 198
individual possibility 186
individual rights 184
individuation 15
information and communication technologies (ICT) 6, 14, 18–20, 127–8, 130
inner self 24–5, 36
institutionalization 7, 88, 90
International Chamber of Commerce 2
interpersonal communication 136
intimidation 103
ISO26000 2

Kant 30–31, 159–60, 163, 166, 182, 186
knowledge workers 98–100, 102–3, 105–10, 119, 121

legitimacy 7, 41, 52, 62, 73, 77–8, 85–7
Liberalism 146, 198–9
linguicism 151

local governance 7, 75, 210
London Stock Exchange 198, 203

managerial dignity 168
managerial wisdom 170–71, 176
Marcel 17, 27, 33–7, 59, 60
mediation of rights 46, 199
Menon 34
modernization 76
moral awareness 163
moral human dignity 66
multiculturalism 8, 147, 149, 151–3, 156
multilingualism 8, 147–8
mutual responsibility 9

neo-liberalism 75, 77, 82, 91–2
normalization 82, 92–3

off-shoring 57
Ontario Human Rights Commission 150
ontology 6, 13, 14, 17, 21, 23, 25, 116, 120–21
openness 22, 24, 34, 36–7, 62, 166
Organization for Economic Co-operation and Development (OECD) 46, 79, 84, 96
otherness 24, 33
outsourcing 57, 59

perfect competition 199
persecutive violence 151
personal responsibility 35–7
philosophical education 159, 161–3, 165–8, 170–71, 176–8
pluralism 61
Policy on Discrimination and Language (Ontario, Canada) 150
positivism 67, 186, 188
pragmatism 167

Quebec Human Rights and Youth Commission 153

realism 30, 32–3
reasonable accommodations 8, 154–6
reciprocity 60, 65, 186–7, 189
reflexivity 17, 21, 34, 36–7, 61

regionalization 84
regulatory reform 41
resistance to change 128, 130–31, 133–4, 137, 141

self-discovery 6, 13, 24, 65
self-regulation 52
sensibility 24, 60–61, 66, 173, 175
sensitivity 34–7
Shaftesbury 32, 36–7
sharing 7, 57–61, 63, 65–7, 69, 90, 103, 107, 136, 140, 152
social conscience 29
social contract 145, 208–9
social image 6, 21
social justice 5, 75, 185–6
social performance 4, 5, 208
societal values 5, 184
Socrates 17, 28, 33–5, 43, 59, 164, 175, 185
solidarity 7, 45, 57, 58–63, 65–9, 81, 92, 104, 155
stewardship 32, 197, 206
subconscious 188
sub-consciousness 187
subjectivity 171, 174, 191
suffering 60, 151, 188
sustainable development 2–5, 32, 193–4

Taylorism 99–100, 102
technological change 127, 134
temperance 30–31, 34, 36
temporality 98, 140
Theory of the Firm 199
thoughtfulness 37, 197
transparency 6, 28, 31, 41, 62, 77–8, 85–6, 205

unconscious, the 16
United Nations 2–4, 8, 27, 31–2, 58, 182, 193, 200–201
Utilitarianism 9, 145, 198–9, 210

virtue ethics, modern 30
virtues 6, 17, 27–31, 33–8, 197

well-being 30, 33, 42, 64–5, 67, 69, 167, 186, 190, 207

whole, the 7, 18, 27–8, 59, 60, 62–3, 65, 68, 191
wholeness 7, 17, 27, 28, 32–8, 57, 59, 60–62, 65–8
willingness 8, 17, 28, 36, 45, 59, 176
World Bank 196
World Business Council for Sustainable Development 2
World Commissions on Environment and Development (WCED) 2
World Summit Outcome Document 3–4, 193
World Trade Organization (WTO) 46, 200